CLASSICS IN ENGLISH LITERATURE

By

Dr. Lopa Sanyal, *Ph.D.*

Associate Professor

Dyananda College of Science & Arts

Bangalore

DISCOVERY PUBLISHING HOUSE

NEW DELHI-110002

Published by:
Namit Wasan
DISCOVERY PUBLISHING HOUSE PVT. LTD.
4383/4B, Ansari Road, Darya Ganj
New Delhi-110 002 (India)
Phone : +91-11-23279245; 23253475; 43596065
E-mail : discoverybooksindia@gmail.com
discoverypublishinghouse@gmail.com
namitwasan9@gmail.com
web : www.discoverypublishinggroup.com

***Edition:* 2020**

ISBN: 978-81-8356-135-8

Classics in English Literature

Printed at:
Infinity Imaging Systems
Delhi

Preface

Classics and English appeals to those with a particular interest in literary and cultural interactions. This book emphasizes the interactions of Classics and English, and provides an opportunity to study classical influence. The key intention of this book is to help students of English literature to form a lucid notion of the influence exerted by the Classics upon English literature. Such a vast subject cannot be covered within the limits of one volume. Main aim of the author is to supply the reader with the kind of information he is likely to want. The book explore links between the Greek and Latin writers on the one hand and the mediaeval and modern on the other; and it shows how the classics have appeared to each age in its turn. For each age has had its own view of them.

It covers tragedy, comedy, pastoral, drama, satire, rhetoric and literary theory in ancient and modern times; the reception of Classical Literature in poetry in English. Literature, especially poetry and drama has this same double, paradoxical nature as classics, that where there is classics there is poetry and drama, where there is poetry and drama there is classics; not two things in close association, but one thing with two names.

Classics in English Literature is designed to cover a wide range of literary and related topics in both English Literature and the classical world, with particular emphasis in the latter field on the language and literature of Ancient times, and to promote consideration of the interrelationships between these two fields. It covers the study of all aspects of the cultures of Greece and Rome (their languages, literature, thought, religion, art, archaeology and history) and their influence on later literature.

Author

Contents

1
Chapter

The Background

INTRODUCTION

English literature, like England, belongs to Europe and its history has been determined by that connection. The invaders of Roman Britain brought with them their language and even some fragments of a literature, of which it may fairly be said that they contained the promise of most that was to come. But this promise would never have been fulfilled, or at any rate would never have been fulfilled in the same way, in isolation from the rest of Europe. The history of our literature may almost be described as the history of what happened when it came in contact with the European tradition, the main current of which flows through Rome from ancient Greece. It is with this tradition, so far as it is classical, that we shall be mainly concerned. And our concern shall be to consider it not so much in itself as in its effects upon our own literature, of which it may be called the background.

Two questions immediately present themselves. What is meant by 'classical', and what is meant by 'background'? The answer to the first question is easy because it is arbitrary. By 'classical' literature is meant, for the purposes of this book, whatever has survived in Greek and Latin from Homer to the beginning of the Middle Ages. That of course is only one of the many ways in which the word 'classical' has been used, and objections may be raised to it. But it is a use with which the ordinary man is familiar and by which therefore he is not likely to be misled. If there is occasion to employ the word in another meaning, that can be explained in its place. It is somewhat harder to defend the metaphor in 'background'.

History, it may be objected, is continuous and alive; and while it is convenient to divide it into eras, the eras are not true divisions. They merge into one another, each causing its successor and caused by its predecessor. For this reason a word like 'background' or 'setting' creates a false impression of permanence. It may be admitted at once that to the history of English literature there is no fixed background, for it is as fluid and changeful as the literature itself. But this is no more than admitting that every metaphor, if pressed too hard, becomes inept. And after all there is a good deal to be said for this one. Where there is change there must be something that changes. This something in English literature can be shown to preserve through all its variations an essential unity. It is what we mean when we speak of a tradition. It is such a tradition that is meant when we speak of the classical setting or background of English literature.

When that literature came into effective touch with the classical tradition is a question not easy to resolve. Certainly before the time of Alfred the vernacular poetry shows little trace of any classical knowledge going beyond the Latin Bible and Lives of the Saints, nor can we assume that even these were read by the poets themselves. It may be argued that even the date of Alfred is much too early for speaking of direct and effective influence. That is true and important. But it is not so important as the fact that English literature grew up in a society where all men who could read and write at all read and wrote and even conversed in Latin. It had to preserve itself in that society. It had to absorb the classical tradition or be absorbed by it. That is the struggle we have to describe. But to do this we must know the combatants or rather, assuming that we know the English side, we must learn what the other was like. And, since the classical tradition is a very old thing, we must go back more than a millennium and a half before Alfred to its source in ancient Greece.

Roman Britain

For it is, originally and essentially, a creation of the Greek spirit. It is not like anything else in the ancient world, and it is only our familiarity with it that disguises its uniqueness. It reveals itself at a surprisingly early date, being fully present in Homer. Earlier than that it is not possible to penetrate because nothing earlier exists in European literature. How or why the Homeric Poems came to embody, and to embody so completely, a spirit which we recognize as essentially European, we do not know. The fact remains, and it is the key and explanation of all that follows. What immediately followed is indeed hard to discern because the record is all but lost. But the sixth century before Christ saw the birth in Greek lands of science and philosophy, and the fifth a prodigious efflorescence of poetic and artistic genius, all of it penetrated by that sense of the reasonable, that dislike of the disproportionate, which distinguishes the Greek mind and distinguishes the European, so far as it has absorbed the Greek tradition. This culture, brilliant as any in history, came to be concentrated more and more in the city of Athens, where in the fifth and fourth centuries before Christ the classical spirit received its finest and most typical expression. From Athens it radiated through Greece proper and the Greek colonies. Then before this fourth century had ended there occurred one of those events that change the course of history. Alexander, the young king of Macedonia, educated in the culture of Athens, turned his armies to the east and conquered as far as India. The result was that from Marseiues to the Punjab, from the Danube to the Sudan, the Greek language, the Greek way of thinking and writing, spread with an almost incredible rapidity. Much was lost in the process; the fine quality of Athenian culture was sadly barbarised. This was inevitable and the plain condition of its spreading so far and so fast. But one factor of great and almost pathetic interest survived—the recognition that it was indeed the Athenian culture of these two great centuries that must be the model for their successors. One fashion in writing after another would appear and disappear; but Sophocles and Euripides, Plato and Demosthenes remained the acknowledged masters of the classical style. If on this point ancient criticism had weakened or broken down, it is hard to see how the specially classical qualities could have survived. As it was they had time to establish themselves—to become in fact 'classical'. Here the scholars did much to help, especially in Alexandria, where during the last three centuries before Christ a succession of learned and accurate investigators, themselves often men of literary eminence, published editions of the Greek 'classics' for the guidance and inspiration of later antiquity.

Meanwhile, in the west, a new power was gathering strength —the Roman *imperium*. By the end of the third century B.C. the Romans had not only destroyed the power of Carthage but ruled over the greater part of Italy, over Sicily and Sardinia and Spain. This expansion brought them face to face with the eastern or Greek-speaking half of the Mediterranean world. It was not their first contact. Greek colonies had been founded in south Italy at a very early period, and from these the Romans had got much, including their alphabet. But it was not until this later period that an independent Roman literature came into existence. One calls it independent because it had some distinctive characteristics, but it was fashioned almost wholly upon Greek models. And this continued to be largely true of Latin literature through all its history. It was simply a Roman-built channel for the transmission of the Greek tradition. This in no way diminishes its importance or interest; indeed it rather enhances both the one and the other. What happened was that the Greek now became the Greco-Roman tradition; losing much but also gaining something by this extension. *Graecia capta ferum victorem cepit*, said Horace. *Greece was conquered*—he means by Roman arms—but conquered her untamed conqueror-he means by her arts, her science, her literature. It is true. Greece was the civiliser of Rome, and through Rome of her empire, which came to include the whole orbis terrarum, the ring of lands about the Mediterranean, and ultimately a great deal more than that.

The Upcoming

In the reign of the emperor Claudius, that is to say in the middle of the first century of our era, the Romans invaded and occupied a part of Britain. There followed a long process of conquest and pacification. Britannia became a Roman province, and with the Roman administration came as a matter of course the Roman culture. It is difficult in the almost total absence of written records to describe the result, but it is possible to dispel some fingering misconceptions. The tribes whom the Romans thus attacked were not uncivilised, although they differed greatly among themselves in the degree of their civilisation. They were of Celtic origin, and they had even then customs and institutions which were retained into historical times by the ancestors of the present Welsh and Irish and the Scottish Highlanders. They had for instance their bards and story-tellers and orators; and, although such literature as they had was probably all oral, it existed and (to judge by the earliest remains of Welsh poetry) may even have been fine. Materially of course this Celtic culture could do nothing against the Roman power; in all the appliances of civilisation it was totally inferior. But in quality, if not in achievement, it might have been considered to hold its own. For even then the quality of Roman civilisation, always to a certain extent unoriginal and sophisticated, was beginning to decline.

In any case it was impossible for the tribes of Britain to appreciate the fine flower of the classical spirit. They were too far away from the centre, too vitally attached to their own traditions. It would seem that Britannia was never more than half Romanised. Doubtless the process would have extended farther and penetrated deeper, if there had been a considerable influx of men of Latin race as well as Latin speech. But there was nothing of the kind. The province was administered by a handful of Roman officials sent there by the imperial government, and even these were certainly not all of Italian blood. The army of occupation was composed of men of every race. The Roman villas which have been, and continue to be, discovered in England were not occupied by Romans, but by Romanised Britons. These would read and speak Latin, which was also of course the language of the provincial government, the law courts, and the Church. But there must have been masses of population who never learned to speak Latin at all, or never with any fluency. In the mountains of Scotland and Wales, not to speak of Ireland, the traditional Celtic culture evidently continued undisturbed.

On the other hand what the Romans did succeed in giving was of inestimable value. They drew Britain within the orbit of the Greco-Roman civilisation, giving it a measure of settled peace for three hundred years and the opportunity to assimilate what it could. The Romans brought (along with their arms and laws) their language, their literature, their system of education. How many Britons besides the sons of chiefs received this teaching we have not the means of knowing, but we know that the Latin schools existed. We can even say what was taught in them, and that is a matter of extreme importance, because the character of our Western civilisation has been in the last resort determined by the character of our education. It was the Greeks who first conceived the notion that every free-born lad should be taught reading and writing and arithmetic. In other countries in antiquity education, so far as it was given at all, was vocational; that is to say, certain youths were trained to be priests or physicians or bards, and nothing else. That is quite a different thing from teaching everybody to read and then letting him read whatever he liked. However familiar and natural such a conception may appear to us now, it was, when it was first formed, a startling innovation, entered upon no doubt with some hesitation and only gradually extending from the more to the less enlightened communities of ancient Greece. It was however in full force when the Romans took it over, and in due time this 'liberal' education became established everywhere in the Empire, including Britain. It has lasted till the present day.

This however is elementary education, and the Romans had more to offer than that. What they offered may without much exaggeration be summed up in the word 'rhetoric'. No doubt a little philosophy was taught as well, but the Romans never showed much taste or aptitude for philosophy, whereas they showed a great deal of both for rhetoric. We learn from Tacitus that well before the end of the first century of our era there were at least some Britons who showed remarkable proficiency in the arts of oratory. We must be clear however about the meaning of that statement, and we may begin by dismissing from our minds the impression that rhetoric is nothing but the use of flowery and exaggerative language. Tlere was always of course a tendency, at least in the Roman mind, in that direction; but it was a tendency that the best classical taste steadily condemned. One has only to read the *De Sublimitate* to see that. What rhetoric really meant in the ancient world may be well enough understood by calling it the art of stating a case effectively in speech or writing. It is not the same thing as style, on which modern criticism has laid such emphasis. Style was only a part of rhetoric, and scarcely the most important part. Rather it was the clear arrangement of your thoughts that mattered most. Thus considered, rhetoric obviously was a very valuable study.

It had of course its dangers. If your whole endeavour is to convince or at least to persuade, you are exceedingly apt to overstate your case. We need not go to ancient literature for examples of that; we may find them in multitudes nearer home. It is however the great vice of Roman literature and it may as well be noted at once. On the other hand rhetoric did teach the importance of form, by which is meant not a mere decorative pattern, but rational or logical form imposed upon the matter by the simple necessity of making it clear. Since an example is often more illuminating than any amount of description, we may point among English writers to Macaulay, whose rhetoric is very much of the ancient kind.

It is easy to understand how valuable the study of that would be to the Celtic mind with its tendency to the vast and formless, as later to the English mind with its tendency to muddle distinctions. One cannot say as much for the other side of rhetoric, its stimulation of what at its best is eloquence, at its worst rodomontade. It is improbable that the Romans had anything to teach their Celtic pupils there.

There was no direct religious instruction in the Roman system, although it is clear that parents liked a schoolmaster to teach respect for the gods and the emperor. At a more advanced stage, when the schoolmaster or *grammaticus* was superseded by the *rhetor* or teacher of rhetoric, the latter might apparently hold and express any views he liked, so long as they were not treasonable. When Christianity first came to Britain we cannot say, but there is no reason to doubt that it flourished in Britannia as much as in other provinces. In the year 311 it became the state religion of the empire. Thenceforward religion came more and more to influence education, until, when the Engfish invaders had begun their incursions, almost the only people who had any education were in the service of the Church. It is however to be noted that this development changed the direction rather than the character of the old grammatical and rhetorical training.

It simply meant that the records of Christianity were more studied and the pagan masters less. It did not mean that rhetoric—how to state a case effectively—lost its importance. We have indeed no direct evidence to show the state of education in Christian Britannia, but we are justified in supposing that it did not fall seriously below that of Gaul or Spain. We cannot make any sound inference from the *De Excidio Britanniae (Concerning the Destruction of Britannia)* by Gildas; for the author, besides being naturally somewhat stupid, lived at a time when education of any kind had almost ceased to exist. He can tell us nothing, as he had experienced nothing, of Britannia in its prime. His real interest is that of a survivor; he was 'the last of the Britons'. But that interest is great. Here in the sixth century (to which scholars assign him) was a man of British blood educated in the Roman tradition, using Latin as his mother tongue. His book is the relic of a civilisation—of the world into which the English had now broken.

Contact Between Indigenous and Traditional Elements

The invaders seem to have killed and sacked with a frightful thoroughness. Wherever they went the schools and churches went down, and Britain became once more a heathen country. The foreground was destroyed; that is certain. But not the background, and it is that which we have undertaken to describe. There was Ireland, where Christian learning had found a refuge from the storm. There was Italy, beginning to recover from the disasters of the fifth and sixth centuries. Above all there was the Latin-speaking Church. After the English conquest, which took at least a century and a half to complete and could not have been entirely without effect on the conquerors, the old civilisation began to close in again upon its invaders. Under a double stream of influence, one from Ireland, the other from Rome, they became Chrisdanised. Their literature was at once affected. *Beowulf* is or became, at least superficially, a Christian poem. Caedmon and Cynewulf were, not superficially, Christian poets. And with Christianity came back the study of Latin. The schools of England, especially those of York and Canterbury, became even famous; and what they studied was not English literature but Latin. True, they paid little attention—they paid some to the authors we think of as specially 'classical', Cicero, Virgil, Horace and the rest. It was Latin Christian literature which they studied and copied out: the Latin Bible, liturgical books, Lives of the saints, hymns, homilies, ecclesiastical history. This happened because education was yoked to the service of the Church. The consequence was that the vernacular literature had to grow up pretty much as it could. It was produced in the main by men who knew little or no Latin for men who knew little or none themselves. This ignorance is so far from being regrettable that it may have been the only thing that could have protected the native character, and perhaps secured the very survival, of English literature. If a knowledge of Latin had been general, it is almost certain that the English would now be speaking a Romance language like the Spanish and the French. It is quite certain they would have got nothing for many centuries but Latin books. For the prestige of Latin was such that for hundreds of years anything written in the vernacular was scarcely regarded as literature at all. It was supposed to be a concession to ignorance.

What we have then to keep before our minds is a picture of Engfigh literature growing up not merely side by side with Latin but in opposition to it, and sometimes with difficulty maintaining itself against this rival. The feeling among educated persons was that, if a man hoped to produce something of permanent value, he would have to write it in Latin. It is a feeling that persisted much longer than is usually imagined; it was not entirely extinct in the eighteenth century. It was so strong in the Early English period, and then again (with a new rival in Norman French) after the Conquest, that we may almost say that throughout these ages English literature led an underground life. Even after the triumph of Chaucer there was, when the Renaissance began to operate in England, a marked tendency for authors to revert to Latin. Thus Sir Thomas More, who could write admirable English, writes *Utopia* in less admirable Latin. It is alarming to think that, if Milton had lived a century earlier, he would not have written *Paradise Lost* but a Latin epic, perhaps not much more sprightly than Petrarch *Africa*. This age-long rivalry is hardly enough remarked in the more popular histories of English literature. It may have deprived us of some masterpieces in the vernacular, but no doubt it was on the whole an immense advantage. English literature has learned too much from its rival to have room for regrets. The language needed to be enriched by Latin words, the thought by Latin wisdom, the native forms and metres by the varied accomplishment of Latin art. That is the truth, which no impartial judgement will refuse to admit. But for serious students it is not enough to accept the *fait accompli;* we must consider how it came to be accomplished. Having got the problem in its setting, we are in a position to examine the process by which it was solved. But before we do this it will be found useful to disengage the elements of the problem itself, those elements, that is, with which we do not assume familiarity. In other words we must discuss the nature of the classical influence.

2
Chapter

Classical Literature

INTRODUCTION

The spirit embodied in classical literature is too protean to find adequate expression in a word or a phrase; we must pursue it through its various manifestations. But if one had to describe it in a word or two, one might say that this literature is animated in a higher degree than other literatures by a love for, and faith in, reason. This may seem either a platitude or a paradox—a platitude in so far as it may be said that there is nothing exceptional about believing in reason, because we all do that; a paradox if it be maintained that the Latin temperament is more amenable to reason than the English. But neither objection can be sustained. The second may be thrown out at once on the ground that it is one thing to believe in reason and another to be governed by it. The first may be met by the observation that, if a platitude is involved, this is wholly due to the fact that the belief in the supremacy of reason has been so long imposed upon us by the Greeks that it has become a sort of second nature with us. It was not always so. In the ancient world—China, which might put in a claim, being outside European knowledge—the Greeks and the Greeks alone had this devotion to the rational. The proofs of that, if they were necessary, would take too long to marshal. But here is one.

The Old Testament was composed almost contemporaneously with Greek literature from Homer to Theocritus. How much appeal to reason is there in the Old Testament? It is all to faith and the emotions, to the fear and the love of God; almost never to the reason. No doubt we must beware of putting the matter too strongly. All great poetry, even all great prose, must appeal to the emotions; at least they do not appeal to the reason only. What may fairly be said of the ancient Greeks is that they not only trusted reason, they were passionate for it as no other people have been before or since. So far is this from being a common virtue that it is the possession of it which makes Greek literature the highly original and distinctive thing it is.

The reasoning power--not quite the same thing as reason —may be applied in many directions. Applied to nature, it produces the natural sciences; and the Greeks to all intents and purposes created mathematics and the natural sciences. Applied to thought, it produces philosophy; and the Greeks invented philosophy. Applied to human activity, it produces what Aristotle called the practical sciences, such as politics and the art of war; and these too were first worked out by the Greeks. But what concerns us is its application to art, in particular to the art of literature. It may be argued that to describe any art as 'reasonable' or even as 'intellectual' is confusing if not misleading, for art can never be a purely intellectual activity. This is true, and Greek writers on aesthetics are perfectly well aware of it. But it was a Greek conviction that into art there entered an intellectual element, which was essential to it; and this they emphasised and perhaps overemphasised. To that extent Greek or classical art may be described as intellectual. This is at once apparent if one compares Greek architecture or sculpture or pottery with those of some other artistic nation, such as the Chinese, whose art is so much more 'amusing' and fantastical. A Greek had the feeling that a work of art ought to mean something; to him it did not appear enough that it should stir the emotions or touch the imagination. He went further, he did not think it could stir the emotions or the imagination in a genuinely artistic way, unless it embodied an intelligible design. Consequently he would have repudiated as entirely false the doctrine which is in vogue today that a work of literary art need not have any meaning at all. He was convinced that it must be consciously designed from beginning to end, even if its inspiration came from something beyond or below our consciousness.

A work of art so designed will have its parts carefully related to each other and to the whole. This characteristic never fails to strike the student of classical art. Nobody looking at the Parthenon or such a 'Grecian urn' as Keats addresses would doubt that its artistic virtue lay very much in the justness of its proportions. But let us take an example from literature, let us take a typical Greek tragedy. It consists of five 'episodes' or acts, each separated from the other by an ode sung by the Chorus. The episodes will be of about the same length, will be uniform in tone (as distinct from feeling), never admitting prose or comedy, and will be composed in the same strict metre and the same elaborate diction. Each complete choral lyric will be divided into strophe, antistrophe and epode. In its metrical structure the strophe will correspond with the antistrophe not merely fine by fine but syllable by syllable. So will epode with epode. External and internal correspondences so intricate as this simply cannot be reproduced in English. But in Greek the proportions are worked out with a thoroughness that might be called mathematical. One would expect the effect to be mechanical, and no doubt it would be in the hands of lesser artists than Aeschylus and Sophocles and Euripides. But it is not merely not mechanical in them, it is a chief source of their power.

Proportion

The feeling for proportion was evidently instinctive with the Greeks and reveals itself in all sorts of ways. It comes out in the fact that geometry was the science which they first explored and which they carried farthest. No production of the Greek mind is more characteristic in its way than Euclid *Elements*, which exhibits in a particularly clear manner the connexion between reasoning and geometrical form. Or take Aristotle's system of logic, which exerted so powerful an influence upon the later Middle Ages; it has the precision of a diagram. We can see the instinct at work in the development of Greek pottery. The earliest, purely Greek, pottery is actually known to historians of ceramic art as 'geometric' because of the circles and straight lines with which it is decorated. Even when at a much later date the Attic potters were producing their masterpieces of the sixth and fifth centuries before Christ, their pots still depended for more than half their charm upon the exquisite balance of their pure and simple shapes. It is the same with their literature. The example of Greek tragedy has been given from poetry. An example may now be given from Greek prose. Here is the first sentence of a speech by Isocrates, whose oratory was the principal model on which Cicero formed that style which in its turn became the principal model for the prose-writers of the Renaissance.

> *I have often wondered, in regard to those who arranged festival assemblies and instituted gymnastic contests, that they considered bodily prowess worthy of so great rewards, while to those who laboured in their individual capacity for the general good – and prepared their souls in such a way as to be able to help others also – to these they assigned no honour, though it would have been reasonable that they should take the greater account of these, seeing that, suppose athletes required twice the strength they have, the rest of the world would be none the better for it, whereas if one man alone has right thoughts the people as a whole gets profit of it, all at any rate who wish to participate in that individual's wisdom.*

This translation (which is by Edwyn Bevan), is quite literal and suffers, as he himself would have been the first to say, from the clumsiness inevitable in a literal translation. But it has the advantage for us of following exactly the structure of the Greek sentence. Now look at it again. How marvellously it is articulated, how carefully clause is balanced against clause! It may of course be argued that prose of this architectural character is foreign to the genius of the English language with its simplified grammar and invariable order of words. We are not called upon to discuss that point. What we can say is that English literature would be greatly the poorer without the prose of Browne and Burke, of Newman and Ruskin, who would never have written as they did if they had not been influenced by the tradition of the classical 'period' or rhetorical sentence, of which Isocrates has given us this typical example.

To have this feeling for proportion—going so much deeper than a mere taste for regularity—involves the ability of seeing not merely as it were both sides of a work of art but both sides of a question. The Greek mind was profoundly antithetical. That, being a somewhat un-English quality, deserves the more attention from us. Thus it is a commonplace of Greek philosophy that to every proposition it is possible to state a counterproposition. This leads to the making of fine and sometimes over-fine distinctions, of drawing subtle and sometimes farfetched parallels. But that is the defect of a very eminent merit —the faculty of seeing both sides of a question, even when one's own feelings are engaged. This is not the same thing as the British sense of fairness. It is an intellectual not a moral quality, although no doubt the intellectual and moral elements here tend to coalesce. The emphasis with the Greeks was on the intellectual elements. In the ancient world this was quite exceptional—it is exceptional still. The contrast with the Old Testament will again serve. It is everything that Greek is not. It is almost totally unhumorous, undramatic (except incidentally), unphiosophical, unscientific. It proclaims, commands, prophesies, consoles, denounces; it rarely argues. It is the Word of God, and those who do not accept it are wicked. Turn now to the *Iliad*. The poet himself is of course a Greek, but he is not on the side of the Greeks any more than of the Trojans. It is impossible to say whether Achilles or Hector is treated with the greater sympathy; most English readers would say (perhaps mistakenly) that it is Hector. The redeeming feature about Achilles is the depth of his love for his friend and comrade Patroclus, whose death at the hands of Hector he avenges by killing Hector. The story is too well known to repeat. Priam, the aged father of Hector, goes alone and unarmed to the hut of the fierce young hero and asks for the body of his son; and, as Achilles listens, his anger dies away. It is not chivalry that moves him, still less is it sentimentality. It is a recognition of the strength of the old man's case—mixed no doubt with the feeling that both their cases are equally insignificant in face of the universal human tragedy.

It was this power of seeing and feeling contrasted points of view which enabled the Greeks to create their drama. A play in which one side has all the best of it is a bad play. It is often as hard to say who is the hero or heroine of a Greek tragedy as it is to say who is the hero of the *Iliad*. This of course is as it should be; the dramatist must let every character make the most of his case. Shakespeare does this, but the Greeks did it before him, and at a time when, so far as we can see, no other people was in the least capable of doing it. It is demonstrated in the very beginnings of their drama. One of the oldest Greek plays is the *Persians* of Aeschylus. The circumstances in which it was produced are these. In the years 480 and 479 B.C. the Persians, the greatest military power which the world had so far seen, attacked Greece, particularly Athens. By desperate valour the attack was repelled, but not until the city had been destroyed and its temples desecrated. It was shortly after these events—and it is easy to imagine how the Athenians felt about them—that the play was acted at Athens. The scene throughout is the Persian capital of Susa, and no Greek appears in the play at all. The war is viewed entirely through Persian eyes. Although you can feel the pride of the Athenian poet in the achievements of his fellow-citizens, there is not from beginning to end of that drama a word of mockery or insult or even hatred of the fallen foe. It was the tragedy of the Persians, not of the Greeks, and the Greek dramatist sees it so. If it be said this only proves that one man was a great dramatic genius, what will be said of the audience? For it gave the *Persians* the first prize in the annual competition.— Or consider the *Prometheus Bound,* also by Aeschylus. It puts with extraordinary force and sympathy the case of Prometheus against Zeus. But we know that it had a sequel (now lost) called the *Prometheus Unbound,* which gave the case of Zeus against Prometheus, leading to a reconciliation between them. Shelley could not bear this and wrote his own *Prometheus Unbound,* in which Zeus is hurled to destruction. Shelley could see only one side of the case. He lets his feelings overpower his dramatic sense, with the curious result that he, the humanitarian, is more cruel than Aeschylus.

It is perhaps worth adding that this dramatic impartiality has nothing to do with the personal preferences of the dramatist. Because a man sees the pros and cons of a disputed matter he is not thereby debarred from giving his passionate adherence to one side rather than the other. The Greeks were passionately convinced that they were in the right as against the Persians. That did not prevent them from seeking to understand their enemies, and it was largely because they made this attempt that they defeated them. So when Herodotus wrote his history, which was in the main an account of this very conflict between Greeks and Persians, he did not represent it as a struggle between good men and bad, but between good men and better. He has a very considerable admiration for the Persians, and he is keenly alive to certain undoubted weaknesses in the Greek character. That is one great reason why his book is a true history. For a book which gives the point of view of one side only is bad history, or rather it is not history at all but propaganda. This judicial impartiality is still more observable in the History of Thucydides, who was a younger contemporary of Herodotus. Indeed in that particular quality Thucydides excels all other historians, ancient or modern, who are also great writers.

Again, the power of seeing both sides of a question is perhaps the most necessary qualification of a philosopher. It is therefore natural that logical and systematic thinking, which is what we mean or ought to mean by philosophy, should have arisen among the Greeks. The method in which it arose is significant. It began in mere speculation. But objections were made, and it was felt that the objections had to be answered. Neither the original speculations nor the objections were denounced as heresies. Argument, it was felt, must be met by argument. Socrates was content to spend a long life in talking, and listening to other people's talk, on any question of human interest, professing to have no special doctrine of his own. A signal contrast to a Hebrew prophet. His great successor Plato gave the Socratic method a literary form. That is why his writings are called 'Dialogues'. In the typical Platonic dialogue some question of philosophic interest is raised, different points of view are stated by the various interlocutors, different arguments are adduced. In the end as likely as not no definite conclusion is reached, but the problem has been examined from every side and at least a number of fallacies exploded. After Plato came Aristotle, who was able after all this practice to work up the rules of argumentation into a logical system. It is hardly possible to exaggerate the influence which Aristotelian logic has had upon the mind of western Europe, including the English. The English, as contrasted say with the French, have rather a distrust of formal logic. It was all the more important for them to learn that, if you do present an argument, it is best to construct it on sound principles.

Now this has a bearing upon literature, for a logically constructed sentence will be a formally correct sentence, and such sentences must be the framework of all good prose. It is worth while to consider a simple illustration. The typical form of logical argument according to Aristotle is what he calls a 'syllogism'. Of this the stock example is: 'All men are mortal. Socrates is a man. Therefore Socrates is mortal'. These three statements form what might be called the disjointed members of a typical Greek sentence. The Greek felt, and felt rightly, that they were not unrelated statements; they have to be put together in order to show their organic connexion with one another. Consequently he would express himself somewhat like this: 'Since on the one hand it is true that all men are mortal, and on the other hand it is true that

Socrates is a man, we may conclude that Socrates is mortal'. This kind of sentence was called a 'period', which is the Greek word for a circle, because like a circle it is self-contained, whereas the clauses of which it is composed are not. It is the characteristic sentence of Greek and Latin prose, the masters of which could make periods of the most elaborate pattern, such as that already quoted from Isocrates. The history of English prose might almost be called a record of the struggle between the native idiom and this classical model.

Sophrosyné

Why should it be thought so important to understand one's opponent in a conflict of will or opinion? What special virtue resides in a balanced statement? These questions raise a moral issue, and it is one which we must understand if we are to understand the classical spirit at all. We have heard so much about classical restraint that we are apt to assume that there was not very much to restrain. That may be true of some imitators of the pure classical style; it is eminently not true of the style itself. The restraint there is due not to the absence but to the presence of strong feeling. It is the counterpart in literature of the virtue which the Greeks called *sophrosyné*. We translate it by words like 'temperance' or 'self-control', but such translations are utterly inadequate. They are so because they are merely negative, whereas *sophrosyné* is a positive virtue, being in fact according to the Greek conception of it the virtue that rules all the rest. It may be thought of as the direction of all the moral energies into the proper channel. We are concerned with it here only as it bears on Greek literature, although it may be well, in view of some modern misconceptions, to affirm that no Greek ever thought that ethics could be entirely kept out of art. Applied to literature, *sophrosyné* brings with it a hatred of excess in statement, in colour, in ornament. It is to be feared that on the whole the modern world rather likes plenty of colour and assertion. Why did the Greeks object to it? Because they thought it weakened the total effect of a work of art. It dissipated instead of concentrating the inward fire. It sacrificed the part to the whole. Classical art in the age when it most completely realised itself, the age of the Parthenon and the dramas of Sophocles, subordinates everything else to purity of form, to singleness of artistic purpose. That is classical art in its essence, as it is distinguished from romantic art—so far as the two can be distinguished—and from earlier and later stages of ancient art itself. For all ancient art is not in this restricted sense classical. Indeed when one looks closely one finds that the actual volume of ancient art which is thus classical is not very large. It is too difficult to produce for a great mass of it to be produced. But, however far short ancient writers and sculptors and architects might fall of the classical ideal, they never doubted that it was the ideal. For ourselves we may say that whoever understands it can understand the quality of Greek art; whoever does not, never will.

Creative Economy.

It was not arrived at in a flash of inspiration. No doubt it expressed a deep instinct of the Greek spirit, but it needed long and varied experiment to find it. When for instance pottery-any kind of pottery that can be recognised as distinctively Greek—appears in the Aegean world, its forms are heavy, thick, with a sort of honest but uncouth solidity about them, and they are covered, densely as a carpet, with geometrical patterns. Gradually the shapes become more slender and refined, the simple designs of line and circle give way to a new style of decoration inspired by Oriental art—zones of feeding or fighting animals, borders of lotus or palmette; there is a fairly lavish use of colour; and with this decoration the surface of every vessel is fully occupied. But as we approach the age of the Parthenon a revolution is accomplished. It may be seen in two directions. On one hand the vessels assume a perfection of form such as has never been surpassed or equalled. On the other hand the colour has gone. Nothing is laid upon the natural clay except a thin coat of black, broken by a single figure or group of figures in red, this red being nothing but the natural colour of the clay left untouched when the artist covered the rest of the vase with his black. Economy of means to obtain singleness of effect—that was the idea.

This development in a minor art is paralleled in literature, although it cannot be traced with such continuity there because so much of the evidence is fragmentary or missing. As we approach Aeschylus and Pindar however the evidence does become fuller. These two very great poets, belonging to the generation just before Sophocles, are not quite 'classical'. They are for instance, in the proper sense of the word, obscure; that is to say they often veil their meaning in allusive or highly figurative language. Aeschylus in much of his finest work is as labyrinthine as Shakespeare in his later manner; while Pindar is almost as rich in colour as Keats. But when we come to Sophocles we find him writing in a style that is almost crystalline in its absence of colour and, though exceedingly subtle, never cryptic, never deliberately obscure. Prose was later in developing and has a somewhat different history. But it moved in the same direction. If scarcely in the fifth century before Christ, which was that of Sophocles, at least in the fourth the 'classical' style prevails as much in prose as in verse. It has become the standard. Some applied it too rigidly, making their work thin and insipid; others applied it not rigidly enough, so that their work appeared florid and verbose. Like all ideals it could not be perfectly realised.

It is so important to grasp its real nature, and this has been so often misrepresented, that something more must be said on the subject. Perhaps the best way of making the issue clear is to bring Matthew Arnold in evidence, for Arnold was, in theory if not always in practice, the great champion of the classical style in literature. He commends it for its absence of 'caprice', of provinciality, of exaggeration—admirable qualities no doubt, but all negative. The result is that Arnold has given many readers the feeling that he regarded the classical style as above all the expression of good taste, which it would be vulgar or 'Philistine' not to admire. For this he is largely himself to blame, although it must be remembered that he thought the ancients were great masters of what he called the 'grand style', the merits of which he certainly did not consider to be purely negative. He nowhere distinguishes clearly between the styles and perhaps he is guilty of some confusion between them. At any rate some of the instances of the grand style which he quotes from the Greek are not instances of the classical style in its special and limited sense. Thus he regards Pindar as an eminent master of the grand style; but Pindar, as we noted, is not classical in the sense that Sophocles is. The general trend however of Arnold's criticism is clear enough. The ancients are better models for us to follow than the moderns with their vulgarity of taste and violence of assertion. To this must be added that the ancients, at least the best among them, are superior in what he calls the 'architectonics' of poetry. They do not sacrifice, as the moderns are apt to do, the whole to the parts, but in all their art they keep the end in view from the beginning.— Yes, it may be answered, but do they move us so profoundly? Because a work of art that fails to move us, however well-designed it may be, has not succeeded in its proper function. That Sophocles did move Arnold is certain; but he has hardly explained why. He does not make it clear enough that the sparing ornament, the economy of line, the logical form concentrate, or are meant to concentrate, the utmost intensity of fife and meaning. The important thing, if we are to write in the classical style, is not merely to employ these effects, but to employ them in the right way. It has to be confessed that in general English writers who have deliberately attempted the classical manner have failed to employ them in the right way. Hence a certain coldness or deadness in their work. There is nothing cold or dead about Sophocles or the Parthenon.

The Kinds of Art Forms

Another characteristic of ancient literature is the importance it attached to the 'kinds' (Latin genera, French *genres*). It was assumed that there were certain kinds of art-forms into which an artist was bound to cast his material according to the nature of his subject. These forms had been discovered by experiment, by lucky accident, by the instinct of genius; but they were not man-made; Nature herself had decreed their existence. They existed by themselves, they were limited in number, and they must not be confused or intermingled. For example, the epic is such a genre. It was not just invented out of his own head by Homer. He had, as the Greeks believed and we can see, a long line of predecessors. These had felt their way ever nearer to the perfect form of the epic, until at last came Homer and achieved it. Beyond that it was not possible or right to go; the character of the epic form had been fixed once for all. If a later poet wished to compose a narrative of a heroic story he had to do it in the Homeric manner or not at all. He must use all the 'epic machinery' of Homer, write in his metre, employ his very diction, though he might be writing a millennium after. Similarly Greek tragedy attained its full development in the fifth century B.C. upon the Attic stage. After that all through antiquity nothing was allowed to be a tragedy that was not constructed upon the Attic model. And so with the other genres.

The genres were not to be mixed. This is a cardinal point in ancient aesthetic theory, formally stated by Aristotle and steadily observed in practice. It is not observed in modern practice. It might even be said that modern literature takes a pleasure in mixing the kinds. We have 'dramatic lyrics' like Browning, and lyrical dramas like the *Prometheus Unbound* of Shelley. Fielding himself described *Joseph Andrews* as a prose epic. To a Greek that would seem a contradiction in terms. Is The Dynasts an epic or a drama or both? Examples might be multiplied. The Shakespearean drama is in this respect particularly instructive. On the Attic stage there was a rigorous distinction drawn between tragedy and comedy. Milton approved of this and condemned the 'error of intermixing comic stuff with tragic sadness and gravity, or introducing trivial or vulgar persons'. But he was too late. The thing had already been done and done too well—in *Hamlet* and *Macbeth* and elsewhere—to permit reversing the engines. For all that it is not certain that Milton (although his view was undoubtedly far too narrow) was entirely wrong, or that the Greek method of relieving the tragic tension by lyrical interludes was not artistically at least as sound as relieving it by broad comedy. The epithet 'broad' is not otiose. There is no objection to evanescent touches of humour even in the most sombre of Greek tragedies. And it is to be noted that Euripides, although the 'most tragic' of the dramatists, led the way to a kind of comedy, in which the happy ending comes only after scenes which threatened tragedy. A Greek would not have objected to a play for ever trembling on the verge of tears and laughter like *Twelfth Night* or *As You Like It.* At least he would not have objected to it on that ground, so long as it was called a comedy and not a tragedy. But even in a comedy he would have objected to the mixture of prose and verse.

Tradition in Ancient Art

The conception of a limited number of self-contained forms is naturally accompanied by a profound respect for tradition. Indeed the tradition is largely concerned in maintaining them. Here is another point of difference between ancient and modern. To the classical as to the mediaeval artist the tradition seemed of priceless value; his aim was to make use of it, to be in it, if possible to carry it a little farther. To break with the tradition merely for the sake of that gesture, in order to be thought original, would have seemed to him not so much wrong as foolish. Why should he throw away the instrument already made to his hand? He had no respect for 'originality' of that kind. And here no doubt he had much of the truth on his side, for true originality does not consist in breaking rules. It is a quality of the mind and will come out just as clearly in playing upon an old theme or an old instrument as upon a new one. There is no poet who is more traditional in his art than Milton, yet he exercises it in the highly original manner we call Miltonic. Take by way of contrast his younger contemporary Dryden. Dryden follows up most of the new experiments and tendencies of his age; but no one could say that his work has the intense idiosyncrasy of Milton's. So far then the ancients would appear to be right. It is a fair generalisation to make that the greatest poets, the modern as well as the ancient and mediaeval, have been entirely content, Shakespeare among them, to make all the use of the tradition they could. Yet it does not follow that everyone can use the tradition rightly.

It may save a second-rate man from disastrous failure; it will not save him from being dull. It was the dullness of the secondraters as much as anything that led to the 'Romantic' rebellion at the end of the eighteenth century. The inference is—and the ancients certainly drew it—that whoever is to follow the tradition successfully cannot dispense with originality. Rather he needs it more than another.

Where it was thought so important to cherish the traditional elements in literature, it was inevitable that literature itself should be regarded as the result of a continuous process. It was a tree continually putting forth new flowers and fruits, not a store to which you made contributions. Here again the ancients, and the mediaeval writers, who on this point were entirely in agreement with the ancients, were clearly right or at any rate more nearly right than we. The student of literary history must in any case adopt their conception, and it shall be adopted throughout this study.

Humanism

One other note of classical literature must be touched on—its almost exclusive concern with the human. *The proper study of Mankind is Man* is a very Greek, and for the matter of that a very Roman, sentiment. While other nations were preoccupied by considerations of God and the supernatural or by the beneficent or hostile aspects of nature, it was man himself that interested the Greeks. This may be seen as early as Homer. In the poetry of other peoples the further back we go, the more exclusively it seems to deal with supernatural beings and events; it is full of monsters and magic. Now it is true that in Homer there are frequent appearances of gods, there are even monsters and magic. But the gods look and behave like human beings, the monsters are as far as possible humanised, the magic is touched in very lightly. As the author of the *De Sublimitate* has said, in Homer the gods are men and the men are gods. As for monsters, one has only to think of the Cyclops in the *Odyssey*. For all his grotesque eye and his cannibalism he is so human that we understand and perhaps even sympathise with him. Circe is a goddess and a witch, but she looks and conducts herself like a woman, though a rather alarming one; the goddess Calypso is not even alarming. The world of Homer is as credible to the modern man as the world of Chaucer—which is saying a great deal. And Homer gives the note for later Greek literature. It is not that the Greeks had little sense of religion or small appreciation of nature, but they could not help relating all that they thought and felt and saw to the human thinker and observer. Accordingly nature is rarely if ever described for its own sake. There is nothing in ancient literature corresponding to the poetry of Wordsworth or even of Thomson. Nor has nature any of that power over the minds of Greek poets that the sea, for example, has over the minds of the Early English poets. The sea was just as familiar to the Greeks as to the tribes that invaded England, and they saw its beauty, but to them it was just the violetcoloured sea.

This 'humanism' of the Greeks entered into all their thinking and feeling, of which their literature is merely the expression. The saying of Protagoras 'Man is the measure of all things' might be taken as the text of all their philosophising. Their ethical systems all inculcate the importance of developing the personality. This side of the old Greek culture imposed itself almost irresistibly upon the men of the early Renaissance, particularly in Italy. But, as always happens, what was only one side was emphasised at the expense of others. The Greek ideal was never immoral or even non-moral. On the contrary it was recommended and pursued because in the Greek view it was especially moral. But it was readily misunderstood by men still under the influence of mediaeval Christian ethic, for it urged the equal and harmonious development of all the faculties of body and mind as well as of soul. It did not like Christian asceticism condemn the flesh. But it did condemn sensuality. What it particularly deplored and distrusted was excess, because that ruined the bodily instrument, on which as on a lyre we have to play. It does not do to stretch one chord to the breaking point and leave the rest unstrung. The Greeks would not sacrifice the body to the soul any more than the soul to the body; at least that was the normal Greek sentiment, although even antiquity had its puritans and ascetics. Let a man, they said, remember that he is a man, that is a compound of soul and body. And let him remember that he is a man among other men, a citizen of a city, nay a citizen of the world. He could not contract out of that double obligation. He could only perform his duty to himself by performing it to other people. If there was one character that the Greeks detested more than another it was the 'super-man'. They knew too much about him.

It may appear surprising that so much has been said in this chapter about the Greeks and so little about the Romans. The reasons for that however are simple enough. The Romans, although they made an immense and valuable contribution to ancient culture, were not originators. They were inheritors. To begin one's explanation with them would be to begin at the wrong end. It was the great historical role of the Roman people, so far as their literature was concerned, to act as transmitters of the Greek literary tradition to western Europe, in which capacity they will be found to occupy a large amount of our attention. But except in the limited field of verse satire we shall find that they had almost nothing of their own to give. They dealt best, as was natural, with whatever in the Greek tradition suited them best. They had little turn for speculation and none for science, in both of which the Greeks were eminent. On the other hand they were strongly interested in rhetoric and they acquired an astonishing mastery of that. Their finest work shows an exquisite sense of form. The notion, a good deal encouraged by the Romans themselves, that they were deficient in art but strong in the substance of what they had to say, is just the opposite of the truth. It was the Greeks who had something to say, not the Romans.—But in literature it is the form that remains, and it is the admirable form of Virgil and Horace, of Cicero and Tacitus that has kept and keeps them alive.

These then are the broad characteristics of classical literature. It is humanistic, with an especial value for the distinctively human faculty of reason; its sense of form is rather stronger than its sense of colour; it loves—not always, but in its finest expression—severe, pure, economic lines; it has a power of seeing both sides of a question, which has enabled it to invent a true form of drama, a true kind of history and philosophy; it respects tradition. We have now to pursue these general traits into their particular manifestations.

3

Chapter

Greek and English Tragedy

The right way to meet a great work of art is not to come with fixed expectations and demands of your own, but simply to listen and allow it to speak. And we believe that any sensitive person who comes to a Greek play with his imagination fairly alert and his mind ready to accept what is given him, will generally feel keen enjoyment in both the drama and the poetry. But the trouble is that we cannot rid ourselves of our preconceptions. We come full of expectation that it will be like Shakespeare or like Racine, or like church, or like some private *a priori* notion of what a Greek play ought to be, and when it proves different we are disappointed and spend our time in searching for something that is not there, and not observing what is.

We wish merely to discuss the first fundamental contrast between Greek and English tragedy, that the English tragedy is primarily an entertainment, the Greek a religious ritual. True, the entertainment has gradually become ennobled: its 'true intent' is for something higher than the mere 'delight' of the audience; and the religious ritual has been transformed by many influences, chiefly by the simple fact that it was conducted by born artists and watched by sensitive spectators, till it became also an artistic entertainment. But something of the origin remains.

We will take for granted a certain archaeological account of the birth and nature of Greek tragedy. Its details will be questioned by many scholars, but its broad outline admitted by almost all; and it is only the broad outline that matters for our present purpose. Fundamentally Tragedy was the mimetic dance of the Dionysus Religion developed and transfigured by certain influences that we shall consider later. It was a ritual dance, a *Drômenon*, or 'Thing Done', a *Sacer Ludus;* under slightly different circumstances it would have been a mystery.

It was a dance; not of course a dance like our dances, a mere gay movement of the feet. A primitive dance was the use of the whole body, the whole being, to express that overflow of dim thought or emotion which could not express itself in articulate speech. The dance is a rhythmical yearning of the whole body towards the emotion that we cannot define, the desire that is beyond our power to compass.

And it was the dance of the Dionysus Religion. What was that Religion? Let us not confuse the issue by asking 'Who was Dionysus?' To that question there is no answer, because of course there was no such person. Dionysus was a fiction, the ritual of Dionysus a reality – the reality in fact out of which the fiction was developed or projected. It is the ritual of the Spring, of the New Year, of '*le Renouveau*' – the Renewal after the dead winter of all the life of the world. Such rituals regularly generate out of themselves shadowy daimones or spirits or gods. This vegetation ritual is so widespread that the so-called 'vegetation-spirit' – the personified life of the world which fades, dies, and is reborn: the 'he' that we call 'it' when we say that 'it' is raining or fine or cold – has many different names and constitutes an element in innumerable worships. We have tried elsewhere to show how deeply the external form of Tragedy has been affected by the ritual of this worship and the recurrent life-history of this Year-spirit, who meets his enemy, dies, and is announced as dead, is wept for, rediscovered, and revived in glory.

Tragedy, then, is the dance of this religion of the Renouveau, developing under three main influences. First, like all Greek literature and art, it fell under the sway of the Epic, both the poems that we call 'Homer' and the lost poems that were so called in the sixth century B. C., an influence rich in legendary and romantic material, secular, aristocratic, and, as Eratosthenes observed, written for entertainment. Tragedy extended its subject-matter, beyond Dionysus or any mere Renouveau-spirit, first to other vegetation-heroes of divers sorts, then to all the heroes of Epic. A second influence came from the great figures or events of recent or contemporary history, provided only that they were sufficiently inspiring or 'tragic'. We must remember that there was then no distinction between history and myth: the death of Agamemnon was as much history as the defeat of Xerxes. But of course contemporary history seemed as a rule comparatively near to prose and unheroic; it needed tremendous events like the sack of Miletus or the repulse of Persia, or great permanent issues like the struggle against tyrants, to win their way into tragedy. Most of all tragedy was influenced, like other forms of art, by its own inherent nature. When you have once begun to act, and to act great themes of life and death, you cannot, if you are an artist, help moving in a particular direction. You are in the world of drama, and things that are dramatic will seize you and carry you along. Greek tragedy as we know it is drama, and intense drama. That indeed is obvious. The thing that we have to realize is that through it all there remains the spirit of the *Sacer Ludus*. It is drama, but it is also religion.

But, you will say, is this not playing with words? In what sense does this dance of Dionysus deserve the name of religion at all? It is a point that we must exert our imaginations a little to understand. We think of religion as something moralized; we have even had it defined, inadequately enough, as 'morality touched with emotion'. Now this religion of the Renouveau is not, in our sense of the word, much moralized, but it has at least this of religion about it: that it is always concerned with our relation to great world-forces. It brings human life into contact with something tremendous that is outside human life; it is a striving towards some sort of harmony of man with his whole unseen environment; it aims at that great prize, or great illusion, the being at peace with God. Further, if we would understand Dionysus-worship, we must realize that these vegetation-cults amid all their grossness were bound up with the things that are most beautiful in the world. It is true that there is little description of scenery in the literature of the ancient Greeks. They did not describe forests and mountains; they worshipped them and built temples in them. Their love for nature was that of the mountaineer or the seaman, who does not talk much about sea or mountain, but sickens and pines if he is taken away from them. And even the literature, if free from actual descriptions of scenery, is full of flowers and garlands, and shot through by the light of the stars and the moon – things that we have superseded and seldom even see, but that were familiar if half-divine companions to every Greek.

This religion had the element of beauty; it had also that of mystery. It was born of primitive wonder and desire, and it moved in a region which is still perhaps the most mysterious of all that are forced upon our daily attention, the region of growth and of renewed life. It had, lastly, what we are apt to forget, the element of peril, peril common to the whole community and ever recurrent. Even in the eighteenth century the ancient feeling about this might have been understood. Now, when the agriculture of the world is open and trade international, we have almost ceased to notice the harvests of the year in any particular place. But in early Greece every little community depended on the produce of its own small plot of land; its agriculture was timid and helpless; it had hungry and more or less hostile neighbours on every side; the autumn store of food was usually eaten before the next harvest. The poet Alcman, describing the seasons, mentions spring as the time 'when the world is budding but there is not enough to eat'. It is worth remembering, too, that primitive men draw no very clear line of demarcation between themselves and their animals and even vegetables, and Greek is full of words which can apply to all three, the thing that is common to them is that they are all young and all children of Earth the Mother. Every autumn these men would see the crops cut, the fields bare and hard, the trees without leaves, a dead world everywhere round them, and the year's stock of food beginning to dwindle inevitably away. Every winter one thought would be in all minds, the longing that the spirit, whoever he was, Dionysus, Osiris, Adonis, would be duly reborn and bring Sotôria – Deliverance, the dread that he might fail to return and the world remain dead. And probably every few years, if we knew the unwritten history of these centuries, we should find that for some little community the dead god did not rise again, and they would wait wondering, full of the sense of horrible and unpardoned sin, despairing or performing ghastly rites, waiting till famine finished them off, or their neighbours discovered that they were weak enough to be safely enslaved.

We must not forget, too, the personality, definite and almost human, of this Rebirth in the mind of primitive man. Primitive man needed so very little to create a person from; he needed no human shape, indeed no shape at all: that thing, whatever it was, that was in the new trees and flowers or the new vintage, that thing itself was a person – it might be Dionysus; it might be the Korê or Maiden – and, what is more, it was the same person who had been here at the beginning of last year and then had died. It was always a return, a rebirth. Just so the new generation of tribesmen were the old ancestors returned, safe from the keeping of Earth the ancient Life-giver. They looked forward normally not to some remote heaven, but to a cycle of life, death, and return from death, a return on which everything depended and for which the tribe prayed as their salvation.

There is obviously religion in this, and it is a religion that branches off into various other forms. For instance, tragedy is full of the religion of the Suppliant, the man or woman who is stricken down by the world and has no help left but prayer. This conception seems very probably to be somehow associated with the suffering and dying god. At any rate Greek tragedy is full of suppliant plays, or plays which at least centre upon some altar of refuge. There is perhaps no other single motive so prominent; and it is worth realizing that often when this power of the suppliant, this compulsion upon the most high gods to avenge the wrongs of the helpless, is not insisted upon, it is at least passionately denied. Tragedy is haunted by the atmosphere; for to cry bitterly that the sun will not turn back in heaven.

> *For the wrongs of man, the cry of his ailing tribes assembled, To do justice ere they die, is, as far as atmosphere goes, much the same thing as to assert that he will.*

And is the Year Ritual after all so non-moral? It looks so at first sight to one who comes to it with modern or Christian expectations. Things that seem to us gross and licentious are actually among its prescribed rites. Yet in reality it is moralized through and through, moralized to excess. The very things we complain of are proofs of this. The natural world is conceived throughout as framed on the same model as the human society, and responding to the same motives as the tribe itself. Consequently actions which in general tend to stimulate human fecundity are ritually desirable as increasing the fertility of the fields. On the other hand, offences against marriage laws and sexual taboos are severely punished: they will bring blight and famine. It is the same with greater issues. The whole process of nature was regarded as moral and human. When the summer was too hot or the winter too cold, it was 'injustice' and sure to be punished. Every year the Sun himself regularly committed 'Hubris', the sin of pride, and that pride was chastised by a proper fall. The early philosophers are full of this moralized physical science. 'The Sun shall not transgress his measures: if he does, he shall be pursued by Erinyes, ministers of Justice.' It is the law of all existing things: 'they all pay retribution for injustice one to another according to the ordinance of Time.' The life-history of each Year-Daemon was an example of this refluent balance. Each in his turn came as an avenger -or, what amounts to the same, as the wronged one re-risen; each slew the slayer, then waxed great in his pride and must in the end himself be slain. It was all as it should be, all as the eternal cycle had ordained. Conceptions like this are very clearly religious, and we all know their profound importance in Greek tragedy. They may almost be said to form the general ground-scheme on which each particular tragedy is built.

These considerations lead us straight to one great contrast. In all Greek tragedies, even those that are full of free thought, the whole permeating atmosphere is that of religion. What is it with us? The answer is not difficult. Our stage demands beautiful women as actresses; the shopwindows are filled with their portraits; our lighter and more popular stage lives by its sexual appeal. The Greeks had no women on the stage and their men wore masks, masks that never had aimed at being particularly beautiful, but were first magical, then sacred, and in the end at least a matter of dignified convention. The same lesson is taught by the almost invariable presence of a pair of lovers in all modern works of fiction. Our permeating atmosphere is that of love between the sexes. We are the descendants not of the tracedians but of the *scriptores erotici*. No doubt we have plays on the most varied subjects, plays of intrigue or adventure – subjects which are akin to romance and in which the love interest is generally strong – plays of war, of patriotism, of social reform. A few peculiar plays sometimes succeed in escaping altogether from the pervading atmosphere, but they only do so by a deliberate and anti-popular effort. Now of course the love motive occurs in Greek tragedy again and again: Euripides is predominantly interested in it; so do the motives of intrigue, adventure, or war; but observe in each case how it is coloured by religion. When we moderns introduce brave warriors we mostly think of them as winning or failing to win the love of fair ladies; when Aeschylus speaks of war he speaks like this: -he tells how the city-sacking hosts of Persia have thrown a path, and nailed it with many nails for a yoke upon the neck of the sea.

The fierce lord of multitudinous Asia driveth the flock that god hath given him forth over all the world; in his hard true captains he hath put his trust, the man like unto a god, of the seed of the shower of gold. His eyes shine dark with a bloody serpent's glare: with many hands and with many ships and the sweep of the chariots of Syria he bringeth down upon brave spearmen the bowman's battle that quelleth from afar.

Who shall be trusted to stem the great stream of men? Who with strong bars to prison the swell of the uncontrollable sea? For none may come near to the army of Persia; and courage is in the heart of her people.

For a doom from God hath prevailed from long ago, and hath laid for a charge upon the Persians the wars that strike at towers and the noise and gladness of battling horsemen and the turning of cities in the dust. And they have learned, when the wide sea grows grey with the wrath of the wind, they have learned to look upon the holy places of the deep, trusting in their cables subtly-built and engines that carry nations.

Yet the deep thought and the guile of God, what mortal man can hide therefrom? Who is he of the nimble foot, who is master of such light leaping? For with love and false smiling at the first Ate brings him to the net, whence it is not for mortal man to climb over and flee away.'

When our heroines die for love they do it in a personal and sentimental way, because their feelings are more than they can bear. When Phaedra dies for love it is in part a definite attempt to save her honour, in part almost a yielding of herself upon an altar.

Let me be To sate the Cyprian who is murdering me! To-day shall be her day; and, all strife past, Her bitter love shall quell me at the last.

And the temptress who leads her into her troubles has spoken very little about Phaedra's feelings: she has dwelt on love not as a personal emotion but as a world-power.

A most strong Goddess hath swept down on thee . . . She ranges with the stars of eve and morn; She wanders in the heaving of the sea; And all life lives from her.

Similar passages might be cited by the score. The rule is that in Greek tragedy every great emotion is treated as an instance of a world-force: its background and atmosphere are made by Religion.

Of course there is development in all art. We start here with a sacred ritual and we end with an exciting drama. The most essential part of the ritual is the dance, the collective or communal dance of a band of worshippers, and this actually survives throughout the whole growth of tragedy. But here, too, there is development, from the first stage of pure magic, where thirsty tribesmen dance the rain-dance to fill the wells, not thinking at all about their appearance, only straining every nerve to get water, to the last stage in which the accomplished professional dancer simply comes forward to exhibit his or her gracefulness. Neither of these extreme stages is found in Greek tragedy; tragedy moves somewhere between the two; and it is obviously somewhere between the two that the right artistic point lies. There is probably no extreme beauty in the first stage, except in fragments; and the last is, We think, clearly condemned by the mere directness of its attack. Any work of art which confessedly comes before us saying, 'Just look at me! See how beautiful I am!' must in some measure fail of its effect. For one thing, it utters a challenge and suggests a repulsion; for another, there seems to be almost a law that beauty should always be a bye-product, the mere result of doing a thing right or trying to express something as well as you can. In Greek tragedy one can see clearly the remains of the magic dances: there is a chorus in Aeschylus' *Suppliants* where the Danaids call upon the divine cow their ancestress and imitate the way she cropped flowers in a meadow (ll. 40 ff.); and the play ends with a lovely and almost undisguised rain-dance. In the *Oedipus Rex* the first chorus represents a magic dance, full of hoots and shouts, for driving away pestilence. The chorus in the *Medea*, on the other hand, has nothing magical about it:

its chief use is purely dramatic, to sympathize, to soften, to shed over the play its lyrical splendour, and at one supreme moment to beat vainly upon a barred door behind which a woman is murdering her child.

Tragedy developed, as we have said, under various influences. But most of all its own inherent instinct led it steadily in the direction of drama. It ceased merely to wail for a death and dance for a resurrection. It began to study character and human feeling: to think what sort of person died and what sort of person killed him, and why he did it, and how they both felt and what things they may be supposed to have said to express their feelings. It developed the interest in character as character and in situation as situation. Now the psychology of a divine being is almost inevitably monotonous and uninteresting. Consequently the stories were humanized. The old gods were made into human heroes. When we think of Agamemnon and Oedipus, of Clytemnestra and Phaedra, it is hard to realize that they were ever mere gods or daimones. Yet we know that they were. It is the hand of the dramatist that has drawn them down from heaven and made them living and human and full of character.

But here comes a remarkable fact. The instinct for drama is notoriously a dangerous guide. It leads most stage-writers to look out for the effect, not the truth; to write with a view to exciting or amusing the audience rather than expressing some real thing which they have to express. It leads to staginess, to the stage hero and heroine, the stage villain, to stage psychology in general. In Greek tragedy this kind of falseness is almost entirely absent. It has no utter villains, no insipidly angelic heroines. Even its tyrants have some touch of human nature about them: they have at least a case to state. Even its virgin-martyrs are not waxen images. The psychology is not the psychology of melodrama, specially contrived so as to lead to 'situations'. It is that of real human nature imaginatively observed or profoundly felt. Even if we leave Euripides out of account, what poet until quite modern times would have dared to make us sympathize with

Clytemnestra, the bloodstained adulteress, as Aeschylus does? Who would have dared, like Sophocles, to make Antigone speak cruelly to her devoted sister, or Electra, with all sympathies concentrated on her, behave like a wild beast and be disgusted at herself for so doing?

What makes this psychological sincerity the more striking is that it exists in the midst of such elaborate and severe convention, in such utter absence of realism. People sometimes suppose that a rigid convention implies insincerity, or, more absurd still, a slack and careless convention truthfulness. Consider George Meredith's sonnet-sequence, *Modern Love*; that is all written in a stiff sonnet-like convention, in verse, in rhymed verse, in verse that has to rhyme in a peculiar and elaborate manner. Yet the great quality of the poem is its subtle and sincere psychology. And take on the other side a sloppy melodramatic novel, in which the convention is as slack as can be, but the description of character may be quite false and 'conventional'. Convention in artistic form has nothing to do with conventionality of thought. The Greek poet when describing his heroine's state of mind may have to do so by putting into her lips a long formal speech on the subject, beginning – in the language of our translations – 'In the first place on the one hand . . .' That is a convention of form. But what she says in that set speech will be not only beautiful in thought and language, but curiously truthful also, instinct both with sympathy and with ruthlessness.

But we think you will find, if you compare the Greek drama with the modern, that while the false elements in modern plays are due to the amatory or romantic atmosphere and chiefly affect the character drawing, in Greek they are due to the religious and chiefly affect the background of the story. Almost all the recorded history of the past was, in the fifth centuryx, a tissue of myth and fable. The heroic saga, the normal stuff of tragedy, was all more or less supernatural; and the Greeks accepted, and even enjoyed, the intrusion of frankly supernatural beings, of oracles and *hieroi logoi*. Clytemnestra was the daughter of Leda, bride of the divine

Swan; her half-brothers were thoroughly miraculous demigods. Electra was betrothed in marriage to one of these demigods. Yet when you study the characters of Clytemnestra and Electra in all three tragedians you will find them both human and severely true.

Aristotle observes, in speaking of the gradual development of tragedy, that 'after passing through many changes it found its proper form and there stopped' (*Poet.* 49A 15). The words have a curious truth. Its 'proper form' was a very strange one, unlike that of any drama before or since. It never forgot its origin; it moved, as it were, in two planes, keeping always present, in the very heart of its action, the sacred Chorus of fifteen, shadowy persons, in part human creatures, in part incarnate shapes of meditation and emotion. It kept its gigantic masked figures, its long formal speeches, every speech beginning at the beginning of a verse and ending at the end of a verse. It kept its messengers, its prologues, and its divine epiphanies. And inside this grandiose shell it created a peculiar kind of beauty, a rhythm of high yet intoxicating emotion, a religious and poignant sincerity, which no other form of drama has quite attained. At one period indeed it looked as if tragedy was beginning to move away from its stiffness. When Sophocles reminds modern critics of Shakespeare it is in part because he began, very cautiously and delicately, to do to tragedy just what we ourselves, nourished on the Elizabethan tradition, would naturally do. We should cut down the formal speeches. We should not compel every speaker to finish his verse. We should unhesitatingly drop the god and the prologue and sometimes do without the messenger. As for the Chorus, since we do not know how to use it, we should cut it out altogether, or, if that were impossible, cut it down to narrow limits. We should work up the drama pure and simple and forget the fixed lines of the ritual. We should get rid of the monotonous shadow of death. We should intermix tragedy and comedy. We should aim at entertainment, at variety, not at worship.

There arose, after the fall of Tragedy, and of the old unmixed Comedy, a form of drama which did all these things. The New Comedy of Menander and his predecessors introduced all the simplifications and improvements which seem to a modern so obviously desirable. It developed an easy colloquial language, a flexible and unexacting metre. It left the Chorus quite outside the play, a kind of *entr'acte*, not worth writing down. It frankly abandoned religious ritual and heroic saga. It drew its material from the adventures and emotions of contemporary middle-class life, and boldly invented its own plots. And, as often happens in matters of this sort, Fate was ironical. Every single change seemed an obvious improvement and the total result was an incomparable loss. It led from the *Agamemnon* to the *Epitrepontes*.

When the end approached tragedy would make no compromise. It turned its face deliberately back towards its origin. Its last effort, the *Bacchae*, reads almost like a defiance. It is a play drawn upon the oldest and most rigid models; all about Dionysus, all supernatural, all charged with ritual and mystery. The speeches are long and formal, the scenes sharply disconnected. The prologue, the god, the two messengers are specially emphasized. Above all the Chorus is the most dominant, the loveliest, the most unearthly that had been seen on the Attic stage for some two generations. The whole atmosphere of the play is archaic; yet it was the last work of the last master of Attic tragedy, and he was dead when it was first acted. Its drama was not the drama desired or understood by the younger generations, yet when they looked at it they were fascinated. It sprang at once into fame and held the stage continuously to the end of antiquity, seeing other and easier forms of drama rise and triumph and at last fall, a thing never to be done again, scarcely to be understood, recognized as the last witness to a beauty of which the secret was lost and the ancient mould broken.

4
Chapter

Poetry

INTRODUCTION

We may now deal with the principal kinds or genres of classical literature in so far as they have influenced English literature. It is natural to begin with poetry and with the oldest poetical kind, which is the Epic. The Epic is Homer, that is to say the *Iliad* and the *Odyssey*, with whatever is akin to or modelled upon these. The many difficult questions suggested by the history of the Homeric poems do not concern us. It is Homer and not Homeric scholarship that has influenced later poetry. We are bound however to take notice of the fact—the most extraordinary and the most important in the whole history of European literature —that at the very threshold of this literature we encounter two poems of great length, which in perfection of style and mastery of design have never been excelled and rarely equalled. It is only a very simple-minded critic who could imagine that these astonishing masterpieces came into the world without ancestry. The art of Homer is not experimental but mature. Both his manner and his matter are traditional. That is the first point to observe; the second is this. Even if Homer as we now read him always existed in writing—a statement impossible perhaps to prove or disprove—his art can only be understood as a development of oral poetry. This is the same thing as saying that it cannot he understood apart from its audience.

It is only too easy for us to forget that the printed book did not exist until a few centuries ago. To say that after all it is only the manuscript stereotyped is not a helpful remark. The printing makes a great difference. For one thing all copies of a printed book are identical, but no two copies of a manuscript are the same. Hence a confusion of various readings and various spellings which vexes the text of all ancient and mediaeval books. With this uncertainty of the text goes a general disposition to think it does not matter. Only scholars verified their quotations, and popular misquotations often drove out the original reading. If it be true that the printed book is only the manuscript stereotyped, it is equally true that the manuscript is only the spoken word committed to writing. That at least may be said of ancient and mediaeval literature in general, and it may be said with particular confidence about Homer. Now in the days of the printing press an author can choose his own subject and treat it in his own way. He may not find—he may not even expect to find—more than a tiny minority of appreciative readers; but at least he has said his say and got it put on permanent record. His position would be totally different if he had, like Homer, to deal with an unlettered audience. If they do not wish to hear what he has to say, there is no appeal; his work perishes with him. In other words it is the audience that chooses the subject and even the general manner of treatment. Of course a minstrel of great power and boldness may win an audience to accept something Father different from what they have been accustomed to hear. If it were not so, progress in his art would be nearly impossible. But this does not alter the broad situation. Thus *Beowulf*came into existence because people wanted to hear about Beowulf and to have his story told much in that way. It is in a sense the result of a co-operation between poet and audience. And the same is true of the *Iliad* and the *Odyssey*.

We cannot say, although we can easily guess, why the tale of the wrath of Achilles and the tale of the return of

Odysseus made a special appeal to the Homeric audience. It is sufficient for us that they did so. It is understood by the poet and his auditors that these are old stories, although no doubt he hoped to tell them better than they had been told before. The style like the stories is traditional, and being traditional it is impersonal. This statement should not be misunderstood. No one denies, or at least ought to deny, that it is possible to use an impersonal style with personal mastery. Thus the ballad style is impersonal, but in *The Ancient Mariner* Coleridge uses it with personal mastery. We may say if we like that Homer raised the traditional epic style to a higher power by his individual genius. But it remains impersonal. This is a point of great importance as well as interest. For the style of Virgil, the style of Milton, the style of Tennyson in his *Morte d'Arthur* is very far from impersonal.

If it be asked how Homer produced this effect of impersonality, we may answer that it is by two principal means: a traditional poetic diction and an objective manner of narration. Let us consider the latter first. In telling his story Homer is not concerned to give his own point of view. His attitude is that of the monk in Scott.

I cannot tell how the truth may be;
I say the tale as 'twas said to me.

He was not engaged in introspection or self-analysis, knowing that it was not in him that his public was interested but in his story. There is no indication that Homer felt this to be in any way a check upon his inspiration. But this single-minded concentration upon the story makes Homer different from his great successors. Thus he has nothing like those passages in *Paradise Lost* in which Milton speaks of himself and which, however interesting they may be—and they are among the most moving in our literature—undoubtedly interrupt the flow of the narrative. In fact they tend to be more interesting than the narrative itself—which surely is a somewhat grave artistic fault. In Homer on the other hand the story is always predominant. Both listener and poet were equally lost in it, and the style is, by the listener at least, not thought of at all. This brings us to the first point, the Homeric style. In spite of what has been said let it not be supposed for a moment that it is artless. If it has a fault it is a certain overfacility, a tendency to let the enchanting diction run on without an adequate body of thought and feeling to express. There are perpetual epithets, ready-made phrases, even whole lines and passages at the disposal of the poet in the inexhaustible stock of his inherited material, and there is always the temptation to use them somewhat automatically. This is true of all traditional oral poetry-think of the Ballads—and is less true of Homer than of the rest. There is no poet, who has written so much, who has written so little that falls short of excellence. It is not that his style is at all an easy one to handle. No later Greek poet was able to recover its charm. The very metre is difficult. The technical accomplishment of Homer is one of the most astonishing things about him.

In Matthew Arnold *Lectures on Translating Homer* there is an admirable analysis of the Homeric poetry, of which he thinks the four cardinal qualities are these: plainness of thought, plainness of style, nobleness and rapidity. The reader will find there explanation and illustration of these points. But Arnold (as was somewhat his habit) is a little too absolute now and then in what he says, so that it is permissible to add some comments. Plainness of thought or directness, plainness or simplicity of style, are best considered together. They are natural in a poet addressing a simple audience—Arnold never thinks of the audience—and so not much need be said of them. There is in Homer little subordination of clauses—few complex sentences, if that is a clearer way of putting it—and almost no involution; one simple statement follows another, independently or in apposition. This of course is quite un-Virgilian and un-Miltonic. Efforts have been made in modern times, including a fine one by Arnold himself in *Balder Dead*, to reproduce this Homeric simplicity. But all are more or less self-conscious, which Homer never is. It is very difficult to be utterly simple in English poetry for more than a line or two without being silly or prosaic or both; but Homer does not find it difficult in his Greek. The fact is that he is not plain in the sense of eschewing all ornament; he is for example fond of decorative epithets. He can be simple and gorgeous at the same time, and that is hardly possible in modern English.

As for the rapidity of the Homeric style, it is certainly very notable in the Greek. In translation it is apt to disappear, or if not to disappear to lose volume, to do what it never does in Homer, degenerate into a mere gallop. Rapidity is a rarer quality in narrative poetry than might be expected. It is deplorably absent from the metrical romances in Middle English, and it is not conspicuous in such masters as Chaucer and Spenser. Much of the Homeric speed is clearly due to the majestic rush of his metre with its predominance of dactyls, its absence of eddy and recoil. But most of the effect is due to the imaginative excitement of the poet himself burning up his subject like a forest fire.

Then there is the nobleness. Homer according to Arnold writes always in the grand style. There has been a good deal of discussion as to what the grand style exactly is, but we have a fair enough idea of what Arnold means by it, and what he says about Homer's possession of it is substantially true. It is however a little misleading in so far as it suggests that Homer is always exerting his muse to the utmost, like Virgil or Dante or Milton. The truth is that, although he is never undignified, he is often familiar. He sometimes admits expressions which were excluded, as too colloquial, from the diction of Attic Tragedy. Like all good narrators he knows that he must not always be at the full stretch of his powers, but must reserve that for the great moments. It is largely because he did not know how to rise and fall with his subject that Milton can hardly be read continuously without fatigue. With this qualification however Arnold is quite right in stressing the pervading nobleness of the Homeric style. Of the four qualities he enumerates it is the most distinctive. It was Homer who decided once for all that an epic must be written in the grand style.

But at least as remarkable is the constructive art of Homer. It affords perhaps the conclusive argument against the view that Greek poetry began with the *Iliad*, for such art implies very extensive experiment. We will suppose that in Greek as in other languages the poetry about 'heroes', which ultimately developed into the Homeric epic, consisted of 'lays' of brief or moderate length; there is in fact evidence in Homer himself for the existence of such lays. Now the obvious thing for the poet to do who wanted to compose a poem of epic proportions would be to string a number of lays together on some principle of arrangement or none at all, like a jeweller making up a necklace. This in fact has been on the whole the general practice. It is the method followed by Hesiod, who was regarded by the ancients as more or less contemporary with Homer, although modern scholarship would place him later. It is the method of Ovid in his *Metamorphoses*, where story follows story for no better reason than that they all describe transformations. It was the method followed by the poets who wrote *Heracleids* (epics about Heracles), *Theseids* (epics about Theseus) and so on, who are criticised by Aristotle for thinking that their poems were artistic unities because they were all 'about one man'. Organic unity is not created by singleness of subject; it is something far more profound and vital.

This organic unity Homer produces by what is perhaps the only possible method. Choosing a central theme, he adds nothing but what naturally or necessarily leads up to that or flows from it. Thus the connexion is not merely apparent but real. The *Iliad* begins by stating its theme—the wrath of Achilles. Observe that Homer does not profess to sing about the Trojan War from its beginning to its end. Nor does he, like the poets whom Aristotle criticised, give us the lifehistory of his hero. With an art that can never be sufficiently admired he begins at a point in the middle or rather towards the end of the Trojan fighting. The poem opens with an account of the origin of Achilles' feud, which was his quarrel with Agamemnon, in consequence of which he withdraws from the war. Zeus, at the instance of Thetis the mother of Achilles, decides to avenge him. He persuades Agamemnon in a dream to lead out his forces to do battle with the Trojans. This battle lasts a long time with ups and downs of fortune until the Greeks are routed and driven back to their ships. Agamemnon then humbles his pride and offers to make restitution to Achilles. The offer is refused. After a night of contending emotions the fighting is renewed. The battle continues to go against the Greeks until at last Achilles, although he will not fight himself, gives permission to his friend Patroclus to do so. Patroclus, to whom Achilles has lent his splendid armour, drives back the Trojans, but is finally met and slain by Hector of Troy. This does at last arouse Achilles, who, clad in a new suit of armour made for him by the god Hephaestus, goes out to seek Hector, finds and kills him. The dead body he throws to the dogs in the Greek camp, but the gods preserve it from mutilation and decay until Priam, the old king of Troy, divinely encouraged makes bold to visit the slayer of his son and wins back from him the body of Hector, which is then solemnly burned amid the lamentations of the Trojans.

That is the barest outline of what happens in the *Iliad*. An outline but continuous, unbreakable, not a succession of independent or detachable happenings. It is what we now call a plot. Within this outline is massed an extraordinary profusion of relevant detail. There are no doubt what might be called digressions. But it will be found that these are not casually introduced. They help to build up that picture of the heroic world which must be given by the epic poet if his work is to have epic scope and significance. The wrath of Achilles would be a mere incident, the proper subject for a lay, if it were not framed in this larger setting.

The structural art—what Arnold calls the architectonics- of the *Odyssey* is even more remarkable. It is not like the *Iliad* concerned with a single episode, but with a series of episodes covering a period of ten years. The obvious way of dealing with these was to begin at the beginning and work through the events in their chronological order. But that, as we have seen, is the inorganic method, and the *Odyssey*, if it had been constructed on such a plan, would have resembled a metrical chronicle. What Homer actually did is so well described by Horace in a famous passage of the Ars Poetica (148), that his very words may be quoted. He is always pressing on to the final scene and whirls the listener into the heart of his story (in medias res) just as if the listener knew it all; leaving out what he has no hope of burnishing into splendour, and so employing his creative imagination, so mingling fancy and fact, that the beginning, the middle and the end of his tale are brought into harmony.

Everyone knows the story of the *Odyssey* and it cannot be repeated after Homer without annoying the reader. But some observations are permissible. The first few books set the stage for the return of the long-lost Odysseus to his native island of Ithaca. Then we embark on the last great adventure before he reaches home. He is shipwrecked and driven, alone and naked, upon the coast of Phaeaecia, where he is kindly received at the court of its king Alcinous. To appreciate what follows it must be remembered that it has always been a part of primitive hospitality not to press a stranger for his name and history until there has passed an interval, of hours or days or weeks, during which he is entertained. It would seem quite natural to Homer's audience, however odd it may seem to us, that Odysseus was so long a time eating and drinking at the expense of his host without mentioning who he was or what he wanted. The interval is very skilfully employed by the poet to heighten the suspense of the Phaeaecian audience, so that it is at its greatest when Odysseus begins to relate his adventures. This relation occupies four books (IX-XII) and is the most famous part of the *Odyssey*. It enables Homer to bring the whole story up to date in a highly compressed but extraordinarily vivid personal narrative, which omits, as Horace observed, whatever was comparatively uninteresting. This method of telling a story by introducing at appropriate moments a passage of retrospective narrative is a very great artistic invention. But it is enhanced by another, which may be equally effective, namely prospective narrative, which reveals what is to come.

A good example of this occurs in the eleventh book, where Odysseus consults the shade of the prophet Tiresias, who reveals to him certain events that lie hidden in the future. It is devices like these, all designed to heighten the suspense and interest of the story, which induce in an attentive reader some conception of the maturity and accomplishment of Homer's art. His successors can only imitate; they cannot improve.

In any account however succinct of the Homeric epic we must at least mention two elements which it possesses but are not found, at least in the same abundance and perfection, in any other narrative poetry not influenced by it. These are the Homeric epithet and the simile. Apart from merely traditional or 'stock' epithets, such as we find in the oral poetry of all peoples, there are others which often seem purely decorative, and are of an enchanting beauty; *rosy-fingered dawn* is a famous example. These are the specially Homeric epithets and they have been imitated, with varying success, ever since. The similes are even more characteristic. One calls them similes because they start at any rate from a point of resemblance. But they have a way (which only a pedant would object to) of wandering from the point. Here is an example, chosen for its brevity. Penelope opens a door which has been shut for a long time; when the key is applied the door *bellows like a bull feeding in a meadow.* The words *feeding in a meadow* are of course entirely irrelevant; they are added by the poet simply because his imagination has passed from the door to the bull, and he sees that bull feeding in a meadow. The similes of Homer are an exceedingly delightful part of his poetry, and as he scatters them in great profusion they give a wonderful richness of texture to his material, since he draws them from almost every part of ancient fife. They have been imitated of course by subsequent epic poets, by none more magnificently than by Milton, who has recently been criticised on the ground that his similes digress from the point. The same might be said of Virgil's similes. It simply means that Virgil and Milton knew their Homer, while the recent critic was ignorant of the epic tradition.

To trace the influence of Homer would be an endless task, but it is not difficult to recognise, for no literary kind except the Pastoral has maintained its conventions so steadily through the ages. Not but what it has admitted of important variations or developments. Much was done in this direction by Apollonius Rhodius, who about the beginning of the second century before Christ produced his *Argonautica* and provoked thereby a furious controversy in that very literary age. His subject was one of the great romantic stories of the world, the voyage of Jason in search of the Golden Fleece and the love that fell between him and Medea. Apollonius is an example of the *doctus poeta*, the poet who draws his matter and most of his inspiration from books. The type was common enough in that Alexandrine age to which he belonged.

Apollonius is a very unequal poet. He has little of Homer's narrative skill, and his style lacks freshness or natural charm, which is not surprising, because he writes not in the Greek of his own day but in the diction of Homer, which he has got by heart. But his services to literature are very great. He introduced into the epic psychological analysis, the epic heroine and the theme of romantic love. In all this Apollonius no doubt is less original than might appear. His psychology he learned in great measure from the Attic dramatists, especially Euripides. Where he was (so far as we know) original was in applying this psychology to the epic. The characters in Homer, both human and divine, are drawn with excellent clearness and naturalness. But they are drawn in outline. That is inevitable in oral traditional poetry, in which the characters acquire traditional, that is fixed, traits. There is nothing in Homer like the detailed study of a human soul in the grip of an overmastering passion that we find in the Medea of Apollonius. It may perhaps be questioned whether such minute and intimate psychology is not more appropriate to drama than the epic with its convention of heroic simplicity. But a poet is always justified in doing what he can do best, and that in the case of Apollonius was feminine psychology. It was a natural and almost automatic result that Medea became the central figure in his poem. She is the true heroine, although Jason is the nominal hero. The women in Homer are all secondary, even Penelope, and never impassioned. A woman like the Medea of Apollonius was an innovation. Here again he pretty certainly got his cue from Euripides, who in certain of his plays, such as the *Medea* and the *Hippolytus*, had treated the tragic love of a woman for a man with singular power and sympathy. There is a passage in Plato in which he argues that 'a woman in love' is an impossible subject for the nobler kinds of literature. By the time of Apollonius no doubt feeling on this point had changed or begun to change. For all that it needed a certain boldness to give so important a place to love in an epic poem, and to make the 'woman in love', what in effect she is, the central figure in it. The results have been remarkable, not so much perhaps directly as indirectly through the Dido of Virgil, who is confessedly modelled upon the Medea of Apollonius.

This brings us to the *Aeneid*, which in its influence upon English literature far excels Homer or any Greek poet. But, since the *Aeneid* in its turn is under an immense debt to Homer and Apollonius, much that has been said of them need not be repeated of Virgil. It is more illuminating to remark the differences. Thus the *Aeneid* is a national epic but not in the same sense as the *Iliad*. The *Iliad* is history, the *Aeneid* is fiction; or to put it in a less controversial way, the *Iliad* deals with a living tradition, the *Aeneid* with a dead or moribund past. The world of Homer is (no doubt with some touches of conscious archaism) the existing world of himself and his audience; the world of Virgil exists in his imagination. How then can the *Aeneid* be a national epic? Because it is the projection into an ideal past of what Virgil believes Rome might and ought to be—perhaps believed to some extent that it really once had been. Into the framework of Aeneas's wanderings the poet contrives to pack all the treasures of his lore, the result not merely of his reading—for Virgil is eminently the *doctus poeta*—but of his love and knowledge of Italy'. It is in this sense that the *Aeneid* is a national epic.

Virgil

Virgil has mastered the secrets of Homer's constructive art and employs them in his own poem, a little mechanically perhaps but with fine effect. It has been said that the first half of the *Aeneid* is modelled upon the *Odyssey* and the second half upon the *Iliad*. This is only broadly true, but it is true enough to be worth remarking. The poem begins like the *Odyssey* in the middle of the action. Aeneas is shipwrecked on the coast of Carthage as *Odysseus* is shipwrecked on the coast of Phaeaecia. He is entertained by Dido as *Odysseus* is entertained by Alcinous; and, as *Odysseus* at the Phaeaecian court, so Aeneas at the Carthaginian relates the story of his past adventures. That brings us to the fourth book, but this, which tells of the fatal love of Dido, is based not on Homer but on Apollonius. The fifth book, containing the funeral games in honour of *Anchises*, is imitated not from the *Odyssey* but from the twenty-third book of the *Iliad*. The sixth book reverts to the *Odyssey* and is suggested by, one cannot say modelled upon, the eleventh book in the Homeric poem. The seventh book of the *Aeneid* brings the hero to Italy, and thenceforward it is chiefly the *Iliad* that is Virgil's model. This suggests a somewhat crowded and involved composition, especially when one remembers that the *Aeneid* is not so long a poem as the *Odyssey*, let alone the *Iliad*. Yet the story is not difficult to follow and it would seem that Virgil has not quite had the credit due to him for conducting it so skilfully. If it is not so interesting as it might be, that is due to another cause.

That cause is the hero. The *Aeneid* is a poem with a purpose —the justification of the Roman imperium—and it has not escaped the fate that dogs poems with a purpose. It was essential for it, or so Virgil thought, that its hero should be the embodiment of all the public and private virtues. The consequence is that Aeneas is not a man but a paragon, in whom nobody can take any real interest because nobody can really believe in his existence. It is different with Odysseus, who is a credible human being, whose behaviour is not always defensible. This central weakness in the *Aeneid* gives a certain unreality even to the most impassioned episodes. We believe that Dido was in love with *Aeneas*, but not that Aeneas was in love with Di'do, and it is this, not his leaving her, that damages him with readers. In the same way one's sympathy is apt to pass from Aeneas to Tumus, who was at least in love with Lavinia, while Aeneas has no feeling for her one way or the other. It was fortunate perhaps for MIton that the notion derived from the *Aeneid* and strongly urged in his time by Rymer and others, that the epic hero must be a perfect being, could not be applied in *Paradise Lost* from the very nature of its subject.

The desertion of Dido was brought about by the intervention of the gods. This invites us to say a little about 'epic machinery', which mainly consists in such intervention. That gods as well as men did battle about the walls of Troy was doubtless part of the tradition received by Homer, and he makes use of it to obtain certain effects which are of great importance to him. It would be interesting to study these in detail, but one can only say here that when a god intervenes in Homer it is either to create a dramatic situation or to break an impasse. More than that, the plan or purpose of the gods, especially of course the supreme god Zeus, is of immense value to Homer as giving unity and direction to the whole action. Virgil sees these advantages and employs them freely. But here again there is an important difference. To Homer and his audience it seemed quite natural that the gods should intervene in human affairs. But in Virgil's day men had ceased to believe such things. So what in Homer is at worst a convention is in Virgil little better than an artifice. This then is another source of unreality in the *Aneid*. It must be remembered however that it is no objection to a poet that he is dealing with incredible things, if he can make them seem credible. It is a question how far in this particular business of divine intervention Virgil succeeds in producing that suspension of disbelief which Coleridge desiderates in poetry. The divine interventions in *Paradise Lost* were justified to Nfilton and his contemporaries by what they read in the Bible. He is therefore with Homer in this matter and not with

Virgil, though he certainly learned much about the use of epic machinery from the *Aeneid.*

It was the element of conventionality or overhterariness in the *Aeneid* which led to a reaction against it towards the end of the eighteenth century when the claims of a more 'natural' kind of epic, which Homer was taken to represent, were asserted against Virgil. There was some prejudice and much misconception in the attacks then made, although it is hard to believe that Virgil will ever again be placed on a level with Homer. The danger now is that he may be underestimated. We find Coleridge for instance saying 'If you take from Virgil his diction and metre, what do you leave him?' One feels the temptation to retort 'If you take from *Kubla Khan* its diction and metre, what have you left?' But a mere *tu quoque* is not an answer to criticism and it is at least worth while considering what Coleridge meant. If he wished to deny to Virgil the possession of any native force of thought, passion or imagination, he was almost demonstrably wrong. But so far as he meant that the great source of Virgil's power as a poet lay in his use of language and metre, he was unquestionably right.

The appreciation of Virgil's style is the last fruit of Latin scholarship, and this makes it next to impossible to describe to the ordinary English reader in what its charm consists. But some points may be noted. He constantly uses words with a slight strain or rather extension of their meaning so as to get a new value out of them—a thing most dangerous to do unless you know exactly how far you may go. Then he uses language to suggest one meaning behind or beneath another. Shakespeare says of daffodils that they *take the winds of March with beauty.* Consider how much meaning or suggestion lies in the single word take. It is words of that kind that Virgil is always seeking and often finding. Then he understands, as hardly any other poet has done, that diction and metre are indissoluble. Coleridge, who was always interested in metre, may have observed this. Not every critic does. For instance in the sixth book of the *Aeneid,* in the passage where Aeneas plucks the Golden Bough, almost every editor is distressed by the word *cunctantem*, 'lingering', because the Sibyl has recently told *Aeneas* that the branch will come away easily in his hand, which is incompatible with 'lingering' or 'reluctant'.

Virgil has absolute mastery of the verse-paragraph, complete in itself and so constructed that the beginning looks forward to the end, and the end looks back to the beginning. The reader has not only to keep the meaning of the often long and complex sentences in mind, but his ear has to follow the metrical scheme which accompanies the meaning. This leads the poet to use *enjambement*—the overflow of one line into the next—to an extent and with a variety quite foreign to Homer. He checks the too rapid flow of the dactyls by a very free use of spondees and elision. The result is an altogether different movement from that of Homeric verse and a verbal music that no other poet in antiquity has altogether equalled.

But no style is perfect, and that of Virgil is to a certain extent marred by too conscious a rhetoric. The Latin races rather expect a man under the pressure of a strong emotion to employ, consciously or not, the arts of the orator. Apart from this consideration there is another and special one. The epic style can hardly avoid being at least tinged with rhetoric. For the epic began as oral literature, and after it had ceased to be this the convention remained that the poet was addressing a listening multitude. That accounts for the fact that Virgil's style—and the same may be said of Milton's—is fundamentally oratorical. One can hardly blame either for that, especially when the results were so magnificent. But rhetoric is always a dangerous element in poetry. It may seem to us, though perhaps it would not to an Italian or an Elizabethan Englishman, that Dido's agony would be more moving if she were less well equipped with the weapons of the public speaker. It is certain that in some places, where he is trying as it were to go one better than Homer, Virgil falls into bombast. For all that he is one of the most perfect of poets, and his style one of the most wonderful achievements of ancient art. That style was his great contribution to literature; the decisive proof of his originality.

Lucan and Statius

Of Virgil's successors in Latin epic poetry little can here be said; but the influence of at least two of these, Lucan and Statius, has been such that they cannot be passed over in silence. Lucan, who died at the same age as Keats, left behind him a poem, about half as long as the *Aeneid*, to which was given the title of *Pharsalia*. It may or may not be the work of a true poet; the intellectual power of it, the brilliance and force of the rhetoric, are undeniable, and remarkable in so young a man. It shows besides a considerable degree of originality. Lucan takes a subject—the civil war between Pompey and Caesar—from recent and documented history, and he gives it a modern treatment. He felt that it would be absurd to represent the gods as personally intervening in the affairs of Julius Caesar. So he leaves them out. Even his style is totally unlike that of Virgil, although naturally he has some echoes or reminiscences. It is rhetorical through and through, sometimes quite silly, sometimes rather sublime; a restless, brilliant style, over-strained, over-coloured, over-emphatic. Its showy qualities made a strong appeal to ages with a taste for them and led in these to an overvaluation of Lucan, just as he is now probably a good deal undervalued. For his poem is at least alive, which is more than can be said of most second-rate epics. It is more than can be said for instance of the *Thebais* of Statius, which is a long epic on the subject of the Seven against Thebes. Statius, who wrote in the generation after Lucan, had a slender vein of genuine poetic feeling. But it is not apparent in the *Thebais*. With obvious sincerity he professed himself a humble follower of Virgil, but his work is not at all Virgilian. It is full of pedantry and empty rhetoric, at once noisy and tiresome. The *Pharsalia* does offer a 'criticism of life'. however crude, and Lucan has a real, if somewhat Macaulayish, grasp of human character. But the persons in the *Thebais* are like phantoms gesticulating in a dream. How then was it that the Middle Ages loved the poem, almost more than the *Aeneid* itself? It was because of the story, which is full of 'strong' situations, of gigantic warriors and horrific witches. The improbabilities did not disturb the Middle Ages, which were ready to believe anything in that line, especially if it had ancient authority behind it. What they took they transformed, so that for instance the Knight's Tale in Chaucer, which comes through Boccaccio from the *Thebais*, is full of truth and humanity. Yet the fact remains that Statius furnished the story, and we must recognise in him one of the main sources of mediaeval poetic lore.

The Didactic Epic

The Homeric epic was not the only sort invented by the Greeks. They produced another, usually called the 'didactic' epic. Its reputed founder Hesiod employs a diction from which the freshness and vigour of Homer have largely departed, but which otherwise is Homeric, and this consideration has convinced most scholars that Hesiod must have been a good deal the later of the two. We cannot involve ourselves in that uncertainty or in the other, how much of the poetry attributed to him by the ancients was authentically his. In effect we are concerned mainly with the *Works and Days*, and it so happens that the authenticity of the *Works and Days* has hardly been seriously questioned. It consists in the main of instructions and advice to small farmers, but does not confine itself to agriculture, having a good deal to say about lucky and unlucky days. It will be seen at once that Hesiod is content with a subject of a much humbler and, if you like, more prosaic order than Homer's; it must be added that, compared with Homer, he was a comparatively humble bard. Nevertheless he has great merits even as a poet, while his subject, with the light it throws upon rural life in early Greece, has rather gained than lost interest by the lapse of time. In the Alexandrine age, when poets had more learning than invention, it became a literary fashion to compose didactic epics on a great variety of subjects. The fashion spread to Rome. Virgil himself was so far influenced by it as to write his *Georgics*, which acknowledges the *Works and Days* as its exemplar. No doubt the poet had in his mind a great deal more than advice upon the raising of crops and of cattle, the keeping of vines and bees. The *Georgics* carried also an exhortation to a simpler, more hard-working, more patriotic fife than was common then in Italy. That does not prevent it from being in form a didactic epic. It showed what could be done in this genre by one of the supreme artists in language. Some good judges, including Dryden, have considered the *Georgics* a finer work than the *Aeneid.* It is a more finished work, not a finer; but the mere fact that the comparison could be made shows how great is the attraction of the *Georgics.* In England the attraction was most deeply felt in the eighteenth century; but it was felt both earlier and later.

Ovid

But in influence if not in merit the great poet of the didactic tradition was Ovid. His most important work, the *Metamorphoses,* is an epic of the Hesiodic type as revived by the Greek poets of the Alexandrine school. In this case however the original model is not the *Works and Days,* but other parts of the Hegiodic corpus which may be described as versified catalogues. The English reader will get a fair notion of them from the *Legende of Good Women* and the Monk's Tale in Chaucer. The *Metamorphoses* is very long—there are fifteen books of it—and in the course of it a very large number of stories tell how this or that god or man was transformed into this or that beast or bird or flower. It is proper to add in this place certain other works of Ovid, especially the *Art of Love (Ars Amatoria),* the title of which sufficiently describes it, and the Fasti, which gives an account of the numerous festivals of the Roman year together with the legends of their origins. It is true that these poems are not epics, and are written in a different metre and style from the Metamorphoses. But they are at least equally didactic, and to make a separate section of them would not help the student at all. The important matter to understand is the didacticism, which is a very different thing in Ovid from what it is in the *Works and Days* or even in the *Georgics.* For the real purpose, not only of the *Art of Love* but of the *Fasti* and the *Metamorphoses,* was not to give information but the pleasure of good writing and the amusement of wit.

The influence which Ovid has exercised upon European literature is quite disproportionate to his present fame. As his name will be found recurring frequently, and not merely in connexion with his didactic or pseudo-didactic poetry, we may restrict ourselves here to a few general observations. The first has regard to his subjects. Whatever one may think of his treatment of them, one can hardly deny that Ovid deals with interesting matters. This will only be doubted by those who have not read him. The *Metamorphoses* is a treasure house of 'Greek mythology', and Keats is not alone in thinking that a poet could not have more delightful material. The Fasti, a poetical calendar, sounds as if it might be dull. It is very far from that, partly because of the quaintness of its antiquarian lore, chiefly because like the Metamorphores it is full of stories delightfully told. But the extraordinary prestige and popularity of Ovid in the Middle Ages was due not only to the stories and his skill in narration, but to the fact that his poetry is as easy as it is possible for artistically wrought Latin to be. Virgil was revered as the prince of poets because the ancients had insisted that he was such, but he was more revered than understood. It is obvious from the Divina Commedia that Dante himself did not always understand him. But Ovid could always be understood, at least well enough to follow his stories. It was these the Middle Ages fell in love with, not so much for their telling, wherein Ovid, admirable though he be, had nothing to teach them, as for their matter, which they took as we say for gospel. That Ovid no more believed his own stories than did Keats or Morris—rather less in a way, for Keats and Morris at least treated them seriously-never occurred to the Middle Ages. To them they were true stories and Ovid an almost sacred authority. This explains their regard for the Art of Love, which is just a *jeu d'esprit*, but was accepted by them as a dissertation by one of the Masters upon a subject which they invested with a mystical significance that would have seemed very odd to the Roman wit. To the men of the Renaissance on the contrary Ovid was the typical 'pagan' author, delightfully amoral, the poet of the senses, the lover of the physically beautiful. But there is more to say than that. They appreciated, as the Middle Ages had never quite had the scholarship to do, the brilliance of Ovid's style. This enchanted them and set them all busily imitating it.

Of this style, because of the influence it once had, it is necessary to say something. There is no denying its brilliance, its almost incredible deftness and resourcefulness. Moreover it is rarely or never fatiguing, as brilliance sometimes is; Ovid is one of the most 'amusing' of poets. The 'wit' for which he was famous in the seventeenth and eighteenth centuries does not appeal to us as much as it did to them, but that is a matter of taste. It is certain that he has wit in almost all the senses of that long-historied word, and this may keep his fame alive as it has kept alive the fame of Pope. His style no doubt has serious faults. It is too facile, too voluble, too evidently delighted with its own ingenuity; it is not a style in which the greatest poetry could be written. But it does what it sets out to do with inimitable ease and grace. It is not to be sure a natural, it is an acquired and studied grace, but this makes it the easier to imitate. His rhetorical and metrical devices can all be reproduced by any competent craftsman, and perhaps no poet, certainly no ancient poet, has been so effective an instructor in the technique of verse. He taught the Latin poets of the Renaissance and they, more than is perhaps generally recognised, taught the rest.

Tragedy

Anyone who looks at an ancient tragedy is at once struck by its differences from tragedy of the Shakespearean type. It is much shorter; it has never more than three characters speaking in one scene; it has never any admixture of prose; it has never any admixture of comedy; above all it has a Chorus, at regular intervals chanting elaborate odes. The impression is of something highly formal, conventional, almost ritualistic. And this impression seems to be confirmed when one begins to read and thereby to discover that every character speaks in a diction as majestic and remote from ordinary conversation as that of Paradise Lost. All this makes it difficult for the modern reader to understand what the ancient dramatist was about. At least it is difficult without some preliminary explanation.

The differences we have mentioned—and we have not mentioned them all—are due in the main to Greek religious conservatism. If this appears an odd remark, we may remember that for the ancient Greek art and religion went together; so that it comes to much the same thing if we say that the differences are due to, artistic conservatism. This however applies only to the form of ancient drama—its structure and style. It does not apply to the thought that informs it. That is bold, progressive and daring to an extraordinary degree. The thought of Euripides for example is often—not always, and this makes him the more interesting—more 'advanced', more disturbing to accepted views, not merely than Shakespeare's but than Ibsen's or Shaw's. But at present we are concerned with the form.

Attic tragedy, the origin and model of all ancient tragedy, began in a particular ceremony or ritual in the worship of the god Dionysus. The evidence is scanty and hard to interpret, but it strongly suggests that this ceremony was a representation of the death, resurrection and apotheosis of the god. If this be so, it will be observed that Greek tragedy preserves only the first stage of the complete original performance. We must suppose that Greek artistic feeling came to revolt against the breakdown of a solemn lament into clownish and probably indecent buffoonery, and developed the lament by itself. What was the nature of this lament? The question can be answered more definitely then might have been expected. It was a choral performance of a special kind—the old Greek name for it was a *molpé*—and its business was to 'imitate', that is to re-enact the thing lamented, which was the death of some god or hero, originally, we must believe, Dionysus himself. The student must of course keep it clear in his mind that we are not yet speaking of Greek tragedy in the developed form in which we know it, but merely of the performance out of which it grew. But it is necessary to have some idea of this performance if we are to understand the nature of the finished product.

A *molpé* is performed by a company, called in Greek a Chorus, of persons who sing and dance to the accompaniment of some music, of the harp or the flute, in the case of the tragic *molpé* the flute. Neither the singing nor the dancing had a very strong resemblance to what we now regard as such. The emphasis of the singing was on rhythm without melody, while the dancing was largely a matter of gesture and formal movement, and must often have resembled a highly conventional style of acting. In any case the dancing was dramatic or, as the Greeks said, imitative—a fact to remember when the student of Aristotle finds the critic describing poetry as a form of imitation. Here then we have three points, all of essential importance, established about the tragic *molpé*: (a) it was choral (b) it was dramatic (c) it bore a religious character. Greek tragedy retained those features to the last, although their relative importance changed. The dramatic element gained at the expense of the others; but it never destroyed or came near to destroying them. The Chorus is always an essential feature of ancient Greek tragedy; and always there is the sense of a solemn occasion. This is not the place to describe, even if we knew more about it than we do, how the dramatic element gradually obtained the predominance. Perhaps it is enough to say this. It is almost a regular feature in a singing and dancing company of the kind we have been considering that there should be a passage of question and answer designed to explain more clearly the nature of the performance. This comes out strikingly in the ritual play from which sprang the mediaeval drama. Something of the sort can be assumed to have been normal in the original Greek ritual, and it explains why *hypocritês*, the Greek word for an actor, means in the first place an 'answerer'. No doubt the leader of the Chorus was the first 'answerer', the Chorus putting the questions. Sooner or later the idea suggested itself of having a second actor, and this step was the easier to take because a Greek Chorus had a natural tendency to break up into semi-choruses, each of which would have its own leader. Two actors are the minimum, but they are an adequate minimum, for a true drama. It was some time before a third actor was added, but with that addition Attic tragedy remained content.

The subjects were regularly drawn from the legendary past; especially that part of it which recounted the fortunes of the House of Atreus and the House of Labdacus. To the former belonged Agamemnon and his queen Clytemnestra, their son Orestes and their daughters Iphigenia and Electra; to the latter belonged Oedipus and Jocasta, with their sons Eteocles and Polynices, and their daughter Antigone. Almost equally important was the House of Priam, with the Trojan cycle of legends told about him, his queen Hecuba, and their descendants. No doubt the tragic poets often went outside these three cycles for their subjects, but there was a marked tendency to keep to them. Aristotle, observing this, approved of it on the ground that the number of subjects meet for tragedy was severely limited. He had in mind two conditions: first, the subject should be drawn from the heroic past; secondly, it should be familiar to the audience. These would seem to the modern dramatist not advantages but serious disadvantages. His aim therefore, at least his method, must be different from that of the ancient dramatist. The difference may be expressed in this way. The modern method is to work upon the ignorance of the audience, the ancient was to work upon its knowledge of the story. We need not discuss which is the better, that is the more dramatically effective, method; but we ought to note the difference, because the failure to understand or apply the Greek method is what is chiefly responsible for the lack of dramatic interest in Samson Agonistes and other English attempts to compose tragedies upon the Greek model. In the typical Attic tragedy the hero walks unconsciously to his doom, the audience watching him in helpless foreknowledge. The art of the dramatist is employed in arousing and maintaining this suspense—this waiting for the blow to fall without knowing just when it will fall—until in Aristotle's phrase the soul of the spectator is purged by pity and terror. Nor is it simply a matter of stage-craft; the effect is enhanced by the language of the speakers. To take a simple example, in the Oedipus Rex of Sophocles the hero is known by the audience to be the son and unwitting slayer of his father; it knows also that this will come to light and that in consequence he will fall under a terrible curse. Sophocles makes a scene in which the hero pronounces upon the murderer of his father a curse, every word of which, the audience realise with a shudder, will be fulfilled upon Oedipus himself. That doubles and more than doubles the impression that would be made by the curse upon an audience that was not in the secret. It is by such arts that the ancient dramatist works upon the knowledge of the spectators. And that is why the old tragic legends were so useful, for they were at once familiar and removed from contemporary history, which could not be treated in such a way without becoming too painful for art.

But to look merely at the differences between modern and ancient drama is to get a one-sided view. There are remarkable and significant resemblances between Attic and Shakespearean tragedy. Take this matter of tragic irony as it was produced by the Greek tragedians in the manner we have been describing. It is employed by Shakespeare too. Thus in Macbeth he takes occasion at the very beginning of the play to bring in the witches, who prophesy all that is to befall Macbeth in the sequel. The story was not, like that of Hamlet, already familiar to Shakespeare's audience, and so he makes a point of telling them beforehand what it is. And, as one prophecy after another is fulfilled in the course of the action, the artistic purpose becomes plain. The audience has been moved from the state of mind in which it would simply have wondered what next would happen to that in which it watches, a man struggling vainly in a net of destiny. In other words the dramatic interest is not in what will happen but in how it will happen; and this is exactly the dramatic interest of the Oedipus Rex or the Agamemnon. The same may be said of Hamlet. There is no doubt that Hamlet will kill and be killed. But how and where? From this it will be seen how mistaken is the view of those who think Hamlet's delays are undramatic. They are on the contrary the very thing that makes the suspense almost unbearable.

There are other similarities due in the main to resemblances in the structure of the Greek and the Elizabethan theatre. Neither had any scenery worth mentioning; neither possessed a drop-curtain. The first deficiency made it necessary for Shakespeare as for the Greeks to indicate the scene of the action by allusions or even set descriptions put in the mouths of the persons of the play. The second deficiency raised technical problems of a kind that may be illustrated by an example. In the Ajax of Sophocies, where (by a remarkable exception to the Lireek rule) the hero kills himself upon the stage, the dramatist contrives a scene in which the body is carried off to honourable burial. The same situation is found at the end of Hamlet, and the problem is solved in the same way. Shakespeare is not here imitating Sophocles, of whom he knew nothing, but adopting like his predecessor an obvious way of getting the corpse removed from the stage. The modern dramatist lowers the curtain—an easy device, which has done more harm than good to dramatic poetry. The particular difficulty in the Ajax is normally resolved in Attic tragedy by having the death of the hero reported by a messenger instead of enacted before the audience. The method is adopted once at least by Shakespeare, in Macbeth, where the killing of Duncan occurs off the stage. Many critics have thought the scene between Macbeth and Lady Macbeth when the deed is doing or done the most powerful even in Shakespeare. At any rate it is a complete refutation of the notion that a death that is unseen is necessarily less dramatic than one that is thrust upon the eyes. Consider how much more disturbing is the reported murder of Duncan than the public murder of Julius Caesar in Shakespeare's play. It will be seen that the Greek dramatists knew their business.

Seneca

It has sometimes been thought that there must have been some direct influence upon Shakespeare from the Greeks.

That is excessively improbable. Indirect influence is another matter. This came, so far as tragedy is concerned, through the Roman poet Seneca. He was a very distinguished person in more ways than one; but we are not here concerned with his political career or with any of his voluminous writings except some eight or nine tragedies written in his youth, at least with all the marks of youth upon them. They were hardly meant for the stage, but most probably were composed with an eye partly to future readers and partly to their representation in some large Roman house in what used to be called Sprivate theatricals'. The subjects were all drawn from the Attic tragedians, chiefly Euripides, who ever since his death four centuries and a half before had been by far the most popular and influential of the Greek tragic dramatists. The plays of Seneca are not translations, and he writes freely enough out of his own mind. But if they are not translations they are imitations. In other words the Senecan drama is just Greek drama in a Latin dress. That is why we must begin our study of him with the Greeks.

The faults of the Senecan tragedies are gross and palpable. They are full of blood, cruelty, natural, unnatural and supernatural horrors. There is hardly any truth to fife either in the incidents or in the character-drawing, and there is a great deal of rant and bombast in the style. These vices reappear in the 'Senecan' plays of the Elizabethan theatre, such as Titus Andronicus, and the result has been a tendency to regard the influence of Seneca upon English drama as mainly if not wholly bad. But there are things to be said in palliation and even in commendation. It might indeed be argued that it did not need a Roman playwright to make the groundlings of an Elizabethan theatre fond of melodramatic horrors; they had that taste already. But that, while it mitigates the effects of Seneca's offence, does not excuse the offence itself, On the other hand it is a thing positively in his favour that he had an unexpected vein of lyrical inspiration, not very abundant or original but genuine enough, which is revealed in the choral odes that divide in the Greek manner the acts of his dramas—a vein worked later with considerable effect by writers like Fulke Greville and Sir William Alexander. It might even be maintained that his characters, though mere types and shadows, move and express themselves with a certain tragic sublimity. But the best way to appreciate what Seneca did for English drama is to think of the mysteries and moralities and miracle plays which he helped so much to supersede. The mediaeval drama has merits which Seneca could never have attained or even perceived, because he was too sophisticated for that. But no one could fairly deny that it tends, broadly speaking, to be formless, and that the ideas it contains are few and of an elementary simplicity. Seneca more than anyone else changed all that.

In the first place he influenced dramatists in the direction of constructing a regular plot worked out through a series of compact, organically connected acts and scenes. That was no small service, although Seneca must share the credit here with the Roman comic poets. His other services were even more important. He raised the intellectual level of the drama. The undeniable fact that early imitations of the Senecan manner, such as Gorboduc, are dull is not the fault of Seneca, who was not only a very clever man but had a brilliant gift of aphorism. The Elizabethans admired the 'sentences' of Seneca at least as much as his fustian. What it all led to may be seen in Hamlet, which, though its subject is not classical, is a 'Senecan' play improved out of all recognition. There is a ghost crying for revenge and, at the end, an orgy of bloodshedding. But there is also a more than Senecan play of mind. The To be or not to be soliloquy is not less in Seneca's way than the ghost; to the classical scholar it reads like a poet's rendering of a typical Stoic—and Seneca was a Stoic—discourse on suicide. Such boldness and freedom of thought on such a theme is not mediaeval but classical. Even in point of style the influence of Seneca was by no means wholly bad. He taught correctness—impeccable grammar, impeccable metre, in neither of which could our native drama be regarded as strong. And, although he overcharged his own style with rhetoric, he taught us that a tragedy must be composed in language of appropriate grandeur.

Ancient Comedy

Classical Comedy like classical Tragedy was developed in Athens, and like Tragedy it had its origin in the worship of Dionysus. Dionysus being a god of wine and of fertility generally, it was natural that his worshippers should on certain occasions form themselves in a *kômos*, or band of revellers, who sang and danced and sometimes dressed up as animals. It was out of some such performance that 'Comedy', the song of the *kômos*, arose. It may be that originally this was little more than a fertility charm. But, if so, that stage was quickly outgrown, and by the time we come to Aristophanes, who wrote at the end of the fifth and the beginning of the fourth century before Christ, a comedy is a finished work of art. It should not be inferred from this that the construction and diction of a comedy were ever elaborated with the same degree of care and finish as in a tragedy, although in his own style there has never been a greater master in any age or country than Axistophanes. Even in his comedies the scenes are very slightly connected, there is hardly such a thing as a plot, and the language is simpler and more colloquial. The Chorus is however just as important, singing choral odes between the episodes much like the tragic Chorus, from which perhaps it learned this arrangement. But it has one special feature. At a certain point in the comedy the Chorus advances to the front of the stage and directly addresses the audience, offering it advice mixed with banter and on occasion with an unmistakable undertone of serious admonition. The Chorus in fact represents the original *kômos*, and when it died the Old Comedy died with it.

But Comedy itself did not die. It survived, though in a greatly modified form, and the vitality of this offspring is one of the most wonderful things in the history of literature. The scholars of the Alexandrine age, surveying the whole range of ancient Comedy from its beginnings to their own time, divided it into three parts, which they called the Old Comedy, the Middle Comedy and the New Comedy. The Middle Comedy passed insensibly into the New, and the real difference is between the New and the Old. Our knowledge of the Old Comedy is practically confined to the eleven surviving plays of Aristophanes, and, since Aristophanes is a unique writer, our view of it is no doubt coloured by his genius. But certain broad distinctions between the Old and the New Comedy are not affected by that. The most obvious distinction is this, that the Chorus, which plays a vital part in the Old Comedy, is absent from the New. Thus the lyrical element, which is particularly delightful in Aristophanes, disappears, and with it most or all of the poetry, or what romantic taste regards as poetry, disappears as well. There is another difference, equally important. In the Old Comedy the satire is personal and attacks individuals; in the New it is directed against types. That is to say it is a Comedy of Manners. The New Comedy produced no genius like Aristophanes; but if much was lost much also was gained. For instance the Old Comedy never was serious; everything and everybody is held up to ridicule. But in a typical play of the New Comedy there may be whole scenes which are entirely serious and may even threaten to become tragic. That development was destined to have important and splendid consequences. Again the Old Comedy had been content with the merest skeleton of a plot; the plots of the New Comedy are skilfully complicated, and—almost a new thing in ancient art—they often startle or surprise. This development also was pregnant with the future.

The effect of the Old Comedy upon English literature has been almost negligible; that of the New has been great and protracted. But it has not come directly. The actual remains of the New Comedy are inconsiderable, and we should know very little about it but for the fact that it was acclimatised in Latin. Of these Roman comedies a fair number have survived: twenty-one from the hand of Plautus (254-184 B.C.) and six by Terence, who died a young man in 159 B.C. They are nothing but free translations and adaptations of Greek originals, and there is nothing Roman about them except the language and a certain blunting or coarsening of the Attic spirit.

We have seen that the New Comedy operated with types of characters, and such are the persons in Plautus and Terence. The range of types is considerable, but limited by convention. The convention found visual expression in the masks which were worn by the actors. Thus the audience knew at a glance if it had before it a stupid old man or an impudent slave or a young lover or one of the other types, say a quack or a parasite or a courtesan or a modest maiden. It might be supposed that this limitation must be a severe handicap to a man of original genius. But it has not proved so. Each type may be freshly studied in an endless variation of detail and with ever-renewed delicacy of observation. This is demonstrably true of Molière and it was evidently true in the case of the chief Greek master of the New Comedy, Menander of Athens. As for Plautus and Terence, it is not possible to rank either of them among the masters of Comedy; their influence has been in excess of their merits, although these are not small. The cause of their influence is simple they provided the only models readily available when modern Comedy began, in Renaissance times, to take shape. They were easy to read, particularly Terence, and they gave exactly what was wanted, a lesson in the art of the comic dramatist. When they had learned this their modern pupils went on to surpass their instructors.

Ancient Lyric

It as thought important in antiquity to distinguish between two kinds of lyric poetry, the Choral Lyric and Personal Lyric. These terms perhaps explain themselves, but they do not tell us very much. It must be remembered that in its early stages poetry, and especially lyrical poetry, is associated with dancing. What is more, the words have to be fitted the dance, not the dance to the words. So far as the Choral Lyric is concerned, it continued through most of classical antiquity to be danced as well as sung. The Personal Lyric followed a different fine of development. It was sung or chanted by the poet himself and by him alone. He did not in historical times dance, although it was long before he ceased to accompany himself upon the harp. Yet his metres too were originally dance-measures. The English reader may be helped by an analogy. We now read ballads in printed books; not so long ago they were recited from memory; originally they were danced and sung, as the etymology of 'ballad', as well as historical evidence, proves. Its characteristic metre was imposed upon the ballad not by accident or the genius of a particular balladist, but by the rhythm of the dance. No doubt in process of time, as poets more and more asserted their freedom from the communal dance, many metrical variations were invented. The history of the Personal Lyric in ancient Greece cannot have been very different. But, as the Greeks had a passion for dancing and an extraordinary refinement of ear for rhythmic intervals, we find that their lyrical metres have a greater complexity and stricter rules than ours.

No difference between ancient and modern, especially perhaps contemporary, poetry is more important than this of metre. It is well enough known of course that ancient verse is scanned according to the quantity of the syllables, while English verse is scanned according to stress. That statement is made in all the handbooks and need not be dwelt upon here. But what is often not sufficiently remarked is this, that quantity and stress, although they can be brought into effective relationship, can never be assimilated to one another. Now, since it is the nature of ancient lyrical poetry that it must produce its effects through metre and in no other way, and since this metre is strictly quantitative, it differs from modern lyrical poetry at the very heart of its being. This is the ultimate reason why the one has been so little influenced by the other. It is illuminating to see what happened in Latin literature. The Latin language was originally almost as much of a stress language as English. But very early in the history of its literature the Roman poets began to treat it as a quantitative language like Greek. They borrowed the whole Greek metrical system and forced it upon Latin. In time they succeeded, and Roman ears grew accustomed to the quantities assigned to syllables by the poetic convention. When this had happened it became possible to reproduce in

Latin the effects which had been naturally produced in Greek, Latin being helped in this by the possession of so many of those long words which are necessary to steady and sustain the weight of quantitative scansion. But the Greek lyric metres were never quite at home in Latin. Catullus and Horace can use them, but almost nobody else. And when lyric poetry revived in mediaeval Italy it reverted to stress.

But if the classical lyric cannot be successfully reproduced in English it has been full of stimulus and suggestion for English poets. To make this clear it is necessary to cast a glance at the Greek lyrists, although what remains of their work, if we except Pindar and the choral odes in the Attic dramatists, is exceedingly scanty. But of Pindar a good deal might be said, while the name of Anacreon recalls a curious strain of influence in modern literature. As Anacreon was the earlier poet, he may be dealt with first. Only snatches of his genuine work are left, but there has survived a substantial number of little lyrics attributed to him, and it is this pseudoAnacreontic poetry that proved so popular. The reason for that popularity is clear. The language of Anacreon was simple, his metre easy, his usual topics, which were love and wine, not difficult to handle in his light and superficial way. It is a fascinating, though not a great, style, and more perhaps than any other known to us it lends itself to imitation. These Anacreontea, as scholars call them, to distinguish them from the authentic work of Anacreon, belong to all ages from the Alexandrine almost to the Renaissance, and vary greatly in merit. But the best of them are so pretty in fancy and expression that they captivated men of letters when they were discovered at the end of the famous *codex Palatinus*, which contains the Greek Anthology. They were translated into English verse in corresponding metre by Thomas Stanley, a celebrated seventeeth century scholar and not at all a bad poet. A new field was added to the domain of English lyricism, and for a considerable period it was quite a fashion to write 'Anacreonticks'.

The influence of Pindar has been very much more profound and fruitful. He is a difficult poet, to be read in the original only by scholars, and it must not be assumed that the many moderns who have written Pindaric odes derived their inspiration from the source. What inspired them was a conception of poetry derived from Pindar. We have seen that a Greek chorus went through certain evolutions as it sang, during which it divided into two semi-choruses and then reunited again. These evolutions might be repeated an indefinite number of times. We need not describe them further, but they explain the division of Choral Lyrics into strophe, antistrophe and epode. The strophe corresponds metrically to the antistrophe fine by fine and syllable by syllable; the epode will be similarly matched by another epode as the composition proceeds. Such is the aspect presented by a Pindaric ode; it is not composed in a single repeated stanza, but in this triple grouping of stanzas. Moreover these are larger in scale and generally more elaborate in design than any stanza normally used by the Personal Lyrists.

Pindar composed in many varieties of the Choral Lyric, but only his work in one variety has survived entire. This is the victory-odes, which he composed in honour of the victors in the athletic contests held at Olympia, at Delphi, at Nemea, and at the Isthmus of Corinth. This explains the division of these odes into *Olympian*, *Pythian*, *Nemean* and *Isthmian*.

They were judged, especially the first two divisions, to exhibit the poet's genius in its utmost splendour, while Pindar himself was held to be the chief lyric poet of Greece. This verdict of the ancient critics has not been shaken, nor is it hard to understand why he has made so great an impression on those who have read his difficult words. He is like no other poet, ancient or modern. Later classical poets, including Horace, imitated him; but it could not be successfully done, as Horace himself frankly admits. It is hardly then to be expected that he could be imitated with success in English. The *Pindarique Odes* of Cowley have nothing Pindaric about them but the name. Even the two odes of Gray do not produce the effect of Pindar, the English poet being content to carry on the CowleyDryden tradition with a better knowledge of the ancient model, but not caring to imitate the exact architecture of Pindar's verse. He was however aware of the qualities which make the true Pindaric style unique, and these he certainly hoped to reproduce. Two in particular he has remarked and imitated: Pindar's abrupt transitions, and his concise and allusive manner of narration. He has also in mind Horace's comparison of Pindar to a mountain torrent (*Odes* IV, 2), and he tries to give this sweep and rush to his own stanzas. But in truth the simile of Horace is not very apt. Pindar's verse undoubtedly moves with an irresistible impetus, but it is not a wild, disorderly rush. That is an error which these seventeenth and eighteenth century poets inherited and spread. For Pindar's form is never 'irregular'. His inspiration never overflows its channels in the manner of a swollen stream.

On the other hand he is of all ancient poets the most daring in metaphor and the most gorgeous in colour. Gray had a real perception of this, although it evidently did not suit his temperament, for there is a suspicion of factitious enthusiasm in his Pindaric verse. But it was a side of Pindar which did suit the tempers of the Romantic poets of the next generation.

How great and fruitful the influence of Pindar, direct and indirect, has been upon English poetry will appear to anyone who considers the long line of odes from *Alexander's Feast* to *Intimations of Immortality* and later. The actual history of this influence is too involved to be traced at length, though the historian must take into account the influence of the French *Pléiade*, which did so much to resuscitate the classical ode, and in this at least was followed by the school of Malherbe. It is also difficult to disentangle the influence of Pindar from that of the choral odes in the Greek dramatists, which powerfully affected Shelley, for example, and Swinburne. But though the facts are involved they are not doubtful and their importance is very considerable indeed.

Horace—for to him we must pass at once—is in his own way no less unique than Pindar. He has constantly been imitated but never, even in his own language, with much success. A main reason for this failure is that no poet in ancient, and not many in modern, times has put so much of himself into his writings. A man's style may be reproduced, but not that which makes him essentially different from other men. There are however special difficulties confronting the English writer who translates or imitates Horace. Two have been alluded to already as generally applicable to ancient poetry: the difference in its metrical system, and the abundance of long sonorous words at the disposal of the Greek or Latin poet. But they have a special applicability to Horace. The poetical value of a Horatian ode depends to an extraordinary degree upon the beauty of its metre, and the metres of Horace cannot be reproduced in English. Tennyson's alcaics and Swinburne's sapphics are *tours de force*. Even if they moved with complete ease and naturalness their effect would still be different from the alcaics and sapphics of Horace because of their poverty in echoing polysyllables. But there is a third and even more fundamental difference, which comes out with unusual clearness in Horace and may therefore be appropriately mentioned here. Latin has a very complete and elaborate grammatical structure, while it is notably rich in the number and variety of its case-endings in the nouns, and distinctions of mood and tense in the verb. On the other hand English has lost nearly all its grammatical forms. The result is that the order of words in an English sentence is fixed, and cannot be changed without producing nonsense or contradiction. But the liberty of a Latin author to vary the order of his words is almost unlimited, because the grammatical forms prevent the possibility of mistake. This liberty Horace exercises with an art that cannot be too much admired, and it puts him totally beyond the range of English imitation. We may do other things better, but this we cannot do at all.

The fact however that the Horatian lyric is a thing *sui generis* does not mean that it has had little or no influence upon English poetry. The admiration which could not but be felt for the perfect finish, the concise elegance, the 'curious felicity' of the odes was a natural stimulus to aim at like qualities in our own lyric verse; and they are qualities that can be imitated. The lesson Horace had to teach was the more valuable as English poetry has been generally somewhat impatient of formal graces. Moreover the range and variety of his subjects, which include not only love and wine, youth and age and death, but even politics and religion, greatly extended the field of possible themes. Thus Marvell could write an *Horatian Ode upon Cromwell's Return from Ireland.* While it may not be easy to point out clear instances of Horatian imitation, there is no doubt that the example of Horace was constantly before Jonson and Campion, before the Jacobean and Caroline lyrists generally, as well as later before Collins and Landor and many others, though they might not all be avowed Horatians.

Pastoral Poetry

Pastoral or, as the Greeks called it, Bucolic poetry did not come into existence, or at least into reputation, until the Alexandrine age. Its origins are obscure and our real knowledge of it begins with the Sicilian poet Theocritus, who lived between the fourth and the third centuries before Christ. He had some reputation in his own day and set a fashion that was followed by a fine of contemporary and subsequent poets, none so great as himself, but two of them, Moschus and Bion, poets of real distinction. Two centuries after Theocritus an anthology of the pastoral poets was made by a scholar called Artemidorus, whose son reissued it in an annotated edition. The book was called *Eclogues,* which is simply *Greek for Selections.* It had an immediate success and established the fame of Theocritus. Among the admirers was the youthful Virgil, who was fired with the ambition to become the Latin Theocritus. This was the origin of his first notable work, his *Eclogues.* The name was borrowed from the Greek but was a misnomer, since Virgil's book was not an anthology. It had a flattering reception in Roman literary circles and never lost its popularity. Perhaps no book has been so frequently imitated. In fact it was Virgil and not Theocritus who gave the Pastoral its vogue in European literature. But, as the *Eclogues* are written in confessed imitation of the *Idylls* of Theocritus, it is necessary to say something about the *Idylls.*

The word 'idyll' does not mean 'a little picture' but rather 'a little poem', and does not by itself indicate one kind of poem rather than another. In fact the poems of Theocritus are far from being all 'idyllic' in the modern sense; even the strictly pastoral do not always give an 'idyllic' picture of country life. Theocritus, though one of the least voluminous, is one of the most versatile of ancient poets, and the student may well begin by rejecting the over-simplification of his art which is a mere reflection from the pastoral convention of a later day. There are at least three sorts of poetry in which Theocritus has written masterpieces: the Pastoral, the Mime and the Epyllion or 'Little Epic'. It will be convenient to take the last two first, as the Pastoral is to some extent conditioned by them. The Mme is a closely and often satirically observed study of a scene from ordinary fife, and has always a dramatic or semi-dramatic character. The best known example in Theocritus is his *Adoniazusae,* in which two Syracusan women, staying in Alexandria, go to see the festival of Adonis there. It is extraordinarily vivid, amusing and 'true to fife', and it is now more popular than any of his Pastorals; it is a kind of thing we understand, and it is natural that we should admire it as it deserves. It is however inferior in the finer qualities to another mime—the wonderful monologue in which Simaetha tells of her betrayal in words which express, all these centuries before the romantic movement was born, the essence of romantic love. As for the *epyllia,* they are short or shortish poems of a quasi-epic character. Tennyson *Idylls of the King* give a very fair notion of what they are like, Tennyson recognising that here Theocritus, and not Homer or Virgil or Milton, was his true master. In his *epyllia* Theocritus takes for his subject some episode in the life of a hero--his preference is for Heracles—and, while using the Homeric diction and metre, nevertheless treats it in a different way from Homer. He does not aim at sublimity but at an effect like that sought by a painter, even a painter of vignettes or miniatures.

We are now in a better position to understand the art of the pastorals. Theocritus has an eye for the actual manners of his rustics and the actual circumstances of their life, and he, can and frequently does describe these with unsparing exactness, embodying sometimes, though not often, what are euphemistically called realistic details. On the other hand there was so much natural charm in that fife, and Sicily is so lovely, that the picture Theocritus gives is irresistibly engaging. This is a great advantage he enjoys over the pastoral poets of less happy climes and less artistic races. At the same time it cannot be denied that his work contains a large element of idealisation, even of sophistication. It was not unnatural to represent Sicilian shepherds as singing of their loves and sorrows, for there is evidence that they did so; but it was only by a poetic fiction that they were made to sing in the style and diction of Theocritus, for those were his own invention. The shepherds themselves must have sung, as they spoke, in the Sicilian variety of Doric; but the language of Theocritus in his pastorals, while it admits a considerable number of Doric words and forms, never was spoken by anybody. It is a special diction invented for this kind of poetry much as Spenser invented a special diction for the *Faerie Queene*. It is indeed a lovely thing, but it is a work of art not of nature, and later Greek pastoral poets had to learn it from Theocritus. Again, he was not always content that his shepherds should be shepherds; he would sometimes represent his friends as such, these friends being no more shepherds than himself. He does this in some of his most charming pastorals; but perhaps it was a pity. At any rate it started that habit of pretending to be a shepherd which in less skilful hands has done more than anything else to make the Pastoral look ridiculous. But even this convention may be so lightly touched as to be inoffensive, and where it is not obtruded it may add a strong personal interest. And if it had never existed, the world would, so far as one can see, have been deprived of *Lycdas* and *Adonais* and *Thyrsis*.

The *Eclogues* of Virgil are in form pastorals and all have Theocritean models with the exception of the fourth, which has the character of a prophecy, although even that is derived from the 'Sicilian', that is the pastoral, Muses, the inspiration of Theocritus. We do not know what model Virgil had for this eclogue, but it is probable that he had one, for prophecies were common in Greek poetry. The event prophesied is the birth of a child at whose coming the Golden Age will return. What child the poet had in mind is a question that modern scholarship has not yet solved. The Middle Ages however had no doubt upon the subject at all—the child was the infant Jesus. Since they knew that Virgil lived before Jesus, they drew the conclusion that Virgil was a prophet, whose evidence must be taken along with that of the Sibyl, who makes an appearance in the sixth book of the *Aeneid* but in particular was the author of the Sibylline books, a collection of prophecies which came to comprise many of a Christian tendency. This is the reason for the awe (as distinct from admiration) in which Virgil was held in the Middle Ages. It gives an adventitious importance to the fourth eclogue, which however has great intrinsic interest. It is distinguished from the other eclogues in attempting a more epic strain, and in the young poet of the fourth eclogue we recognise the future author of the *Aeneid*.

The *Eclogues* like all Virgil's work have an indefinable charm. But this should not blind us, as it was apt to blind the critics of the Renaissance and indeed of much later times, to their deficiencies. Nothing could exceed the sweetness of their versification and the daintiness of their phrasing; but they are immature, over-literary, and sometimes downright silly. Virgil knows the country, no ancient poet better, and when he has in Wordsworth's expression his 'eye on the object' he describes it with admirable fidelity. But usually he is thinking of a passage in Theocritus or some other poet, and that comes between him and his personal observation. You never quite know where he is—in Italy or Sicily. You never quite know whether he is being allegorical or not, whether he is speaking of a real shepherd or of some friend in the guise of a shepherd. His rustics have not Latin but Greek names, thus leading to another convention of pastoralism, followed by Milton and others, so that King becomes Lycidas, Keats Adonais and Clough Thyrsis. There is talk of nymphs, satyrs and the like, in whose existence Virgil can hardly have believed-whence another convention, which Doctor Johnson never tired of denouncing. It will be seen that Virgil at least sowed many of the seeds of that artificiality which infested so much of the pastoral poetry of the seventeenth and eighteenth centuries. In the very first eclogue the poet introduces allusively a piece of his own biography. His father, the owner of a farm near Mantua, had been expropriated in favour of a demobilised soldier, whom Octavian, the future emperor Augustus, had no other means of rewarding. Virgil, whose verses and personal character had already found favour with the statesman Maecenas, was recommended by him to Octavian, who restored the property. How is this represented in the eclogue? Virgil appears as a shepherd and ex-slave called Tityrus, who tells his story to another shepherd, not so lucky, called Meliboeus. It is all a little absurd.

The eclogue which, next to the fourth, is the most famous and has been far the most influential upon English pastoral poetry is the tenth. It is a lament for Gallus, who is represented as dying of unrequited love. Gallus was a real person who had written a number of love poems expressing his devotion to an actress, who had tired of him and followed Mark Antony into Gaul, where he was fighting under Julius Ceasar. The young woman is called Lycoris in the eclogue, which shows us Gallus wasting away because of her cruelty. The scene for some reason is laid in Arcadia, and this is a circumstance of the greatest interest, for it seems to be the first mention of Arcadia in pastoral literature. Gallus keeps his Latin name, although surely, if there could be an excuse for calling an Italian by a Greek name, it was presented here. He is visited by the Arcadian god Pan, which in the circumstances is natural, but also by the Italian god Silvanus, who has no business in Arcadia at all. Throughout the eclogue Gallus keeps changing his character; sometimes he is a soldier serving in Italy, sometimes he is a swain bemoaning himself in Arcadia. Such are the inconsistencies of the pastoral Muse in Virgil. We move in a world of make-believe.

But does it matter very much? It was scarcely possible for Virgil to treat pastoral life in Italy with the same fidelity as Theocritus in Sicily, where conditions had been so different. Roman industrialism, especially the exploitation of slave labour upon the great estates, had made the world of Theocritus seem almost as remote from Virgil as from us. In fact it was in some degree that very remoteness that attracted the later to the earlier poet. For Virgil Arcadia is already Arcady, a country existing only in the geography of romance. It was a sound poetic instinct which led him to recognise this, and his failure, so far as he did fail, came from his inability to do it consistently. His real shepherds get in the way of his idealised shepherds, and are not very real after all. But it is not hard to think them away and to dwell only upon the beauties of the *Eclogues*. They are not to be compared in freshness, variety and vigour of imagination to the *Idylls* of Theocritus, and their art is less accomplished. But their words have a sort of enchantment about them, giving wonderfully melodious expression to the nostalgia for a lost and lovely past.

One of the striking differences between ancient literature on the one hand and mediaeval and modern literature on the other is found in their conception and treatment of love as a subject for poetry. It is not necessary to consider how far if at all the ancients understood or accepted the ideals of chivalrous or romantic love. But we are bound to note that Attic literature—the 'classical' literature *par excellence*—did not consider sexual love to be a possible subject for high poetry.

This was the prevailing view throughout antiquity; and, however much Sappho or Anacreon or Catullus might be admired, their kind of poetry, which was the Personal Lyric, was not supposed to rank, not merely with the Epic or with Tragedy, but even with the Choral Lyric, which confined itself as much as Epic or Tragedy to heroic themes. This may surprise us, but it is perhaps not more surprising than the ancient choice of a vehicle for the expression of love. To us it may appear that the only possible choice was the Personal Lyric. The ancients did not think so, although even in antiquity love, if not the only, is the principal theme of the Personal Lyric. But from the first the Lyric had a rival, and this rival finally won all along the line. It was Elegiac poetry, and about this we have now to say a little. The mere name is nothing. Although for us an elegy means a lament for the dead, and that in fact seems to have been its original meaning, when it enters Greek literature not later than the seventh century before Christ it has become a form of war poetry. It bad a characteristic metre of its own, the 'elegiac couplet', consisting of a dactylic hexameter followed by a pentameter. This metre was found suitable not only for war poetry but for poetry of a reflective or 'gnomic' kind and for love poetry; and this last kind gradually came almost, though never altogether, to supersede the others. It was rather a new sort of love poetry, very modern in some ways, though in others it recalled the amatory verses of old Ionian poets, who had written before the austerely 'classical' period of the fifth century B.C. It was a favourite form of the Alexandrine poets, from whom it was eagerly taken up by the Roman poets of the Augustan age, of whom three have had their work largely preserved to us, namely Tibullus, Propertius and Ovid.

It is unnecessary to deal with Tibullus and Propertius because, however modern criticism may rank them, their fame and influence were swallowed up in those of Ovid. Tibullus indeed was at one time imitated a good deal, much more than ever was Propertius, a poet with far more genuine passion, imagination and intelligence but less easy to read and less normal in temperament. Yet even the influence of Tibullus did not penetrate to any depth. It is quite different with Ovid. He has such ease and fluency of manner, he is so sympathetic and quick-witted, so witty and so audacious that he was irresistible. Ovid was at all times a master of the mechanical part of verse, but his mastery is most complete in the elegiac couplet. It is not perfect, for it does not succeed in concealing itself. It is possible to analyse and expose all the artifices of Ovid's prodigious virtuosity. But of course that only makes him the more imitable. The positive indebtedness of English poetry in the Middle Ages and up to almost recent times to the poetry of Ovid in general and to his love poetry in particular is an important fact of literary history, which can be plainly observed and estimated. But it is hardly more important than the influence of his example. There can be little doubt that the development of the so-called heroic couplet in English poetry, at least from Waller to Pope, owes a great deal to conscious, and perhaps unconscious, efforts to obtain the effects of the Ovidian elegiacs. The regular beat of the Popian couplet, its snap and glitter, its formal graces are classical, are Latin, are Ovidian. Since the time of Burns and Blake we have felt that the couplet is not a suitable medium for the expression of love, which seems to us a more lyrical emotion than it did to the Romans. But the author of *Eloisa to Abelard* agreed with the Romans, and so perhaps did the author of *Venus and Adonis,* one of the most Ovidian poems in the language. It is a point of view. One superficial evidence of it is all these Cynthias and Delias and Corinnas who flit perpetually through the love poetry of the sixteenth, the seventeenth and the eighteenth centuries. Our present feeling is against it. Indeed it is hard to read the *Amores,* which describe passages in the wooing of Corinna, and the *Heroides,* which are imaginary letters from heroines in love, without feeling that Ovid was not looking into his own heart so much as following, though with great brilliancy and psychological insight, a literary fashion. The effect on his imitators was lamentable. Their verses became a pot-pourri of loves and doves, of Venus and the boy Cupid, and all that pretty pretence which has come to look so insincere. Ovid cannot be blamed for the feebleness of his modern disciples, otherwise he must be given credit for those who, without being disciples, nevertheless owed more than a little to him, one of them being John Milton. But no doubt if he had been a more serious artist these regrettable consequences would not have followed.

Satire

While the Romans admitted their indebtedness to Greece in all other forms of poetry, they were not willing to admit it in the case of satire, which they claimed as their own invention. It is enough for us that Roman satire is or became a thing *per se*, which is the only kind of originality that matters in literature. It was first brought effectively into Latin poetry by an interesting man called Lucilius, who wrote in the second half of the second century before Christ. He had certain advantages for a satirist, for he was in easy circumstances and enjoyed the friendship of people influential enough to protect him. He may have needed this protection, for his satire was generally, though by no means always, of a bitterly personal order. The vices which most aroused his indignation were those that seemed most injurious to the state; in that respect he was, though not of Roman birth, a genuine Roman. About himself he was always ready to discourse, thus bringing into satire an autobiographical element, which again is rather Roman than Greek. (The impersonality of Greek art is a thing the Romans like the English were never quite content to accept.) He did not trouble much to polish his verses, but poured out a stream—a muddy stream, Horace calls it—of comment on almost every aspect of contemporary fife. The combination of personal invective with a good deal of learning and a great deal of self-revelation proved congenial to Roman taste, and Lucilius maintained his popularity for some centuries. Ms importance for us lies in the effect he had upon Horace and Juvenal.

It may seem odd that the poet of the exquisite *Odes* and the urbane *Epistles* should have begun his literary career with satire of a personal and occasionally offensive kind, as Horace did in his *Epodes* and in what is now the first book of his *Satires*. But young men often fancy they have a talent for satire, although to be really good it requires a deeper knowledge of human nature than they are likely to possess. Not but what there is excellent writing in both of these volumes; but personalities and mere invective were never in his line, and when he indulges in them he falls below himself. In 'this he was following tradition—Greek tradition in the case of the *Epodes*, in the case of the *Satires* Lucilius. The tone is greatly modified in a second book of satires, which he published after some interval. Ultimately it disappeared altogether, or nearly so, in the two books of his *Epistles*, which, though not professedly satirical, have a spiritual continuity with the second book of the *Satires*. This continuity is indicated by the name which Horace gave to his satirical writings—*Sermones* or "conversations'; for the difference between a conversation in verse and a letter in verse does not amount to very much. It is in the *Epistles* that Horace is most completely himself, and in discovering himself he has discovered a new kind of satire. Personal invective has passed into a generalised criticism, in which certain types of character are viewed with a detached irony. The change is comparable to that of the Old Comedy into the New; and it is significant that Horace was aided in his development by study of the New Comedy, which, it will be remembered, was a Comedy of Manners. He found much to help him too in the more dramatic dialogues of Plato, who had shown how formidable a weapon irony can be in the criticism of ideas. Horace does not fail to admit his debt to the philosophers, who in antiquity were not as a rule unworldly recluses but public characters with a passion for converting fools. His *Sermones* are on the way to becoming 'sermons'. We are moving from personalities to a discourse on morals, with of course a satirical flavour. There was a great future for this manner of writing, and not only in poetry, for it affected prose. After all there is more of the true Horatian spirit in Addison than in Pope.

The admiration of Horace for Lucilius was qualified by a sense of the old poet's artistic defects. Lucilius, perhaps because he did not care about literary finish, perhaps because he wished to produce the effect of natural talk, was prolix without being always clear. From the first Horace avoided that, certainly grave, fault; from the first he aimed at being terse without becoming obscure. Of course terseness and lucidity were never his sole aims. The perfect felicity of his phrasing, the perfect modulation of his metre are the results of an almost unexampled concentration on the mere art of writing. He is the apostle of what Pope called 'correctness, and it is to Horace that we must trace that whole theory of the poetic art which governed so much of the practice of the eighteenth century. But no poet was ever saved by 'correctness' alone, and this comes out when we compare Horace with Pope. In mere wit, in point, in *deadliness*—and it is a virtue in satire to be deadly—Pope has greatly the advantage; nor can it be said that he has less understanding of the human heart, at least in its weaknesses. But the charm of Horace he does not attain.

Horace perceived that his satiric style—which of course is totally different from that of the *Odes*—must be kept on the level of conversation, but it is conversation at its best. He is never boring or pretentious or self-conscious or crude. At the same time, as conversation must have an unstudied air if it is to seem natural, he is careful to avoid the appearance of too fine a polish. He therefore introduces an element of colloquial roughness and metrical harshness into his verse, but with a tact and discretion quite foreign to Lucilius before him and to Persius after him. The latter died a young man much less than a century after the death of Horace, whom he regarded as his master. He not only exaggerates the studied carelessness of Horace but is moreover obscure, which Horace is not, and pedantic, which Horace is if possible still less. But his style caught on. Probably the taste of the day was satiated with the impeccable verse of the *Aeneid* and the *Odes* of Horace and the elegiacs of Ovid, somewhat as a later generation resented the accomplishment of Pope, and a still later generation the accomplishment of Tennyson. It is only fair to say that in spite of the imitativeness natural in so young an author Persius had some touch of original genius. His knowledge of men and the world is drawn from books, but he strikes out occasional flashes of a noble eloquence. We have to mention him because his example was held to justify much harshness and roughness of style and metre in our satirists of the seventeenth century. His influence on Donne is worth more consideration than it has received.

We come now to the striking figure of Juvenal (A.D. 46 to perhaps 130). In him satire exhibits a new character. Where Horace is conversational Juvenal is declamatory; where Horace is carefully unrhetorical, because rhetoric is detestable in conversation, rhetorical effectiveness is the alpha and omega of Juvenal's style. Also their interests are different. Literature, philosophy, social intercourse are what chiefly engage the attention of Horace; Juvenal cares for none of these things. He claims indeed to take for his subject the whole range of human life—*quidquid agunt homines*—but in practice he is content with a few targets of his own choosing, against which he directs every shaft in his armoury. He does not attack any of his contemporaries by name—that might have been dangerous—but he assails the dead, often with extreme violence. Perhaps it does not matter much, because the objects of his attack are merely embodiments of one or another vice, not credible human characters. Juvenal writes as a moralist, as perhaps every satirist is bound to do; but his sincerity has been questioned. In his third Satire for instance he gives vent to his rage against foreigners. If he is sincere in that, it must be said that xenophobia is not a respectable emotion. The sixth Satire is an attack upon the female sex of such a nature that, if it expressed his true sentiments, the proper place for him was a mental home. The defence is that Juvenal is merely stating a case. It was expected of a Roman prosecutor that he should state in the strongest terms at his command all the evil he could think of, true or false, against the accused, leaving it to the defence to set forth his virtues. On this view Juvenal is only counsel for the prosecution and is not bound to believe all he says. But we are still left in the dark as to his real sentiments; and this is one indication how far his kind of satire has diverged from that of Horace, which is a revelation of character.

The style of Juvenal is quite his own and borrows nothing from Horace or Persius. The influence of *declamatio,* the art of public speaking, perceptible even in Virgil, had come more and more to predominate in every form of Latin verse, and it reigns unchecked in Juvenal, who has mastered the art as perhaps no other poet has done before or since. There is no device for obtaining point, colour or emphasis which he does not employ, and employ with an unmatched variety and resourcefulness. It is a style which no doubt a pure taste would condemn; but in mere effectiveness, in the punishing force of his blows Juvenal has scarcely a rival. His descriptions too have a graphic power which makes them unforgettable. It is often employed upon subjects on which there was no particular reason why it should be employed; and this preference of the poet or his readers for the gross and the obscene, though far from omnipresent in the *Satires*, must be noted because it was taken for a justification of similar grossness in the satirists of later ages. Thirdly, he is a master of versification, which is a great weapon in the hands of a satiric poet. The fire and energy of his hexameters is extraordinary.

He has had a great influence upon the history of Satire, greater even than Horace. For one thing he is more imitable, for another his invective has a higher relish. He has not Horace's humour nor perhaps his wit; but these cannot be acquired by study, while much that Juvenal offers can. He shows how to treat men's foibles as if they were vices and their virtues as if they were foibles—a species of misrepresentation invaluable to the satirist. He shows how to awaken horror and disgust by mere vividness of description, in which few writers have excelled him. He draws the reader into a state of virtuous indignation by the force and splendour of his moral apophthegms, which have often the pungency of epigrams. He is one of the most quotable of authors. It is not that what he says is often profound or subtle--satirists are rarely concerned with the subtle or the profound—but he can express an obvious truth more forcibly than it had been expressed before. He uses with great effect the device of illustrating one's theme by means of examples drawn from popular history. Now all these artifices, although no one has used them to quite such purpose as Juvenal himself, nevertheless can be used by others. Consequently this poet has always found his imitators.

The Epigram

It seems natural to pass from satire to epigram. But that is only because we derive our conception of what an epigram should be from the Romans, above all from Martial. The Greek conception (which was the original one) differed remarkably. The word 'epigram' itself is Greek and means no more than 'inscription'. Ancient inscriptions, being for the most part, at least in early days, cut in bronze or marble, naturally tended to be short and concise. Laws were often engraved in this manner, but laws were not usually composed in verse. On the other hand epitaphs often were, and so were dedications of offerings to the gods. Wit is out of place in an epitaph or even in a dedication. So we cannot be surprised to find that the Greek epigrams have rarely anything witty about them. They are content to seek clearness, brevity and dignity. If the occasion was a moving one, the poet might rise to it. That he sometimes did so is proved by a handful of epigrams, most of them attributed to Simonides, who lived at the time of the Persian wars and had his fines inscribed on the monuments of the fallen, which have never been equalled for a noble simplicity. The beautiful verses of Collins that begin *How sleep the brave* are too allegorical, Housman's epigram on a mercenary army is too rhetorical, to equal the Greek. That level however could not be long maintained even in a language adapted by nature for this kind of writing. (The suitability of Latin for inscriptions has long been recognised, Latin being for once on a level here with Greek.) But epigrams continued to be written. Only now they were written as often as not on imaginary subjects. In other words the epigram became an independent literary kind. It came to include not merely epitaphs and dedications but short love-poems. An immense collection of all these varieties of epigram remains to us under the modern title of the *Greek Anthology*. The included poems are very unequal in merit, but the best of them (which are generally the oldest) are charming and sometimes of an exquisite beauty. The anthology has been favourite reading with scholarly poets ever since its discovery about the time of Sir Thomas More, who translated some of the epigrams into Latin. Its influence can be detected or surmised in many English poets since.

A certain number of the later contributions to the anthology are epigrammatic in the modern sense. But the trend in that direction is due above all to one man, the Romanised Spaniard Martial, who did most of his work in the last quarter of the first century. He seems to have discovered quite early in what direction his talent lay. No one has ever perhaps equalled him in the versified epigram as we now understand it, the epigram with a sting in its tail. The Romans have always had a taste for pasquinade, and Martial is pretty sure to have had some predecessors in his art. If so he has eclipsed them all. He has wit and elegance, and he is, what few Roman authors are, genuinely funny. It must be added that he is often indecent, because that explains the grossness of the epigrams in Jonson, Herrick and others of his following. But Martial does not survive merely because he is scandalously witty. He can write when he likes with simplicity and even with tenderness. He is a true artist in his own medium. His dexterity is consummate, his language precise and supple, full of lightness and brightness.

This chapter is not a balanced survey of ancient poetry, nor will the next chapter be a balanced survey of ancient prose. They merely touch on those influences which have been most potent in their effect upon English literature. The absolute values and the relative merits of ancient authors do not come into question. If they did the picture would be greatly changed. Sophocles is a greater poet than Theocritus, but has had nothing like his influence on our literature. Propertius is a truer poet according to modern taste than Ovid, but Ovid is an incomparably more important figure in the history of literature. And it is the history of literature with which we are here concerned.

5
Chapter

Platonism in English Poetry

It is a plot of ground, however, which, we would plead, has two great advantages to set off against its scantiness. First, it is a garden which we all already know and love; and our study of platonism within its enclosure will, at least, be sympathetic – a matter of the first importance where the understanding of an elusive spirit like that of platonism is concerned. Secondly, the platonism which our little garden offers to our study is, for the most part, what we would call 'personal platonism' only slightly affected by tradition; and it is personal platonism which, somehow or other, we must have learnt to appreciate, before we can hope to understand traditional platonism.

Let us begin the preliminary explanations, which we said would be as brief as possible, with what we are sure you wish us to begin with – with a statement of what platonism, as we understand it, is – and, more especially, of what it is as a spirit in poetry.

Platonism we would describe, in the most general terms, as the mood of one who has a curious eye for the endless variety of this visible and temporal world and a fine sense of its beauties, yet is haunted by the presence of an invisible and eternal world behind, or, when the mood is most pressing, within, the visible and temporal world, and sustaining both it and himself – a world not perceived as external to himself, but inwardly lived by him, as that with which, at moments of ecstasy, or even habitually, he is become one. This is how personal platonism, whether in a Plotinus or in a Wordsworth, may be described in outline – and it is in outline that such a mood is best described.

But traditional platonism enlarges, and adds detail to, the outline-description which is sufficient for personal platonism: and we are told that the man, who, in the temporal world, is haunted by the presence of the eternal world, is a Lover – that, from love of the visible and temporal, he is lifted up to love of the invisible and eternal world, of the existence of which his love is itself the sure evidence. Further, we are told that it is with its conjoined Ideas, or Powers, of Goodness, Truth, and Beauty, operating, for one end, through the agency of a hierarchy of dependent Ideas or Powers, that the world invisible and eternal – sometimes called World, sometimes God – sustains the world visible and temporal; sustains it, not once for all, but by continually creating it anew, always after its own likeness, but yet with endless variety, never the same. Further, we are told that the world so created is a living creature which has soul as well as body; and that it is through the intermediation of this created 'Soul of the World', or 'Plastic Spirit of Nature', that the operation of God, or of the eternal World of Ideas, actually reaches matter, and moulds it into the form of the world visible and temporal. Finally, we are told that the exaltation of love of the visible and temporal into that love which is evidence of the existence of the invisible and eternal world is inseparable from 'Recollection': the Lover had experience of the invisible and eternal world in a former life, and now in this life recollects it – sees it again, in flashes, through the darkness of the flesh. This, in brief, is the teaching of traditional platonism.

It is enough for us to know that the mood is a real experience. That it was an extraordinarily vivid experience in Plato himself is plain from the expression which he gives to it in the *Phaedrus, Symposium,* and *Timaeus* – an expression, indeed, so memorable that it arrested and held the attention of disciples almost to the exclusion of the Master's other teaching. Plato, the great man of science, the mathematician, the founder (along with Socrates) of logic and of moral and political philosophy, was exploited and superseded by Aristotelians and Stoics, and soon ceased to be an individual force even within his own Academy. But Plato the prophet lived on in the speculation of theologians, the inspiration of poets, and the lives of religious men, Pagan, Jewish, Christian, and Moslem, through the Alexandrine period and the early centuries of our era, through the dark ages so-called, through the two centuries of the dawning renaissance, till in the latter half of the fifteenth century, with the foundation of the Platonic Academy at Florence, his personality became the object of a cult to which zeal for the new learning, love of earthly beauty, and love of heavenly beauty, all gave fervour. Plato's Dialogues, especially the *Phaedrus* and *Symposium,* as translated and commented on by the chief devotee of this cult, Marsilio Ficino, and the *Enneads* of Plotinus, as translated by the same hand, now began to be read in the West, and, while they influenced philosophy and theology chiefly, also influenced poetry by adding volume and weight to a stream of 'Platonism' which could be traced back beyond Dante, and, in the sonnets of Petrarch, more than a century before the foundation of the Platonic Academy, had already become a classic river which was to flow on through Italian, French, and English love-poetry – Spenser's, Sidney's, Shakespeare's, Jonson's, Drummond's, Donne's – till at last it was' lost in the confluence of other waters.

The platonism which lived throughout these eighteen or nineteen hundred years was, as we have said, not the doctrine of Plato the man of science, but the mood expressed in the *Phaedrus, Symposium,* and *Timaeus,* and that only – the mood of Plato the prophet, Plato's own expression of which, handed down by tradition, appealed to theologians and poets who already knew the mood as a personal experience of their own. Had there not been such personal experience to appeal to in an unbroken succession of men of genius, the platonic tradition could not have maintained itself even for the use of those who merely repeated its letter without understanding its spirit. In the main, throughout all these centuries, the platonism of the *Phaedrus, Symposium,* and *Timaeus* was a genuine faith – as in Philo the Jew, in Plotinus, in Erigena, in Dante, in Ficino himself, in Michael Angelo, in Spenser, in Cudworth, in Henry More. Only here and there, chiefly among sonneteers of the Petrarchan succession, did the platonism of these three Dialogues become a mannerism.

The platonism expressed in the *Phaedrus, Symposium,* and *Timaeus* is indeed a vital spirit not easily quenched. Its vitality seems to us to be bound up with what may be called its duality. It has two elements, logically distinguishable, which it holds in organic combination – love of the visible and temporal, and love of the invisible and eternal, the former love passing into the latter, not once for all, but, as it were, in a perennial stream. If love of the visible and temporal were ever to fail, love of the invisible and eternal would cease. It is only the born connoisseur of things seen and temporal who is likely to aspire to, and is able to attain to, and, without abating his love of things seen and temporal, is able to hold fast by that love, or faith, which is the certainty of things unseen and eternal.

We would ask you to note carefully this quality in platonism. Platonism is love of the unseen and eternal cherished by one who rejoices in the seen and temporal. This is the platonism of Plato himself, and, what concerns us especially now, it is the platonism which is vital in great poetry. But the history of platonism shows us how easily the continuity of the temporal with the eternal, of the visible with the invisible, may be broken, and two one-sided dead platonisms made out of the one living two-sided platonism. There were neoplatonic philosophers and theologians who preached only this: 'Shut your eyes to the visible that you may apprehend the invisible; flee from the flesh that you may find union with God'; and there were amorous sonneteers who were only platonists in manner, but, at heart, disciples of Ovid. After all, it is in the great poets, rather than in philosophers and theologians, that we find the balance of the platonist mood the more justly kept. The philosopher or theologian who is a platonist, unless he is endowed with great sensibility, is apt, as thinker, to treat Goodness, Truth, and Beauty, and the other Ideas dependent on them, as abstractions, for it is with abstractions that we think; whereas the great poet who is also a platonist is saved, by his poet's sensibility, from the extreme of asceticism, or abstraction, into which the theologian or philosopher is apt to fall. As poet, he is one who cannot take his eyes off the things of this visible world; and, as he looks intently at them, or vividly recalls them in solitary reflection, they charm him into dreaming them; he sees them with the eye, not of wayward fancy, but, since he is a born platonist, with the eye of steady imagination – sees them altered, on a sudden, into their own eternal meaning – sees them become vehicles of the unseen and eternal world which is substantially present in them behind the veil of their sensible attributes.

Now we have done with the preliminary explanations. You have we trust, gathered from them, first, that it is to the great poets, rather than to philosophers and theologians (with some notable exceptions), that we would have you go for the finest expression of the platonist mood realized most adequately as a personal experience, and, secondly, that the study of this mood, as a personal experience expressed without the aid of traditional forms, ought to precede the study of it as expressed with the aid of them: for example (to take two platonist poets of the highest rank, Spenser and Wordsworth), we ought to study platonism in Wordsworth first, and then study it in Spenser. We shall take Wordsworth and Coleridge closely together, in order to compare and contrast them as platonists.

In both the platonist mood is a personal experience little influenced by traditional platonic teaching, although, of course, that teaching was matter of knowledge to them. Both are aware of the real presence of the eternal in the temporal; the eternal for them is no abstraction apart, it is concretely present in the temporal: but Wordsworth is habitually aware of the real presence. Sometimes, indeed, it is ecstatically felt by him in 'gleams like the flashing of a shield', but, for the most part, it is apprehended quietly in the actual scenes and occurrences, often quite ordinary scenes and occurrences, of external nature and of man's life directly observed, accurately remembered, and plainly described: whereas to Coleridge the presence of the eternal is only intermittently revealed. The cause of this difference is interesting, and helps us to understand the conditions under which the platonist mood is realized. As Wordsworth saw, Coleridge's was a mind 'debarred from nature's living images' – debarred by 'its self-created sustenance', 'platonic forms', and 'words for things' (Wordsworth is speaking here of Coleridge at Cambridge) – 'debarred from nature's living images' most of all, we would add, by an imagination, weird and romantic, and little moved by passion. 'Nature's living images,' actually existing, ordinary things, seen in mental pictures which fill us with wonder, although they are soberly, even austerely, drawn true to life -such is the world, seen and temporal, in which the mind of a Plato, or a Dante, or a Wordsworth is aware, and makes us aware, of the world unseen and eternal. Debarred from this world of living images by his weird and romantic imagination, Coleridge produced, in the *Ancient Mariner* and *Christabel*, what is, doubtless, great poetry – great, because it translates us, with amazement, from this earth; but not the very greatest poetry, because it is not to the Platonic Plain of Truth, not to the unmoved Empyrean Heaven that it translates us, only to the space, midway between the Earth and the Moon, where the demon-heroes and the fairies are. And Coleridge was a great poet only in his youth – only so long as the pageant of weird images still kept passing before him. The time came to him prematurely when the 'self-created sustenance' of his mind failed, and he could say:

Afflictions bow me down to earth:
Nor care I that they rob me of my mirth,
But oh! each visitation

Suspends what nature gave me at my birth,
My shaping spirit of Imagination.

While Imagination remained he was content with fairyland, and heeded not the world unseen and eternal: but when Imagination failed, then he longed for the world unseen and eternal, and sought it where his memory of rare ecstatic moments told him it is to be found, in 'nature's living images' – in the world seen and temporal pictured, as it is, for our wonder: but he sought in vain, for the Dejection which suspended his shaping spirit of Imagination also killed the inward joy out of which, in the past, these ecstatic moments had flashed:

All this long eve, so balmy and serene,
Have I been gazing on the western sky,
And its peculiar tint of yellow green:
And still I gaze – and with how blank an eye!
And those thin clouds above, in flakes and bars,
That give away their motion to the stars;
Those stars, that glide behind them or between,
Now sparkling, now bedimmed, but always seen;
Yon crescent moon as fixed as if it grew
In its own cloudless, starless, lake of blue;
I see them all so excellently fair,
I see, not feel, how beautiful they are!

To see, and while one sees, to feel Beauty – this is the platonist mood. That the mood which Coleridge here – in *Dejection: an Ode* – so pathetically mourns as gone from him, was his at times, and was experienced in the contemplation of 'nature's living images', let the two following passages testify: This (addressed to Charles Lamb, in *This lime-tree bower my prison*): Ah! slowly sink

Behind the western ridge, thou glorious sun!
Shine in the slant beams of the sinking orb,
Ye purple heath-flowers! richlier burn, ye clouds!
Live in the yellow light, ye distant groves!
And kindle, thou blue ocean! So my Friend
Struck with deep joy may stand, as I have stood,

Silent with swimming sense; yea, gazing round On the wide landscape, gaze till all doth seem Less gross than bodily; and of such hues As veil the Almighty Spirit, when yet he makes Spirits perceive his presence –

and this (in the Eolian Harp):

O the one life within us and abroad,
Which meets all motion and becomes its soul,

A light in sound, a sound-like power in light, Rhythm in all thought, and joyance everywhere – Methinks it should have been impossible Not to love all things in a world so filled; Where the breeze warbles, and the mute still air Is music slumbering on her instrument.

. . . .

And what if all of animated nature Be but organic harps diversely framed, That tremble into thought, as o'er them sweeps Plastic and vast, one intellectual breeze, At once the soul of each, and God of all.

In *The Prelude, or Growth of a Poet's Mind, an Autobiographical Poem,* Wordsworth produced a work which must be regarded as the classic authority on Platonism in Poetry. The essential nature and the necessary conditions of the platonist mood, as experienced by one who is a poet, are set forth by Wordsworth, in the *Prelude,* with so much first-hand knowledge, and with such subtlety of analysis and completeness of circumstance, that, if we might venture to offer advice, we would say that the study of this poem ought to precede the study of platonism in other English poets – especially where the platonism is much influenced by tradition, as it is in Spenser, and his successors, whether leaning to the Ovidian or to the 'metaphysical' side in style. We would have you make the platonist mood revealed as a personal experience in the *Prelude* the touchstone of the genuineness of the platonism ostensibly present in the writings of any one of this line of poets.

Let me, then, put down some of the marks of the platonist mood as Wordsworth helps us in the *Prelude* to surmise its nature.

It is an 'amplitude of mind' – to use an expression which occurs in *Prelude* xiv – which may be called indifferently Love, Imagination, Reason – an amplitude of mind which the eternal world, present within the temporal world, fills with its influence. In the first place, figured as *Love* the mood is an experience in which a Beauty not of this world suddenly flashes. through the transparency of some scene or event of this world, and entering into the poet's heart and cherished there, becomes a habit which disposes him ever after to recall the scene or event, and other scenes and events like it, and see them illumined with 'glory not their own'. But, secondly, thus habitually to recall and see is *Imagination*, which does not change the scene or event, as Fancy does, into something else, but sees it steadily as it is, only illumined: so that, while remaining the same scene or event for description, it is become, for imagination, the symbol of some Power or Virtue, or, as Plato would say, Idea, in which the diffused Beauty of the eternal world takes specific form. And, thirdly, the platonist mood, being Love and Imagination, is also *Reason* – the intuitive apprehension of the one spiritual system of the universe, which Love seeks after as Heavenly Beauty sojourning on earth, and Imagination sees variously figured in scenes and events of this temporal world become symbols:

> *I held unconscious intercourse with beauty Old as creation. All that I beheld Was dear, and hence to finer influxes The mind lay open, to a more exact And close communion. I would walk alone, Under the quiet stars, and at that time Have felt whate'er there is of power in sound To breathe an elevated mood, by form Or image unprofaned; and I would stand, If the night blackened with a coming storm, Beneath some rock, listening to notes that are The ghostly language of the ancient earth.*

Or make their dim abode in distant winds. Thence did I drink the visionary power; And deem not profitless those fleeting moods Of shadowy exultation: not for this, That they are kindred to our purer mind And intellectual life; but that the soul Remembering how she felt, but what she felt Remembering not, retains an obscure sense Of possible sublimity, whereto With growing faculties she doth aspire, With faculties still growing, feeling still That whatsoever point they gain, they yet Have something to pursue.

And not alone, 'Mid gloom and tumult, but no less 'mid fair And tranquil scenes, that universal power And fitness in the latent qualities And essences of things, by which the mind Is moved with feelings of delight, to me Came strengthened with a superadded soul, A virtue not its own.

. . . .

How shall I seek the origin? where find Faith in the marvellous things which then I felt? Oft in these moments such a holy calm Would overspread my soul, that bodily eyes Were utterly forgotten, and what I saw Appeared like something in myself, a dream, A prospect in the mind. This from the Prelude; the following from The Wye above Tintern.

I have felt A presence that disturbs me with the joy Of elevated thoughts; a sense sublime Of something far more deeply interfused, Whose dwelling is the light of setting suns, And the round ocean and the living air, And the blue sky, and in the mind of man: A motion and a spirit, that impels All thinking things, all objects of all thought, And rolls through all things. Therefore am I still A lover of the meadows and the woods, And mountains; and of all that we behold From this green earth.

From these passages (and there are many like them in the *Excursion*, in the *Intimations of Immortality*, and throughout the whole poetry of Wordsworth) we can surmise what the personal platonism of a great poet necessarily is. First, for him the eternal is immanent in the temporal, not transcendent as it may be for the philosopher and theologian, if they lack a poet's sensibility. Secondly, the immanence is at first revealed in flashes to the poet -and here a poet may stop, and yet be a great poet. But, thirdly, the greatest poets are those to whom, as to Wordsworth, the immanence, at first revealed in flashes, becomes, in course of time, the object of an habitual faith, as we may call it, which dominates their lives, so that in the end they see all things, great and small, *sub specie aeternitatis,* as symbols. For them the temporal world is become altogether a scheme of symbols:

Alles Vergängliche ist nur ein Gleichniss.

Here let us say something about symbolism, for we think that, by doing so, we may make clearer to you what we understand by the personal platonism of a great poet.

Symbols are of two kinds: first, those invented and made by the poet himself or his predecessors; and, secondly, those which are not invented and made at all, but come of themselves to the individual poet – spontaneous symbols, we may call them.

The study of invented symbols belongs mainly to the domain of literary history. The main task of the student is to explain the structure of certain similes and personifications, and to interpret certain allegories, as they occur; and this he does by reading the intended 'meaning' of each in the light of its literary history.

As for spontaneous symbols, the symbols which are not invented at all, but come of themselves, the first and last thing to be said about them is that they have no literary history and do not admit of interpretation. They spring, without the poet's conscious aid, out of his emotion. They are of two sorts, according as their form is supplied mainly by external nature, or is mainly the product of the poet's entranced brain: that is, spontaneous symbols – symbols which are not invented, but come – are to be distinguished as nature's symbols, and trance-symbols. Nature's symbols are what Wordsworth calls 'nature's living images' – actual scenes, or events, or persons, accurately pictured by the poet in tranquillity, with the after-light upon them of a vivid emotion which his first seeing or picturing of them kindled in him: it is this after-light which transforms them from mere memoryimages into symbols. Such symbols do not admit of being 'interpreted'. What 'interpretation' is possible or needed of the scene which Wordsworth saw with the eye of Love, or of Imagination, or of 'the morethan-reasoning mind', when he wrote

Flow on for ever, Yarrow stream! Fulfil thy pensive duty, Well pleased that future bards should chaunt For simple hearts thy beauty: To dream-light dear while yet unseen, Dear to the common sunshine, And dearer still, as now I feel, To memory's shadowy moonshine!

This dear image is a symbol which is itself its own meaning, and needs no further interpretation.

And so too it is with the other sort of spontaneous symbols, with trance-symbols, images, like Ezekiel's, or Dante's, or Vaughan's – 'I saw Eternity the other night' – images with no definite external originals, which flash spontaneously out of some tense emotional state of the poet, especially when ordinary outlets are closed, and, relieving for a moment – just as an involuntary cry or gesture may relieve – the tension of the emotion, are accepted straightway as 'interpreting' the mystery with which the emotion is charged – how, words cannot tell: for the tranceimage, thus become a symbol, is, like nature's symbol, itself the 'interpretation' longed for, and admits of no further interpretation; the mere seeing it with the mind's eye, or hearing it with the mind's ear, is the 'interpretation' eagerly expected. The emotional tension is a sort of ineffable question, and here is the answer to it! – this loud shout of praise heard afar, articulating itself, as Dante listens, into melody and words (*Par.*xiv, xxiv); this sudden illumination in which the bright forms shape themselves before his eyes when he first has sight of the Celestial Rose (*Par.*xxx-xxxiii). These are the modes, well known to the psychologist, in which tense religious, or other, feeling expresses itself; and it is in connexion with these experiences that the need of symbolic expression, and its primary satisfaction by means of the spontaneous symbol, must be accounted for. The need of symbolic expression, first naturally satisfied by the spontaneous symbol, and then artificially by the invented symbol embroidered, if it is to have anypoetic value, on the web of the spontaneous symbol – this need of symbolic expression is involved in the very nature of emotion, which is a state of tension always seeking relief in cries, in gestures, or (and it is this that concerns us here) in images, either nature's living images – natural objects seen pictured with the after-light upon them – or trance-images.

The sole meaning of one of 'nature's living images' – Yarrow unvisited, Yarrow visited, Yarrow revisited – is simply itself, as the poet sees it, with 'the hope divine of pure imagination' quickened by it in his heart. Here 'resemblance' between symbol and thing symbolized is not to be thought of, for each belongs to a different world. The symbol is the image of an object of sense in the temporal world, the thing symbolized is in the eternal world, beyond sense, beyond understanding; not seen, not known, but felt: the poet's sole guarantee of its reality is 'the hope divine of pure imagination', felt while he pictures Yarrow, or Wye, The Highland Girl, or Michael building the sheep-fold on the foundation sacramentally laid by his son.

Wordsworth's poetry, then, being impassioned contemplation of 'nature's living images', takes rank as a typical product of the platonist mood. For this mood, Beauty, Truth, and Goodness, and the other Powers or Ideas of the eternal world, are always substantially present in objects of sense, never exist apart as abstractions waiting, like all abstractions, to be personified and to have their parts assigned to them, as persons or puppets, in some elaborated allegory. It is a mistake to suppose, as some have done, that deliberate personification and allegory are of the essence of platonism. They were, indeed, introduced into platonism at an early time -against the precept of Plato himself, and, since his myths are not allegories, against his example too -and became traditional, as exegetical methods in theology, and embellishments in poetry; but they are really, in so far as they are deliberately invented, foreign to its nature. As soon as Goodness, Truth, Beauty, and the other Ideas of the eternal world are deliberately personified, and have parts carefully assigned to them in allegory, they are become mere items in a pageant of the temporal world — objects which Fancy plays with. But for a poet like Wordsworth there is nothing to personify and play with: 'nature's living images', informed with the presence of the eternal world, are already there, and are, themselves, sufficient. The more pressing the platonist mood is in such a poet, the more directly and simply, eschewing simile, personification, and allegory, will he describe the objects and events of the world of external nature and of man's life which constitute the matter of his poem. He will describe these objects and events directly and simply, because they themselves were just what he had before him in sense or memory, when, on a sudden, he felt 'the hope divine of pure imagination' in his heart, and the presence of the eternal world encompassed him. To alter these objects or events by personification, or allegory, or simile, would be to trifle with the august experience which came to him while he regarded them.

Now we come to personal platonism in Shelley; and what we have just said about the incompatibility of allegory and personification with the genuine platonist mood may make you think that we ought to say that there is no personal platonism in Shelley. But we are not going to say that:

> *That garden sweet, that lady fair, And all sweet shapes and odours there In truth have never passed away: 'Tis we, 'tis our's, are changed! not they. For love, and beauty, and delight, There is no death, nor change; their might Exceeds our organs, which endure No light, being themselves obscure.*

These concluding lines of *The Sensitive Plant* breathe the genuine spirit of personal platonism, but such lines are comparatively rare in Shelley; and his poetry, as a whole, with its abounding personification of the modes of human thought, feeling, and action, and of the phenomena of external nature, gives little evidence of the influence of the platonist mood likely, at first sight, to be satisfactory to any one who takes Wordsworth as the Platonist Poet *par excellence.* It is in these modes and phenomena themselves, as they are, not as changed by personification into what they are not, that the platonist mood, as exhibited by Wordsworth finds what it seeks.

But we must not judge Shelley's platonism by the standard of Wordsworth's. There is all the difference in the world between deliberate personification, which is, indeed, foreign to the genius of platonism, as debarring us from nature's living images, and spontaneous personification. Spontaneous personification is simply Shelley's way of seeing nature's living images. Sometimes his visionary personages are tender dream-shapes, dryads and naiads, who for him, as for the old Greek countrymen, at once are, and are not, the very oak-trees and fountains; more often his personification is, like Blake's, of elemental powers, the might of which passes in passion through his sympathetic soul, and embodies itself in Titanic forms. How different is such personification from that which, in the professedly platonist poetry of the Petrarchan tradition, so often but ill conceals the entire absence of personal platonism! Shelley's skilful and learned Fancy, indeed, clothes his visionary personages with newly invented or traditional attributes: but behind the added attributes, the visionary personages themselves are always there, not invented, but come of themselves out of the poet's day-dream or passion; and they are, for him, what images of actual scenes and events and persons are for Wordsworth, visible and temporal vehicles of the invisible and eternal. Read Wordsworth's sonnet beginning, 'Even so for me a vision sanctified,' and Shelley *Adonaïs* together, and you will feel assured that this is so: the eternal world which Love discerns present in this world is not less manifest to Shelley in the visionary personages who throng the Roman chamber where Keats lies dead, than it is to Wordsworth in the face which he describes so simply:

> *When thou, dear Sister! wert become Death's Bride, No*
> *trace of pain or languor could abide*

That change: – age on thy brow was smoothed – thy cold Wan cheek at once was privileged to unfold A loveliness to living youth denied. Oh! if within me hope should e'er decline, The lamp of faith, lost Friend! too faintly burn; Then may that heaven-revealing smile of thine, The bright assurance, visibly return: And let my spirit in that power divine Rejoice, as, through that power, it ceased to mourn.

We may say, then, that personification, which is certainly not essential to platonism, and is a weakness in the majority of platonist poets, is the strength of Shelley's platonism: these visionary personages spring spontaneously out of his ecstatic passion, out of his longing to be made one with the Spirit of Nature, which is the Spirit of Beauty. It is in a fairy chariot, moving in a pageant of such visionary personages, that the ascension is made, in *Queen Mab*, to the Temple of this Spirit, just as the ascension to the Plain of Truth is made by winged chariots in the *Phaedrus*:

Spirit of Nature! here! In this interminable wilderness Of worlds, at whose immensity Even soaring fancy staggers, Here is thy fitting temple. Yet not the lightest leaf That quivers to the passing breeze Is less instinct with thee: Yet not the meanest worm That lurks in graves and fattens on the dead Less shares thy eternal breath. Spirit of Nature! thou! Imperishable as this scene, Here is thy fitting temple!

And in the Hymn to Intellectual Beauty, he tells us that his life was early dedicated to the service of this Spirit, which

– visits with inconstant glance Each human heart and countenance; Like hues and harmonies of evening, Like clouds in starlight widely spread, Like memory of music fled, Like aught that for its grace may be Dear, and yet dearer for its mystery.

Spirit of BEAUTY!. . . .

And just another word more before we end this chapter. You understand, that the distinction which we have so continually spoken of, using Platonic language, between World invisible and eternal and World visible and temporal, is a distinction with which scientific thought has no concern: it is a distinction which is valid only within the region where Poetry reigns: but it is not therefore of less moment to us in the conduct of our lives.

6
Chapter

Prose

INTRODUCTION

Prose literature begins in story telling, which can reach a remarkable standard of excellence among an unlettered people. This excellence, if we are to judge by the stories in the Old Testament and in Herodotus, was strikingly attained among the ancient Greeks and Hebrews. There is no question of mutual influence; the art is traditional. Herodotus is not a very early writer—he was the contemporary of Sophocles-but he is the last of a long series of predecessors, most of whom never thought of writing down their stories at all. He not only thought of this but conceived the design of using the traditions to illustrate a central theme. This was the age-long conflict between Greeks and Barbarians, more especially the two Persian wars. He travelled far and wide to get material, considering nothing irrelevant that had any bearing at all upon the relations between Greece and the Orient. In this way he became not only the first considerable figure in European prose literature but the first true historian, his predecessors and even some of his successors being mere chroniclers or just raconteurs. Herodotus for his part had both a central theme and a philosophy of history. History, he thought, was a record of the punishments inflicted by the gods on human pride and insolence, and of their favour for the little, well-governed state. His material, being mostly based on hearsay, is easily shown by modern critical methods to be full of errors. But the position of Herodotus himself is unassailable.

He does not guarantee the truth of all his stories, but he regards it as his business nevertheless to tell them all, because what people say is itself a fact of historical importance. And indeed if we can judge the value of his evidence better than he, in his day and with his lights, could judge it, it is because he himself has given us the material for doing so. As for the style of Herodotus almost everything that has been said about the Homeric style is, apart from the poetry, applicable here. It is simple, clear, vivid, dramatic, constantly keeping the story in mind. It is one of the most delightful of styles, but the secret of it died with Herodotus. His true successors are the story-tellers of the Middle Ages.

The next great name among ancient historians is Thucydides of Athens, who took for his subject the Peloponnesian War, in which he himself played a part. He was not a great deal younger than Herodotus, but he seems to five in a different world. The older man had not lacked critical insight, and some of his observations are shrewd and pertinent. But he did not regard it as his special business to criticise the traditions; he obviously loves them and wishes to believe them as far as he can. He was not untouched by the new spirit of enlightenment which appeared in Greece after the end of the Persian wars, but his mind turns instinctively to the great generation that had won the battles of Marathon and Salamis, and he has no heart to criticise it for its simple faith in oracles and miracles. He even knows something of the new rhetoric, but uses it very sparingly and with care that it should not complicate or alter the tone of the style he had inherited from the storytellers. Thucydides is the opposite of all this. He will believe nothing on the strength of tradition alone. He applies an intense and searching criticism to the whole of early Greek history, and then gives a brief reconstruction of it in a manner as austerely scientific as the most severe modern scholar would adopt. If he is devoid of credulity he is equally devoid of cynicism. He has a reverence for great men and, if it would seem that he reverences them only for their intellectual qualities, that is no doubt because like Socrates he believed that moral and intellectual qualities are indistinguishable. His own eminent virtue as a historian is his passion for the truth. It was this which chiefly led him to take for his subject the history of his own times, because here it seemed possible to discover the truth. He took infinite pains to ascertain it and, when he had, he set it down with an impartiality as complete as is possible for a sensitive human being. The result is a history which in conception and execution stood unrivalled until modern times and is in some ways unrivalled still.

HISTORIANS

The style of the History was as new as its conception. It has nothing traditional about it like the style of Herodotus, but is entirely personal. The traditional style, Thucydides evidently felt, was no doubt right for the telling of traditional stories but not for a critical history written for the instruction of statesmen and thoughtful soldiers. That clearly required a more modern style of writing. This modern way was already coming into fashion, its chief characteristic being that it was deeply imbued with the new rhetoric. What that was has been to some extent discussed already. Its principal effect was to substitute the period for the simple sentence. This was a natural or rather a necessary development as thought became more complex. A new medium had to be found for the expression of the human spirit in literature, and this was what rhetoric attempted to supply. As might be expected, its first efforts were in many respects mistaken and unhappy. The first exponents of the new style were besotted by their own pleasure in the balanced and complex sentence. Clause must be poised against clause at all costs. An antithetic structure was forced upon every sentence whether there was any antithesis in the thought or not. To point the antithesis they loved to end the clauses with like syllables, so as to get a kind of internal rhyme or assonance. Nay each sentence was composed more or less on a metrical scheme. These devices pleased Thucydides more than might have been expected in a man so reserved and free from childishness, and they often give his style an appearance of artificiality. But they are by no means omnipresent. When he is engaged upon what might be called straightforward narrative he is not much, if at all, more difficult than Herodotus. It is when he reflects upon the causes or effects of the war, or when he puts an oration in the mouth of some statesman, that Thucydides involves himself in these perplexed sentences. It is the new style breaking in upon the old. But everything he writes bears the impress of his personality. Thucydides can never be mistaken for anyone else. Whatever the faults of his style, it has an unforgettable quality. A speech like the Funeral Oration of Pericles makes the eloquence of more facile orators appear superficial, while in his simpler manner the account of the Athenian retreat from Syracuse may well be, what Macaulay, who had read everything, thought it was, the finest piece of narrative in any language.

In Thucydides as in all ancient historians we find a practice which on the face of it seems indefensible. From time to time they insert in their narrative a speech purporting to be delivered by some historical person, but in reality composed by the historians themselves. It must be considered that an ancient author did not have at his disposal an authentic version of what a speaker said, unless the speaker himself published it, which never happened for the convenience of Thucydides. He says that he always tried to give the general drift of any speech he reports. Everyone knows that it is impossible to remember more than a few of the actual words of a public speaker ten minutes after he has sat down. But apart from this there is an artistic problem involved. An ancient history, at least as the Greeks conceived it, was a work of art and therefore, according to ancient notions, must have a uniform tone. In other words it must be written throughout, speeches and all, in the same style; and that could only be the style of the writer. Whatever may be thought of this practice, it continued all through the Middle Ages and modern times until almost the other day.

In the Decline and Fall the speeches are as pure Gibbon as the narrative, for to Gibbon as much as to Thucydides a history was a work of art. And when a contemporary historian analyses the motives and character of Queen Elizabeth or Cromwell, is he not simply doing in a less artistic way what Thucydides and Gibbon do when they make a statesman reveal his character and motives in a speech composed for him?

The work of Thucydides (which he left unfinished) was continued by Xenophon in his Hellenica or 'History of Greece'. That Xenophon could tell a story as few ancient writers have shown the faculty of doing was proved once for all by his Anabasis. But history is something more than a tale of adventures. It requires the power of distinguishing the important issue from the unimportant and that kind of imagination that is called the historic sense. Thucydides possessed that sense as hardly any other man has possessed it, but Xenophon had it only in flashes. He has no large political ideas and does not understand them in other people. It is almost ludicrous to contrast the wisdom and insight revealed in the speeches of Thucydides with the empty volubility of the speeches in Xenophon. Yet Xenophon wrote such an engaging, easy picturesque style that he had great influence, if not at once, upon succeeding generations. Here as in other divisions of his work he stands between the Attic and the Hellenistic ages. For after his time history took something of a new turn. Of the new historians (the most eminent of whom were Ephorus and Theopompus) the primary purpose was to make history readable. In this they succeeded, but their success had some disastrous consequences. They must be given credit for extending the scope of history and assembling masses of information; but inevitably they were less concerned to assure its authenticity than to pick out its high fights. Whatever had dramatic value, whatever seemed heroically noble or scandalously wicked, was set forth by them with the eloquence they had learned from Isocrates but with small effort to criticise their sources, partly from a genuine deficiency in the critical spirit, partly from the feeling that a searching analysis might destroy some of their most sensational material. That historians should behave like this is of course highly reprehensible, but our only business is to understand what happened. This will become easier if we remember that the ancient historian was nearly always animated by patriotic motives. He had formed in his mind an ideal picture of his country's past and this he wished his readers to accept. Evidence that disturbed it was unwelcome and therefore not apt to be diligently sought. An historian who explodes the flattering legends which every people cherishes of its past must expect to encounter a good deal of unpopularity. Thucydides was prepared to risk that; but everybody is not a Thucydides.

The speeches, which were a great feature of the new school of historians, gave their authors the opportunity of displaying their skill in the kind of rhetoric which had been developed since the time of Thucydides, principally by Isocrates. It is probable that no great harm was done so long as the writers were dealing with recent or contemporary history, for most public men speak in the fashionable idiom of their day. But when the matter belongs to a remote past, or to a foreign or backward country, the practice becomes ridiculous. Thus Livy who, though he lived so much later, belongs to the Isocratean school of historians, makes Hannibal, whose native language was Punic, deliver eloquent orations in Latin, and that the Latin of Livy's own day almost a couple of centuries later. Even Tacitus makes the Caledonian chief Calgacus address his men in the kind of Latin no one but Tacitus could write. Nor is that the worst of it, for in these speeches the very sentiments of the speakers are apt to be modernised.

This leads to the mention of another aspect of ancient historiography—its moralising tendency. It was there from the first, for there is a great deal of moralising in Herodotus. But in him it is little more than the age-long reflections of simple generations upon the mystery of human destiny—a shaking of the head over the pride that goes before a fall. Thucydides draws no moral at all. The Isocratean historians however evidently scattered moral judgements right and left. It was the common opinion at all times in Greece that the artist should be a teacher, and history was an art. Therefore historians wrote in a mood—it would not be fair to call it a pose—for the most part of gloomy reprobation of human wickedness and folly, especially as exemplified in their own generation, for there was a tendency to look to the past as a time of greater simplicity and virtue, the contemplation of which ought to make us ashamed of our present degeneracy. This is the dominating tone of all ancient history down to Tacitus, who has expressed it with extraordinary force and intensity.

Passing over the work of the great Greek historian Polybius because it had almost no influence upon literature, we come to the Romans. Of the early Latin historians, among whom the most influential was the elder Cato, we know too little to justify detailed comment. But we can hardly thus dismiss Julius Caesar, whose Gallic War and Civil War are among the most celebrated of ancient books. Neither is, or was intended to be, a regular history; they are meant rather to furnish material for the future historian, at least as pièces justificatives of Caesar's own actions. It is well known that they are written in the third person, and this method is carried out with at least a great appearance of detachment and impartiality. The style of Caesar has always been admired. It is eminently clear and succinct, bare of ornament, of a studied simplicity and male elegance. There is little colour, little glow of imagination; but the very plainness of the style is more convincing than rhetoric.

Among the Roman historians proper the first important name was a lieutenant of Caesar's, Sallust. Two of his books survive entire: the Catiline and the Jugurthine War. They are not so much histories as historical brochures on two episodes, being the Conspiracy of Catiline in 63 B.C. and the campaigns against the Numidian king Jugurtha about half a century earlier. Neither book was written with the single-minded purpose of discovering and recording the facts. The author hoped that they would influence public opinion. He belonged to the 'popular' party, which was opposed to the Senate. So in the Jugurthine War his thesis is that all had been mismanaged by the Senate until Marius, a man of the people and a champion of his order, had got himself elected consul and brought the fighting to a triumphant conclusion. The Catiline is an account of that almost incredible affair when a handful of young nobles plotted to seize supreme power in Rome by murdering the consuls, one of whom was Cicero, and burning the city. The plot was discovered by the vigilance and crushed by the energy of Cicero. But he is not (as he ought to have been) the hero of the Catiline, in which the most prominent parts next to that of the villain Catiline himself are played by Cato, who makes a great speech calling for the death penalty, and Caesar, who makes a great speech condemning the, death penalty as an ineffective deterrent. As there was a strong suspicion that Caesar had himself been implicated in the conspiracy, the Catiline has been commonly regarded as an attempt to whitewash Caesar. But it has perhaps not been sufficiently considered that Sallust was faced by an artistic problem. The speeches which Cicero had actually delivered against Catiline had long been published and were universally regarded as among the masterpieces of Roman eloquence. Sallust could not embody them, as they stood, in his own short study; and to rewrite them in his own style would have exposed him to ridicule and contempt. For that style is almost the opposite of Cicero's. The long, intricate yet smoothly flowing periods of the orator give place in Sallust to a type of sentence which is deliberately broken into short, pregnant clauses; the smooth rhythm is checked and halted, the uniform tone replaced by splashes of brilliant colouring. He is fond of archaic turns of expression, perhaps in reaction against Cicero, but more probably because he felt these went well with his general attitude of old-world austerity. It is a highly effective style, though mannered and somewhat uneasy, and its combination with his highly sensational matter accounts for his popularity at all times and especially in the Tudor and Elizabethan ages.

He was greatly influenced by Thucydides; but, whereas the thought of Thucydides is often strikingly original, Sallust is apt to content himself with the epigrammatic expression of a truism, generally of a moralising kind, for, unlike Thucydides but like Tacitus, he carries very far that tendency to moralise in a censorious vein which we remarked as characteristic of ancient history. There is another point in which he resembles Tacitus—his skill in character-drawing. There is almost none of this in Herodotus and only the beginnings of it in Thucydides. Xenophon does attempt it, particularly in his Anabasis and his Agesilaus. But the traits of character are not very subtly or distinctly drawn, and Xenophon's people remain rather types than individuals. Sallust makes a real advance on this. His bold, vivid, 'impressionistic' sketches of the chief actors in his scenes may not represent the truth about them; but they are true to nature and they stay in the memory. It is unnecessary to point out the importance of this development; one has only to think of the character-drawing in Tacitus, in Clarendon, in Macaulay and Carlyle.

In the beautiful Preface to his history Livy states the motives which induced him to undertake the work of his life. They may be reduced to one—patriotism. In his own lifetime he had seen the vast framework of the Roman power shaken to its foundations by a series of terrible civil wars. In the course of these wars, as always happens, the standard of public and private morals had been lowered. Worst of all to Livy's way of thinking men had lost their libertas, the necessary root of all genuine virtue; the Republic had been destroyed and the Romans were now the subjects of one man, the emperor Augustus. From the contemplation of all this Livy turned to the past and sought comfort there. There he saw the grand forms of the Republican heroes, who never thought of themselves but only of the state. In other words he idealised that part of Román history about which least was known. His politics were a kind of romantic Toryism. He was a student and a recluse in love with a heroic dream.

Of his great work we possess thirty 'books' complete with the greater part of five others. It was designed to embrace a hundred and fifty, but perhaps the author did not get beyond the hundred and forty-first. It is obvious that no man, however diligent and long-lived, could write a history of that compass if he had to do any real research. Livy worked with none but written sources; he did not visit the scenes of battles or other important events; his method was to follow a single 'authority' —meaning somebody who had already written on the period with which he happened to be dealing—and only leave him if he came across another author who seemed to give a more credible narrative in certain points than the first. His inclination is to believe whatever shows the worthies of the old Republic in the best fight. He does not conceal evidence that points in the other direction, but he often tries to mitigate or explain it away. He is sadly deficient in critical acumen, and neither Thucydides nor Polybius was able to teach him better. He often does not understand clearly what he is writing about, especially in his accounts of military operations or constitutional changes. In spite of these very serious defects he achieves his object. He has written what might be called the prose epic of Rome, which he has told in page after page of glowing narrative and ardent eloquence. It is an illustration of what can be done by style, for it is by his style that Livy survives. He must have learned a great deal from Cicero, but his sentences have a different rhythm and modulation; the order of words is bolder, there is more interlacing of phrase with phrase; the vocabulary is more poetical. He is in many ways the most pictorial of the ancient historians, using a broader sweep of the brush than Tacitus, although Tacitus is more vivid. He does not have the speed and brevity of Sallust, but he does not waste words. His artistic conscience is such that it is impossible to find a careless sentence in his work.

The next in the fist of Roman historians is unquestionably the greatest both as a writer and as an investigator of the truth. This is Tacitus, whose life covered the second half of the first century and the first half of the second. If we were to judge by that aristocratic temper of his, we should infer that he belonged to one of the old, politically important families of Rome. What is certain is that he had a very distinguished public career ending in the consulship. The earlier part of this career fell in the reign of the emperor Domitian. It would appear that Domitian administered the empire with ability and success, but in Rome itself he showed himself a gloomy and suspicious tyrant. He suppressed all freedom of speech and writing; he executed or banished the philosophers, who stood for liberty of conscience. Tacitus, who hated this policy, was nevertheless in his official capacity consenting to it. If he had refused he would in all probability have been put to death, and evidently he was not prepared to refuse. That was his personal tragedy, and he as much as confesses it towards the end of his *Agricola*. One does not remember a happy passage in all the extant works of Tacitus.

In the earlier part of his career he was famous as an orator, and the impress of his rhetorical studies is upon his first book, an 'imaginary conversation' between three famous masters of eloquence composed in a style which without being quite Ciceronian is clearly in the tradition of Cicero. This dialogue was produced before the tyranny of Domitian had made itself felt. Then came the years of silence, a great slice out of the best years of the historian's life, *grande humani aevi spatium*, as he says in his sad, impressive way. When at last after the assassination of Domitian men could breathe freely and write what they felt, Tacitus once more took his pen in his hand. But it was a changed man who wrote and he wrote in a changed style. Cicero is now completely rejected as a model. There is no model; for, while Tacitus may have owed something to Sallust and something to the elder Pliny, his manner of writing is henceforth entirely his own. It is still however experimental and in places harsh and crabbed. The subject he chose was the life of Agricola, his father-in-law, to whom he felt that justice had not been done. After the *Agricola* he brought out another little treatise, generally called for short the *Germania*, which reads more smoothly than the *Agricola* but is less moving, being an account of the tribes inhabiting the wide regions included in the Roman Germany.

His next work was on a very different scale. It has come down to us under the title of *Histories* and originally consisted of fourteen 'books', of which we now possess the first four. They deal with the reigns of Galba, Otho and Vitellius, which together lasted only a year; the lost books took the story down to the end of Vespasian. The *Histories* are not exactly easy reading, but the meaning, where the text is sound, is never really in doubt, which is more than can be said of some more flowing and facile styles. The common charge against Tacitus that he is obscure involves an incorrect use of the word. Obscurity is an intentional darkening of one's meaning for artistic or other reasons; but Tacitus is always trying to extract from words the utmost meaning that he can. This concentration is carried a stage further in the *Annals,* a later work than the *Histories* and like them surviving in a mutilated form. It was also when complete somewhat longer, but it dealt with a longer period and took a wider sweep. The *Annals* has made a greater impression on readers than any other work of Tacitus. To some extent this is due to the subject. The early Roman emperors are more interesting to us than their mushroom successors or even the Flavian dynasty founded by Vespasian. We know that Tiberius and Nero were represented after their deaths as monsters of wickedness, and we turn to see what Tacitus makes of them. But after all what enchains the reader is the style. Its effects are more easily described than its elements; the imagination is irresistibly impressed by the vividness of his descriptions, and the judgement is almost overpowered by the seduction of his advocacy. The epigrams for which he is famous are not so numerous as is supposed, for Tacitus was too good a writer to use a style compact of epigrams. Even those he does permit himself owe less to their verbal point than to their psychological insight.

Tacitus has great merits as an historian. He is learned and accurate; he understands affairs and how public business is transacted; he does not deliberately distort the truth; he has the enthusiasm for noble things, the hatred of baseness, without which an historian may easily become blind to the moral significance of history, if it has any moral significance. But the historian must not let his feelings affect his judgement, and this is what Tacitus does. He did not see the good side of the Empire because he thought it had murdered liberty and put back the clock of civilisation. So he is not fair to the emperors. And here his power of characterisation, in which he excels all ancient historians, served him only too well. His picture of Tiberius is painted in the darkest colours with here and there a relieving touch which only heightens the gloom of the total effect. Much the same is true of his portrait of Nero. But however unjust it may be, it is magnificent literature. From Tacitus historians learned that human actions are only fully intelligible to him who understands human motives. And that was a very important lesson.

BIOGRAPHY

Biography might be regarded as a branch of history. But it developed on lines of its own. In a rudimentary form it is found very early—there is for instance a *Life of Homer* which in its original form seems to go back to the sixth or even the seventh century before Christ—but the first regular biography set in a historical framework appears to be the *Agesilaus* of Xenophon. It is a Life of the Spartan king of that name written by one who knew him personally. It is interesting and it is not uncandid, but it has a defect very common in biographies ancient and modern—it is more a eulogy than an impartial account of its hero. Such Lives appear to have been fairly common in the Alexandrine age. They were not confined to statesmen and warriors and kings, but included men of distinction in all walks of fife. It looks as if there had been a special revival of biographical writing towards the end of the first Christian century. At least to this period belong the Life of Apollonius of Tyana by Philostratus, the *Agricola* of Tacitus and the *Parallel Lives* of Plutarch. The book of Philostratus may be very briefly dismissed. He was a clever man of letters who decided (evidently correctly) that there would be a public for an account of Apollonius, a strange figure, half philosopher and half miracle-worker, who made a great stir in his own day. But the *Agricola* is a different matter. It is a thoroughly original work. It has indeed the characteristic marks of ancient biography. It picks out the high lights of the hero's career and leaves the rest in obscurity; it says a good deal about his origins and a great deal about his death, while the space between is chiefly devoted to an account of the special action for which the hero was remembered. In all this, and in the general tone of unqualified (though not extravagant) eulogy, Tacitus is deferring to custom. Yet every page is stamped with the author's personality. It is not clear whether he meant to use the *Agricola* to influence public opinion, or to defend his father-in-law from the charge of too great submissiveness to a bad government, or to tell his readers something about Scotland, or as a safety valve for the escape of his own feelings, or for all these purposes. For us the important thing is that the strong personal note, natural of course in autobiography, seems in biography to be something new.

Tacitus was a contemporary of Plutarch, who spent the later and longer part of his life in the country town of Chaeronea in Boeotia, where he had been born. He was a very prolific author, writing not only biographies but essays on a variety of subjects. As Plutarch is neither a very elegant nor a very accurate author, as he is never sublime or profound or impassioned, it is natural that estimates of his absolute value as a man of letters should vary considerably. But on one point there can be no two opinions. He is simply one of the most influential writers who ever lived. It is hardly an exaggeration to say that at least up to the nineteenth century the picture of ancient Greece and Rome in the modern mind was the picture painted by him. And it was more than a picture, it was a moral force. The best minds of the French Revolution and of the American Revolution before it drew much of their inspiration from the democratic idealism of Plutarch. On the literary side the greatest writers are very much in his debt. In particular Montaigne and Shakespeare (through translations of course) simply pillage him with both hands. And if they improved what they took, they took what they improved.

Plutarch, who was a modest man, would have been exceedingly surprised if he could have foreseen these results. Undoubtedly he hoped to do some good by his writing, for he loved humanity, but his chief motives were to satisfy his own mind and to give a rational pleasure to others. He had always been a great reader of history, but what he liked was not the political and military parts but everything that threw light upon the character of the actors. He disclaims the title of historian. His subject is human nature in history. He considered the best material for such a study was to be found in personal anecdotes, of which accordingly he collected an astonishing number. He knows that such anecdotes are often apocryphal; but even when they are not true they reflect the impression made on their fellows by the personalities of whom the stories are told. It was the belief of Plutarch that great issues often hung upon small traits of character. If Antony had been a different sort of man, if Cleopatra had been a different sort of woman, the history of the world would have been different. Now that was Shakespeare's conception of history and it was Walter Scott's. It is perhaps inevitable that a dramatist or a novelist, treating of an historical subject, should see it as a conflict between characters. But they may and often do see the characters as the victims of destiny or circumstances. Plutarch takes the view that, if they are victims at all, they are the victims of their own temperament or, as Democritus had said long before, character is destiny. That, broadly speaking, is also the view of Shakespeare. So when he came to read North *Plutarch* he found the very stuff he wanted; it hardly needed any more dramatisation; all that was necessary very often was to turn North into blank verse.

Plutarch's essays, which in their collected form are called *Moralia* because they generally have an ethical character, have had a good deal of influence. But they hardly call for separate consideration from the *Lives*, because their tone, and especially their method of illustrating moral qualities by means of anecdotes, makes it possible to deal with both the books at once. Neither has the influence of the *Moralia* been at all comparable with that of the *Lives*. The plan of the latter is not altogether happy. It is to match the Life of a distinguished Greek with that of a distinguished Roman who might be not unreasonably compared with him. So we find Alexander paired with Caesar, and Demosthenes with Cicero. These are instructive parallels, but many of the rest are hardly that. Plutarch however attaches no excessive importance to his scheme, but regards it as a framework in which to place his historical portraits. It is the interest of these that has preserved his work, not his style, which is no more than adequate for his purpose. What makes Plutarch a great, and even a very great, writer is the fact that all his work is a revelation of himself. Though this may be somewhat obscured by his practice of writing about other people, it is not less true of him than of Montaigne that his real subject is himself, and it is not less true because he is entirely devoid of egotism. He thinks he is only giving us his opinions, but in fact he gives us his character-one of the most attractive, it may be added, in literature. That is the true importance of Plutarch, and to us moderns, with a literature drenched in egotism, it will not seem small.

ORATORY

It has been necessary more than once before to stress the importance of rhetoric in ancient education and consequently in ancient literature. The brevity with which the subject must be treated here does not at all correspond with this importance. Let us however, supposing that to be understood, take up the history of rhetoric at the point where we left it with Thucydides. In him we saw a good deal of forced and unnatural twisting of sentences to get antithetic point and even a jingle of like sounds. These novelties did not commend themselves to Attic taste and quickly disappeared. One of the most important agents in this improvement was the advocate Lysias, who made for himself a style almost perfect for its purpose, which was to convince juries. There is no sense of strain at all in Lysias; his sentences are so well contrived that they appear to have formed themselves, and they are as clear as they are natural. His service to Greek, and through Greek to Latin and modern prose, was of inestimable value. He may be considered the founder of that tradition of plain as opposed to ornate style which has run through prose literature ever since. He is not much read now, because he does not stir the imagination or move us deeply one way or another; but he is one of the masters of style. Isocrates, a somewhat younger man, sought to enrich and extend the resources of prose and give it an ampler movement than is perceptible in the elegant but rather thin manner of Lysias. His success is written all over the subsequent history of literature. We have had occasion to remark that already, and we shall have occasion to remark it again. But it may be useful at this point to observe that students of rhetoric in antiquity made a distinction between 'figures of thought' and 'figures of speech'. The figures of thought were various methods of constructing sentences or clauses so as to give the most effective expression to the thought of the speaker; the figures of speech were metaphor, simile and so on—what are sometimes called 'flowers of speech'. The Greeks never had any doubt that the structure of the sentence was far more important than any ornament, and so they regarded the figures of thought more highly than the figures of speech. Lysias carries this preference so far that (like Swift) he will hardly admit a figure of speech at all. This was felt by Isocrates to be keeping prose from achieving the highest level of which it was capable; and, just as Lysias may be regarded as the founder of the plain style, so Isocrates may be regarded as the founder of the ornate style, although it must be remembered that the most ornate style in antiquity that had any pretence to be considered classical is never coloured and gilded like any style that would be thought ornate today.

One cannot mention all the Greek orators, but the greatest must not be passed over. Demosthenes had the imagination, the conviction, the passion that we miss in Lysias; he had the practical experience in public and judicial oratory which Isocrates did not possess. He belongs on the whole distinctly to the school of Isocrates, that is to say he takes over the Isocratean period; but in the hands of

Demosthenes it becomes infinitely more alive and multiform. The sentences of Isocrates are all formed on much the same plan, so that at last we get tired of their monotonous symmetry. In Demosthenes no two consecutive sentences are alike. He is content, like most effective speakers, to drive home a single point in a whole speech, but he very rarely repeats himself. Every speech composed by Demosthenes had in view some practical object, often one of transcendent importance to his country and himself. So all Ms words are addressed with an almost terrible concentration upon carrying the judgement of his fellowcitizens with him. Any word that would not help him to do this he flings away, while he ransacks the whole treasury of Attic speech for the words he wants. He does not mind what they are so long as they are pure Attic and vivid and to the point. The metaphors and similes which Lysias had eschewed and Isocrates used sparingly, he scatters with a free hand. The effect of this upon his hearers was far greater than would be supposed by the reader of a translation. Modern English is terribly infected by the meaningless metaphor, but in Demosthenes all the metaphors are *meant*, that is they were imaginatively realised by himself and his auditors. The only English orator who might be compared to him in literary merit is Burke, but the comparison is not very helpful. In richness of imagination and lavishness of illustration Burke appears superior, but in effectiveness the palm must go to Demosthenes. You admire Burke, but you are convinced by Demosthenes. He is never boring, as it must be confessed Burke quite frequently is. Burke never understood his audiences; Demosthenes understood his to the core. So he is constantly shifting the point of attack; he passes quickly from narrative—he is a wonderful narrator—to argument, from argument to eulogy or invective. And he understands, as Burke never did, the power of quiet statement made under pressure of great emotion; this being one of the discoveries of classical art.

Demosthenes having carried ancient eloquence to a point beyond which it could not go, there followed, as might have been prophesied, a reaction against his style. The possibilities of other styles were explored. There was on the one hand a return to the elegant simplicity of Lysias, and on the other a movement in just the opposite direction to a more lavishly decorated manner than Attic taste approved. This latter came to be called the 'Asiatic' style, apparently because it was practised most in the Greek-speaking cities of Asia. Both styles found their admirers in Rome when, in the first century before Christ, Roman orators began to study and imitate the Greek. Thus Brutus—the Brutus who appears in Shakespeare *Julius Caesar*—was a devotee of the Lysiac or (as it was sometimes called) the Attic style. If anyone wishes to know what it was like, he has only to read the address of Brutus to the crowd at Caesar's funeral. On the other hand Cicero leaned more to the Asiatic manner, especially in his early period, although he never failed to recognise the eminence of Isocrates and the supremacy of Demosthenes.

No other writer ancient or modern is so important in the history of prose style as Cicero. He is not so great an orator as Demosthenes; he is not quite supreme in any branch of literature, unless it be in the minor branch of letter-writing. It is even possible to find some faults in his style. But the influence of that style is an historical fact, and there has been nothing quite like it. It was partly due to accident. He was the first writer of real eminence to employ the medium of Latin prose, and this gave him the opportunity to mould it as he pleased. The success with which he did this is the greatest proof of Cicero's genius for literature. He may be said to have created Latin prose as a vehicle of literary expression. He imposed rules upon Latin syntax, he enormously enlarged its vocabulary of abstract and general terms, he vastly increased its flexibility, adapting it to subjects which had never been treated in Latin before. All the figures, both of thought and of speech, were employed by Cicero with complete and easy mastery. In this way he fashioned a medium of great beauty and versatility, which later writers could and did adapt to their own uses. Through all the history of Latin prose literature the style of Cicero is on the whole the dominating style. Seneca might rebel, but his rebellion had no permanent success. Tacitus rebelled, but he was almost alone in his age; his friend and admirer the younger Pliny did his best to write like Cicero, as indeed Tacitus himself had done at the beginning of his career. At the Renaissance, when there was a demand for better Latin grammars, the scholars based their new grammars on the practice of Cicero, making him the standard of latinity. When they wrote Latin themselves they took him for their model, many for their exclusive model. When Latin yielded to the vernaculars the new prose writers, in English as much as in French and Spanish and Italian, tried to reproduce the effects of the Ciceronian period. Nearly all the more elaborate styles in English from Hooker to Ruskin derive in the last resort from Cicero. These facts concern us more than the comparative merits and defects of the Ciceronian style itself. If we look into these we find that it tends to verbosity, being full of synonyms and parallel phrases. There are too many exclamations and superlatives for our taste. Sometimes the reader feels a certain emptiness in the matter, as if the author were beating out the substance of his thought too thin. Sometimes Cicero strikes us as pompous, sometimes as trite. But the form of his sentences is always impeccable, and that form is certainly one of the highest achievements of literary art.

PHILOSOPHY

The first considerable influence of ancient philosophy upon English literature—and it has been a great and abiding influence—is that of Plato. His writings have come down to us under the title of Dialogues, and the first step towards understanding them is to form a clear notion of what a Dialogue meant to him, for it is not a mere interchange of talk. The earliest Greek speculations on the nature of things were set forth in a kind of prose which seems to have been a blend of the speech of cultivated society in Ionia, where philosophy began, with elements drawn from the diction of poetry, which had hitherto been considered the only fit medium for serious literature. But towards the end of the sixth century before Christ there began a movement of the greatest significance in European thought. It was partly religious, partly scientific, and it shook to pieces the tentative and somewhat complacent theorising of the previous century. Men arose of great intellectual power and intense conviction who spoke with the assurance of prophets. Since the epic hexameter had long been (as in Hesiod's poetry) the accepted medium for the revelation of divinely warranted truth, these men set forth their doctrines in hexameters. Then came Socrates. It was one of the convictions of Socrates that truth was most likely to be attained not by one mind thinking by itself, but as the result of discussion and argument between intelligent friends. It is probable enough that he had an actual prejudice against writing down conclusions. At any rate he never did. Plato, although he wrote so much, perhaps agreed so far with Socrates on this point as to think that absolute or final truth could not be expressed in written words. But at least he could write imaginary conversations between Socrates and others on topics of philosophic interest—imaginary, but based no doubt, at least in many cases, on actual colloquies—and in this way some glimpses of the truth might shine out. The idea was not entirely new, for such dramatic conversations were part of the stock in trade of the Mime-writers. The Mime we have met before in the case of Theocritus, and we found then that it was prone to the satirical and the realistic, and that it had a dramatic quality, making it akin to Comedy. Theocritus to be sure lived a century after Plato and wrote in verse. But the Mime existed before Plato and existed in prose. It is Aristotle who says this and he clearly tells us that the Platonic Dialogue is a form of the Mme. He was thinking chiefly of the earlier dialogues, in which Socrates routs a number of charlatans or entrances his friends, in both cases with an urbanity that appears to be a new thing in controversy. The later Dialogues have lost nearly all this dramatic character and are more in the nature of discourses or disquisitions. Their philosophical value is no doubt greater, but their literary value is certainly less; and our business here is with literature.

A man like Plato cannot take over a form of literature and leave it exactly as he found it. His Dialogues are hardly Mmes, though they might be called a modification or even a transformation of the Mime. The Teniers-like realism of the old Mime becomes in Plato a delicate truth of observation. The dramatic element is raised from a conflict (often abusive) of personal likes and dislikes to a conflict of ideas. Above A we get a new kind of humour—we get irony. Before Plato gave the world his portrait of Socrates irony—for the word existed—meant little more than cunning or slyness; after that portrait irony meant what it means to us. It is in vain that we ask how far the portrait faithfully represents the historical Socrates; all we can say is, it has the truth of art. Here then are two inestimable contributions made to literature by Plato. He has given us the first detailed representation of an historical character as he lived and talked, and he has given us the modern conception of irony.

These are perhaps the two greatest gifts of Plato to literature as an art. But the influence of the Platonic philosophy upon the minds of men, including many English writers, has been so extraordinary that some account of it, however brief and inadequate, must be attempted.

As a young man Plato had been struck by an argument developed chiefly by the followers of Heraclitus. That philosopher had observed that the phenomenal world, that is the things we perceive through our senses, was in perpetual and continuous movement, being never exactly the same from one moment to another. This led to the conclusion that knowledge was impossible, that is knowledge in the full sense of the word. For such knowledge is knowledge of nothing less than the absolute truth, and the absolute truth is unchanging. It cannot be true one minute and untrue the next. 'Twice two is four' is not true today and false tomorrow. If then Heraclitus is right, as of course he is, in saying that all visible and tangible objects are in a state of flux, then of these things there can be no real knowledge. Yet such knowledge, we feel certain, exists. Where then are the objects of it? Since they are not of this world, they must be of another; since they are not on earth, they must be in heaven. This belief that behind the world of sight and sound there is another, unseen by mortal eyes but more true and more real, giving in fact to the objects of sense what truth and reality they may have, is the central doctrine of Platonism. Whoever shares that conviction is consciously or unconsciously a Platonist. The conviction came, as Plato himself believed, from the intercourse of mind with mind when they were attuned to one another. This mutual attraction of kindred spirits eager for the discovery of truth he described by the name of Love. Now the true was, according to the general faith of the Greeks and of Plato in particular, in the last resort also the good and the beautiful; so that to love the beautiful was at the same time to love the good and the true. That is Platonic love; anything else is a misunderstanding.

This teaching was bound up with Plato's doctrine of the Soul. The objects of knowledge he called 'ideas'. These, he maintains, and not the objects of sense are the real, indestructible things. Since they cannot be perceived by the bodily senses, they must be apprehended by something else, and this can only be some such faculty as we call reason. Reason cannot be deceived like the senses or suffer change and decay like them. In other words it does not partake of human mortality, although it is embodied in human beings. It is the immortal part of the human soul. This is equivalent to saying that the human soul, so far as it is reasonable, is immortal. The belief in the immortality of the soul is very ancient, but it was Plato who first made it an essential part of a philosophical system; and it is due to him and not to the Bible that it is now an essential part of Christian theology. Arguments for it are set out in one of the most famous of all his Dialogues, the *Phaedo,* which represents Socrates as discussing them just before he drank the hemlock. They are not all good, and it is not necessary to suppose that Plato himself thought that they were. Good or bad, they made a profound impression both in antiquity and later. But we shall come back to the *Phaedo.*

Two Dialogues call for somewhat special mention, the *Republic* and the *Timaeus.* The first is an account of what a state might be at its best, which cannot happen unless it is ruled by philosophers, by whom Plato means men trained in a system of education such as he then or later instituted in his Academy. The Republic is too well known to permit of general, and too rich in matter to permit of detailed, discussion. We can only remark that it is the first and the most suggestive of all Utopias, being in fact one of the supremely great books of the world. The *Timaeus* is an account of the formation of the world, including man, by the Demiurgus or 'Creator'. The Demiurgus however should not be confounded with the Creator of the book of Genesis. He is divine indeed, but the servant of some mightier Power. This Dialogue has had a strange history. It was almost all that the Middle Ages in western Europe knew of Plato, and they knew it not in the original, but in a Latin version of an Arabic translation. In this defective form it was taken as an authoritative pronouncement on the nature and origin of matter and of the body and soul of man, and what Plato offered as an hypothesis was taken as gospel. Not only so but that part of the *Timaeus* which modern scientific theory regards as particularly profound and valuable was not understood, while the physiological part, which is quite antiquated, was swallowed with eyes shut.

The *Timaeus* has a sort of appendix in the form of an unfinished myth entitled the *Critias,* in which the story is begun to be told of the primaeval island of Atlantis, now sunk beneath the sea. This is the parent of many similar stories, especially in the last hundred years. It gives us the occasion to say something about the Platonic myths, of which most of the more important Dialogues contain at least one. They are not fables or fairy tales. They nearly always have some scientific theory for a basis. Plato did not believe that the natural sciences could tell us the final truth about anything, but he did not despise them on that account. He thought that they enabled us to make a probable guess at the truth; only it seemed to him unscientific of the scientists to state a probable guess in a series of positive assertions. He therefore clothes his own scientific speculations in language appropriate to a divine mystery—the language of the old mythological storytellers. Such are his myths. In them sublimity of imagination, power of thought and magnificence of phrase go hand in hand in a way unrivalled in the prose of any other language.

The *Phaedo* gives the final touches to that portrait of Socrates which is one of the great contributions of Plato to creative literature. It is a portrait as living and almost as detailed as Boswell's Johnson. The latter part of the *Phaedo,* in which the closing hours of Socrates are described, is certainly one of the most beautiful and moving things that ever was written. The portrait is developed further in the *Sympasium,* the most brilliantly dramatic of all the Dialogues. Socrates appears in nearly all of them and each contributes something to the total impression. In the *Apology,* which appears among the Dialogues but is not really a dialogue but the speech addressed by Socrates to the judges before whom he was being tried for his life, we get his own summing up of his career in words which the world has been unable to forget.

Socrates was written about by other philosophers as well as Plato, and one of them was Xenophon. The philosophical works of Xenophon are not now regarded as valuable, but that is a comparatively recent estimate. Few philosophers, indeed few authors, have had a longer run of steady popularity. He had a talent amounting to genius for adapting himself to the public taste, always giving his readers something they could understand or flatter themselves on understanding. He published reminiscences of Socrates—*Memorabilia* is their Latin name—recording conversations of the Master with 'certain people of importance'. Some of the incidents related may have actually occurred, but most of the conversations can only represent the sort of things that Xenophon supposed Socrates said or might have said on each occasion. Unfortunately he is never made to say anything which would lead one to think that he was a man of extraordinary genius, whereas the Socrates of Plato is evidently such. But the *Memorabilia* is readable even now, and was eminently readable to the average ancient and mediaeval student. It is Xenophon who tells us about the shrewishness of Xanthippe the wife of Socrates and thus started a snowball which went on growing and growing. (Xenophon was too young and embarked too early upon his military career in Asia to have known Socrates very well, let alone Xanthippe.) He also wrote a, *Symposium* and an *Apology of Socrates*, both perhaps in rivalry with Plato. The *Symposium* is really funny, but it has no philosophical importance. The *Apoloby* (if it is genuine) is a poor thing after Plato. He also wrote a Dialogue, admired by Ruskin, about the management of a country house, and the *Cyropaedia*, which may call for some notice when we come to the Greek novel. The importance of Xenophon, except for the immortal Anabasis, is now chiefly a thing of the past, but in the past it was very great and we shall constantly find his name pressing itself on our attention.

The later Middle Ages are so full of the fame of Aristotle that more must be said of him than of Xenophon, although his influence on the actual form of literature is much less. It is not negligible because he popularised, if he did not quite invent, the scientific treatise, which in the right hands can be a work of high literary distinction, and because he gave a new direction to the Dialogue which was to have, through Cicero, the most striking consequences. But it was his matter, not his form, that made and makes Aristotle so important. To give an account of his philosophy is out of the question, for it was an attempt to systematise on a scientific basis the whole of human knowledge. Yet we must say that the spread of Aristotelianism in western Europe is one of the cardinal facts of mediaeval history. It was in the thirteenth century that something like an adequate notion of Aristotle's teaching, particularly his logic, made its way into Italy, France, Germany and England, and in a remarkably short time revolutionised its thinking. Platonism, which in its later form as developed by the NeoPlatonists had hitherto given its tone to mediaeval philosophy, was eclipsed by the new enthusiasm for Aristotle. The greatest of the Schoolmen, Thomas Aquinas, built his theological system upon Aristotelian logic. To Dante Aristotle was 'the master of those that know'; and this no doubt was also the view of Chaucer. At the end of the Middle Ages, when Plato came to be more fully known, Platonism came back into favour, especially with men of letters. But it was long before the authority of Aristotle was seriously questioned by the majority of educated persons. It was still powerful in the days of Galileo and Bacon.

The surviving works of Aristotle are nearly all of an austerely scientific character with little or no attempt to give them artistic form. They were in fact not meant for the general public but for students trained in the technical language of his own philosophical school, the Lyceum. Yet Aristotle has genuine literary talent, and this comes out in almost a casual manner in sentences and phrases of a penetrating power. A good deal depends on the subject with which he happens to be dealing. If it is man as a political or moral being, the interest of what he says is intense; and this is true also of his Poetics. But it takes a metaphysician to understand or even to read his metaphysics, and a logician to read his logic. The fact remains that Aristotle did write books for the general public; only they have been lost. But Cicero read them and admired them. He went further and imitated them. These lost works of Aristotle took the form of Dialogues, suggested no doubt by Plato's, but wisely not written in close imitation. Aristotle, who had none of Plato's dramatic and novelistic power, did not attempt the give and take of rapid conversation, but made his speakers address each other at length, each setting forth his own point of view. It is a duller method than Plato's, but more satisfactory to those readers (probably the majority) who want to get a distinct view of what the arguments are. At any rate it was the method generally adopted by Cicero.

The modern world has probably no great regard for Cicero as a philosopher nor did he himself, full of harmless vanity as he was, claim regard in that respect. All he did was to popularise the teaching of the famous Greek sages. But this he did, if not always correctly, with infinite skill and grace; and anyone who thinks this a small or easy service to perform knows very little of the matter. His immense vogue as a philosophic teacher was not undeserved. In this discussion we must confine ourselves to one or two of his writings as having had for one reason or another a special influence on later thought. These are the De Divinatione, the De Officiis and the Somnium Scipionis. The first is a dialogue in the Aristotelian manner. It professes to be a conversation between Cicero and his brother Quintus on the subject of oracles and veridical dreams; but in fact it is a treatise in two 'books', the first being spoken throughout by Quintus, while the second is entirely occupied by the answer of Cicero. In the course of the work a great many anecdotes are told bearing upon the truth of oracles and dreams, and it was these anecdotes that made the fortune of this essay On Divination. The subject—whether it be possible to foresee the future—is of course an interesting one, and Cicero handles it with tact and common sense. But it was the stories that the Middle Ages loved, not the discussion, for they thought they knew the answer to that. (It is given by the Cock in the Nun's Priest's Tale.) These stories are perpetually recurring in mediaeval literature and bear witness to the popularity of the De Divinatione.

Yet its importance is small compared with that of the De Officiis or, as our ancestors called it, Tully's Offices'. It is in three 'books' and took the form of an open letter addressed by Cicero to his son, who was a student at Athens. What it amounts to is a popular treatise on the public and private duties of a Roman gentleman. It does not touch on man's duties to God or the nature of conscience, but merely tries to answer the question of how a self-respecting man, in particular a Roman gentleman, should behave in such and such a contingency. It is necessary to say 'Roman' because every nation has its own conception of a gentleman. But fundamentally the sort of man Cicero has in mind is one with whom we can sympathise. His morals are pretty much our morals. Why is this? Because to a great extent it is this very book of Cicero's that has made us what we are. The De Officiis became a sort of handbook of practical ethics in the Middle Ages. It was of course complicated by Christianity and the ideal of Chivalry, but it was never superseded. Chivalry died away, but Cicero's ethics did not. A Whig statesman of the eighteenth century for example is far more like Cicero's Roman than he is like anybody in the Bible. Nor is there much difficulty about understanding why the De Officiis had such an influence. In the first place the spirit of it is admirable; what the great eighteenth century philosophers called 'the amiability of virtue' was never more attractively set forth. Nor is it a very shallow book-at least these philosophers did not think so. Then it is readable, being full of anecdotes excellently told. In the third place it is interesting because it deals all the time with practical cases, with situations which may confront a man, especially a man of affairs, any day of his fife. Of course everything depends on how the matter is handled by Cicero, and here his incomparable literary skill, which would have enabled him to write finely about a broomstick, served him as almost nowhere else.

None of the dreams in the De Divinatione, though reported as true or possibly true, had anything like the influence of a dream which is not true, the Somnium Scipionis. This 'Dream of Scipio' formed the concluding myth of Cicero De Re Publica, a very important work on the best form of government, of which only a part now remains. The Somnium itself would have been lost, if it had not been preserved as the text of a long commentary by Macrobius, who lived in the fourth century and expounded the Dream in a strange mixture of erudition, pseudo-science and mysticism, which would have much surprised Cicero but immensely impressed the Middle Ages. So far as any single book can be said to have started the mediaeval Dream upon its long and varied career, it was the Somnium Scipionis. it is related by Scipio Africanus the younger, who tells how in a dream he met the spirit of the elder Africanus (now dead) and was shown by the spirit all the stars moving in their courses and the earth stationary in the midst of them. All this the Middle Ages, as was their way, accepted as a kind of revelation, the commentary of Macrobius being also accepted almost without question. Cicero was not the first to bring the Dream into literature. Ancient poetry and prose are full of dreams, beginning with Homer and Herodotus. But the Somnium Scipionis, though quite short, was still the longest and most elaborate dream in ancient literature that was known to the Middle Ages, and it was the more eagerly embraced by them because it told them about the stars and the life after death, two subjects of which they could never exhaust the interest.

The other philosophical writings we must leave undiscussed in order to give some attention to Seneca. Besides his tragedies Seneca was a voluminous author in prose. It was chiefly ethical problems that engaged his pen, although he also attempted 'natural philosophy', by which he meant popular science. Most of what he wrote was addressed to a somewhat exclusive circle of friends and men of some education, for he did not expect either to convince trained philosophers or to reach the lower ranks of the 'general reader'. Seneca was no more than Cicero an original thinker, and his system, if it can be called a system, was a compound of Stoic doctrines coated with sugar. But he was original in his style. Instead of the Ciceronian period he writes sentences that are broken up into brief clauses, full of 'snap' and cleverness. It is a manner of writing which does not, as might at first be expected, tend to greater brevity than the periodic style. And the perpetual strain after brightness quickly fatigues most readers. But there is such a play of mind in Seneca, such a fertility of illustration, such a knowledge of the human heart, that he is almost a great writer. He has always been more admired in France than in this country, but here too he was widely read until the beginning of the last century, when the Greek philosophers began to be better known. He had a great name in the Middle Ages, partly as author of the tragedies and partly as a wise man. There is extant a series of letters purporting to have passed between him and the Apostle Paul. It is a forgery, but the Middle Ages did not know that, and it gave them an additional reason for holding Seneca to be both good and wise. On the other hand it is only in modern times that Marcus Aurelius has had much influence on English writers. Marcus, who was emperor in the latter part of the second century—a period worth noting because it was also the date of Lucian and of Apuleius—had no thought of publishing his book, which was given by others the title of *Meditations*. It is a *journal intime* addressed by the author to himself and discovered apparently after his death. The value of the *Meditations* does not reside in the style, which is awkward enough, though with sudden flashes of eloquence and grave emotion, nor in the thought, which has little originality, though it always shows the marks of independent reflection. It is prized for the revelation it makes of a soul of almost unexampled devotion to duty and of an undramatic heroism. It is the first ' *Confessions*' that has come down to us, and it has had an undoubted effect on many writers, although this is obscured by the fact that the form of the *Meditations* is scarcely imitable. It is the Confessiom of Augustine that is the true progenitor of all that long series of volumes in which authors have explained their feelings to the world, not the *Meditations*, which Augustine could only have condemned. Indeed it is not everybody's book. It owes a good deal to Epictetus, whose *Enchiridion* or 'Handbook' has been often translated into English and was not without effect on English moralists and preachers, especially in the eighteenth century. Both Marcus and Epictetus wrote or spoke in Greek.

THE NOVEL

It looks like an anachronism to speak of the classical background of so modern a form as the Novel. Yet the history of the Novel is not fully intelligible without reference to some remarkable experiments in story telling made in antiquity, without which the Novel would hardly have become what it now is.

If we do not count the stories in Herodotus and the myths in Plato, both of which have often a novelistic quality, the first book that could be with any propriety called a novel, being in fact a *roman philosophique*, is the *Cyropaedia* or "'Education of Cyrus'" by Xenophon. The hero is the famous Persian conqueror Cyrus, and the story has a slight, an exceedingly slight, basis of historical fact. But it is an error to regard the *Cyropaedia* as an historical novel, for it makes no real attempt to reconstruct the past. Cyrus is exactly like what a spirited Greek boy would be in Xenophon's time. The real purpose of the book was to give the world the benefit of the author's ideas upon education and a number of other subjects. But when Xenophon thought of doing this through the medium of an elaborate fiction, full of incidents and speeches, he must be given the credit of starting something which has had almost incalculable consequences in the history of literature. Dull as it is on the whole, the *Cyropaedia* is one of the great seminal books. It suggested the title and in some slight degree the subject of the *Grand Cyrus*, which again is one of the great landmarks in what might be called the prehistory of the Novel. Interwoven with the main plot of the *Cyropaedia* is a romantic tale of parted lovers, Abradatas and Panthea, which is the first of a long succession of such polite romances, which were perhaps the favourite reading of the seventeenth century. But long before that time it had produced its effect upon the so-called Greek novelists.

Of these we have room to mention only two: Longus and Hehodorus. Who Longus was, and when his *Daphnis and Chloe* was written, we do not know, nor for our purpose does it greatly matter. It is best described perhaps as a pastoral in prose. Nothing could be simpler than the story, which tells how a country boy and girl fell in love with each other in the island of Lesbos, were separated by various accidents, but met again and were married. The charm of the story lies partly in the setting of rural sights and sounds and customs, partly in the telling of a history of love gradually realising itself. Longus is not profound or subtle, but his knowledge of human nature is adequate, and the whole book is filled with a sort of smiling grace. This tale of the young loves of a shepherd and a shepherdess—they were really goatherds, if that matters—has exercised a remarkable influence upon literature at more epochs than one. We can observe it at work in Elizabethan fiction and throughout the seventeenth and eighteenth centuries. No doubt there is a touch of artificiality and sentimentality even in the original and these qualities were exaggerated in the imitations, but a certain over-refinement of sentiment probably had a real value in counteracting the brutality of seventeenth century manners; and at any rate *Daphnis and Chloe* opened a new field to the love-romance.

The work of Hehodorus, who is said to have been a bishop about the end of the fourth century, was called *Aethiopica* or *'A Tale of Ethiopia'*. Its subject is the strange adventures of two lovers, he being called Theogenes and she Chariclea. With Hebodorus the story is everything, the characters naught. His technique is equal to that of any modern spinner of such yarns except that he is more literate than these mostly are. His long romance is crammed full of moving accidents by flood and field, pirates, robbers, oracles, prophetic dreams, last-minute rescues and the like. It will be seen at once that Hehodorus is an origin. His literary merit may not be very high, but he makes no mistakes in telling his very complicated story, he has some dramatic skill and the art of exciting and suspending interest. Moreover he knows how to link episode with episode in a manner not understood by the early romancers. The *Aethiopica* was much admired and translated at the Renaissance. It was dramatised in England as early as 1572-3 and had some influence on the Elizabethan novel.

(Shakespeare has an allusion to it in *Twelfth Night v*, 1, 121-3.) No doubt the romance of adventure, with lovers for its principals, would have come into existence if Hehodorus had never lived. But he must not be robbed of his credit on that account.

We must now go back, for they are earlier in date, to the Latin story tellers. The first of whom we need speak is Petronius Arbiter if, as seems almost certain, he was the author of the *Satyricon*. He lived in the time of Nero, whose friend and victim he was. In its complete form the *Satyricon* must have been a very long book, but only portions of it have survived, the most substantial of which is generally quoted under the title of *Cena Trimalchionis*, 'The Dinner of Trimalchio'. If we did possess it complete, we might be able to discern some traces of a coherent plot, but it is more probable that we should find, what the fragments indicate, a rapid succession of incidents leading nowhere in particular. It is perhaps best described as a satire in the form of a picaresque novel. (Observe however that *Satyricon* comes from satyr not satire and presumably refers to the indecent character of much in the book.) The English novelist who most resembles Petronius is Smollett, who knew the *Satyricon* well and was influenced by it. Its vividness and naturalness are astonishing, rivalling the best modern work in these respects, but it would be a greater book if the characters were less uniformly vile or contemptible. It is not a mere adventure story, for it touches on as many subjects as *Tristram Shandy*. It has certainly had a considerable, perhaps not always admitted, influence upon some modern developments of the Novel.

About a century after the *Satyricon* appeared another extraordinary book, the *Metamorphoses* of Apuleius. The author was himself an extraordinary person, combining a number of apparently contradictory characteristics: philosopher, professor of rhetoric, dabbler in mysticism if not magic, man of letters, wandering scholar. These varied interests appear pretty clearly in his book. It is an adventure story related by the hero himself, whose strange fate it is to be transformed by witchcraft into an ass. He is finally restored to human shape—he never loses his human intelligence—by eating rose leaves. It is for this reason that the *Metamorphoses* was also called the *Golden Ass*—golden because of the author's style, which was greatly admired. The protracted search of the ass, constantly baffled and renewed, gives to the story that continuous thread of interest which is lacking to the *Satyricon*. The most famous episode is that which introduces an old woman, who tells a girl the story of Cupid and Psyche, so often translated. The *Metamorphoses* is full of robbers and abductions, of rescues, magic, fabliaux, fairy tales, all the paraphernalia of romance. It is full of exact and picturesque detail, but at the same time it has a curious dream-like quality rather like what we find in *Lavengro*. The style is too jewelled and precious, but does not obscure the fact that Apuleius is a born story-teller. The Middle Ages as usual thought the tale was true and very properly admired it. Besides the exquisite Cupid and Psyche fable the *Metamorphoses* as a whole has exercised a stimulating effect on the development of romance ever since it was written and has not entirely lost its power to stimulate even now.

It is convenient at this point to notice the *True History* of Lucian, who was a contemporary of Apuleius. It is a parody of a kind of literature that had long been popular with Greek readers—the literature of travel. Some of the first stories of this kind were sober accounts of actual explorations. But that love of the marvellous which distinguishes the human race could not remain satisfied with the truth and created a large audience for what are, politely or impolitely, called travellers' tales. The most popular of these was the *Incredible Marvels beyond Thule*, which included among other surprising experiences a visit to the moon. One of the devices employed by the author, Antonius Diogenes, to lend verisimilitude to his narrative was to quote 'authorities' invented by himself. It was this book that Lucian had specially in his mind when he wrote the *True History*. It gravely tells how the hero, who relates the story, was with his fellow voyagers swallowed, boat and all, by a kind of whale in the Atlantic, how they escaped from the whale and visited the moon, what they did and saw there, and so on to increasing absurdities. The narrative is admirably direct and circumstantial, but with an undercurrent of Lucianic satire. The whole is extremely entertaining and brilliantly written, though it is not and was not intended to be more than a *jeu d'esprit*. It has not the intellectual force and savage irony of Swift, and the resemblance to *Gulliver's Travels* is superficial, although Swift of course had read his Lucian. But the *Utopia* owes something to it. Indeed the debt of More, and with More Erasmus, to Lucian has not yet been property estimated. It would also be possible to make out a case for the view that Lucian is the father of the scientific romance, unless indeed the credit should go to Antonius Diogenes.

LITERARY CRITICISM

During the great creative age of Greek literature, roughly the fifth century before Christ, there was not in the strict sense any literary criticism at all. The writers of that age were evidently too busy with creation to consider the principles of their art. It is not until we come to Aristotle that we find true literary criticism, uninfluenced by personal or moral considerations. It is found chiefly in two books, the *Rhetoric* and the *Poetics*. The practical effect of the *Rhetoric* would be difficult to overestimate, for it was the first systematic treatise on the art of prose and set the example for all subsequent works of that kind. The effect was broadly beneficial, but it might have been more beneficial than in fact it was, if Aristotle's successors had been less hide-bound by tradition. It was natural and even inevitable that he should draw the materials for his analysis from the only literature he knew; what his Roman and stiff more his modern continuators failed to do was to think how far his analysis was applicable to Latin and to the modern languages. The natural mould of an English sentence is quite different from that of a Greek one, and the study of classical rhetoric is largely responsible for the ill results of trying to force the one into the other. Still it was a very great service to English literature to impress upon it the value and beauty of a more elaborate type of sentence than English usually affects. This however is rather advice to authors than literary criticism; and that is pretty much all that the *Rhetoric* itself professes to be.

It is different however with the *Poetics*. Although it never loses sight of the actual practice of poets, it has something to say about the nature of poetry, and this is probably the most valuable part of the little treatise. Aristotle accepts from Plato the view that poetry is a form of *mimêsis* or 'imitation'. But, since he does not follow Plato in denying independent reality to the visible world, he is not led to the Platonic conclusion that *mimêsis* of that world is a bad or deceptive thing. On the contrary poetry shows 'the universal in the particular' and therefore unveils reality instead of obscuring it. The reader will find it easier to follow this, if he leaves out of consideration poetry of the descriptive or Wordsworthian kind, which can hardly be said to exist in classical Greek. The 'imitation'—a bad translation at the best—which Aristotle has in his mind is not the imitation of natural objects but the imitation of people. So when he speaks of the 'universal' in the phrase above quoted he really means the universal element in human conduct. He gives an example himself. 'What Alcibiades did' is a particular action; 'the sort of things Alcibiades would do' is not. Particular actions are the subject of the historian. The poet is not concerned with the truth about them but with what we call truth to nature. His business is to divine the character of a man from his actions and to reveal that character in his actions. That is why Aristotle says that poetry is 'more philosophical' than history. It does not matter, he thinks, if the poet describes things that did not happen so long as he makes us feel that they might have happened—that they were, as we say, 'in character'.

It will not escape the notice of the reader that the truth of these remarks comes out best in dramatic poetry. And in fact most of the discussion in the *Poetics* revolves about the drama, more particularly about Tragedy, although a good deal is said as well about the Epic. The omission of any discussion of lyric poetry is disappointing, but we must be thankful for what we have got. Aristotle is the founder of literary criticism, being the first man, so far as we know, to judge literature on its own merits without reference to moral standards. This does not mean that he believed in 'Art for Art's sake'. In the first place Art (with a capital A) is a purely modern conception, and in the second place he would have thought that a poem without any moral significance was of little value, because all great poetry deals with life, and all life except the animal part of it is bound up with conduct.

The influence of the *Poetics* (which is our special concern) has been very great both upon the theory and the practice of poetry. It can hardly be said to begin before the Renaissance, for the book was strangely neglected in antiquity, while in the Middle Ages it was hardly even known to exist. When it came again into note it was often misunderstood or misrepresented. The Greek of the original is very hard and even an accurate English translation is largely unintelligible without elaborate notes of explanation. The result was that even scholars were for a long time content with a Latin version or with what Julius Caesar Scaliger (1484- 1558) said about the *Poetics* in his *Art of Poetry*. From him seems to have come the notion that Aristotle inculcated the observance of the three unities, as they were called, of time, place and action, although in fact Aristotle insists only, and very rightly, on the last. This misunderstanding has a history of its own which cannot be pursued here. Whether, as is often implied, it did nothing but harm—whether parts of Shakespeare himself, say *Cymbeline*, would be any the worse of a stricter observance of the unities —may still be questioned. It is not at all improbable that Aristotle, if it had been put to him, would have given at least a general support to the doctrine that all three unities should be observed if possible, for they suit Greek Tragedy very well. But he nowhere says so. We for our part are bound to take notice of the strength and persistence of the doctrine because, though not actually stated in Aristotle, it was for long attributed to him and therefore must count as an important part of his influence on our literature.

In the first three centuries before Christ, especially towards the end of that period, there was evidently a good deal of discussion as to the best models for writers to follow. This naturally involved a certain amount of literary criticism, some of which has survived, although it never got very well known in England. But few Greek books got to be better known in the seventeenth and eighteenth centuries than the *De Sublimitate*, which contains far more purely 'literary' criticism than the *Poetics*, the subject of which is not poetry but the art of poetry. The *De Sublimitate*, now thought to have been composed about the beginning of the Christian era, was formerly attributed to Longinus, who lived more than two and a half centuries later. The Greek is rather difficult, with many technical terms of which the meaning is not always quite clear. This dubiety extended to the title, which led people to think that the author was discussing 'sublimity' as we understand it when we say that Milton or Isaiah is sublime, and that he was urging writers to aim at this quality instead of others. He has no such purpose and is under no such limitation. He is only trying to answer the question, 'What is it in an author that makes us say of him "This is a great writer"?' His own answer is that you cannot have great literature except from a man who has a great 'soul', which for a Greek always means intellectual as well as moral qualities. 'Longinus' has in his mind a man of genius with an aspiration towards noble things. Genius however is not enough; it must be directed by art. The untaught writer falls into many defects of style. He may be bombastic or silly; he may have purple passages in the wrong place; he may be guilty of many forms of bad taste. This condemnation of bad taste was very much taken to heart by the eighteenth century. But 'Longinus' himself is not content with such negative doctrine. The great writer must have passion and imagination. If he has these, he may be forgiven many lapses of form and taste. Lysias is more faultless than Demosthenes, but that does not make him a greater writer.

The force and eloquence of this unknown author, the aptness of his citations, the critical genius which can see the merits of such varying types of writer could not fail to have a vitalising effect upon modern literature. It was not however edited, and seems hardly to have been known, in England until 1636. Even this edition was soon eclipsed by the prestige of Boileau's translation, published about twenty years later and accompanied by a Preface emphasising the importance of 'correctness', although, as we have seen, this was only part, and the least important part, of the teaching of 'Longinus'. Pope accepted the interpretation of Boileau, yet not so absolutely as is sometimes represented, for Pope never thought that correctness was a substitute for genius. The fact is that the author of the *De Sublimitate* has suffered at least as much from distortion of his meaning as the author of the *Poetics.* The eighteenth century took from him what it liked best and neglected the rest; the nineteenth century admired the rest-the enthusiasm for the heaven-born genius—but passed too lightly over his admirable exposure of the faults of style, because these faults happened to be dear to the Romantic heart.

About the same time as the Greek *De Sublimitate* appeared the Latin *Ars Poetica* or, as it is more correctly entitled, the *Epistola ad Pisones.* It is a versified letter addressed by Horace to two young brothers called Piso, who evidently were ambitious of writing dramatic poetry, more particularly the burlesque variety of it called the Satyric Drama. At least Horace devotes most of his space to Drama, although it would have interested us very much more if the author of the *Odes* had dealt with lyric poetry. Thus his subject is not really the 'Art of Poetry', and Horace would have been the first to repudiate so ambitious a claim. He does not seek even to be original, for the *Epistola* is dependent on a Greek authority. There is actually more of Horace himself in his Epistle to Augustus, so brilliantly 'imitated' by Pope. From these two documents we can make out Horace's critical point of view fairly well. It is in effect a defence of 'correctness'. Having behind it his authority, and being stated with his irresistible charm, this teaching exercised an almost tyrannical influence over some of die best and acutest minds from the Renaissance onwards. Yet in fact it has neither the philosophical depths of the *Poetics* nor the stimulating virtue of the *De Sublimitate.* Horace was convinced that the great defect of Latin poetry had been its refusal to take trouble about its form, and therefore he insists upon the need to take this trouble. It does not follow that he thought nothing else mattered. Yet readers could hardly be blamed if they got that impression. It is the *Epistola ad Pisones* that is the source of that already mentioned doctrine of 'correctness' that was later read into 'Longinus' and prevailed for about a century, beginning in France and thence crossing to England. Its negative and narrowing effects are not matters of doubt. Yet in England at any rate its influence, at and for the time, was perhaps more beneficial than otherwise. It helped to save our poetry from the extravagances of the decadent Elizabethan manner. In fact so far as it goes it can never be out of date.

Literary criticism in antiquity by no means ended with Horace, but no later authority has exercised a comparable influence upon English literature. Nevertheless we cannot ignore Quintilian, whose *Institutio Oratoria* or 'Education of an Orator' carried great weight both in the Middle Ages and at the Renaissance, and still commands respect. His literary criticism is to be found in the tenth 'book' of his large treatise. It is a highly concentrated account of the principal Greek and Roman writers from the point of view of their usefulness to the orator, for according to Quintilian literary culture is an essential part of the orator's education. The judgements passed on each writer show no narrowness or professional bias; they come from a man who had a real taste for literature as such, and for a long time they formed, and deserved to form, critical opinion upon the comparative merits of ancient writers. Quintilian may be little read now, but that does not diminish his historical importance. His views have entered into and profoundly influenced both the theory and practice of education. When it is remembered that for the last four centuries Englishmen have been educated in the main on a system introduced at the Renaissance, and that this system was very largely constructed on the principles advocated by Quintilian, it will be seen that we must count his book as having its place, and an important place, in the background of English literature.

THE FABLE

The Fable is very ancient. It belongs essentially to oral and popular literature; and if, as seems possible, it came to Greece from the East, it was not in written form. When the first Greek fables were committed to writing is not clear, but it must have been before the time of Aristophanes, who knows a book of them. Their author was believed to be one Aesop, a Phrygian slave and a hunchback. This is not the place to question that tradition, but it is clear that he cannot have been the author of all the fables attributed to him. In fact the Greek collection which now passes under his name belongs to a very late age and, as literature, is beneath contempt. However at a much earlier period the fables were rendered into very tolerable Latin verse by a Greek called Phaedrus, who had been a slave at one time in the household of the emperor Augustus. He called his book *Fabulae,* that is 'Stories'; whence our habit of speaking of the 'Fables' of Aesop. It consists of five 'books' published at wide intervals of time. All five together do not make a very substantial volume, and Phaedrus does not seem to have written anything else. It was not mere translation; Phaedrus modifies, adds and probably invents a good deal of his own. These *Fables* have considerable merit. They are told with point and brevity, if not with all the simplicity which is one of the principal charms of the unsophisticated beast-fable. Here appear for the first time the story of the Fox and the Sour Grapes, the story of the Dog in the Manger and others almost or altogether as good. They would be unforgettable in the hands of a much worse artist than Phaedrus. He had successors like Babrius in Greek and Avianus in Latin, who helped to bridge the gap between him and the Middle Ages, but Phaedrus is the main well-head of that stream of fable literature which flowed through these ages, died down a little and then swept on more strongly than ever, reinforced no doubt by the example of La Fontaine, who after all is mainly Phaedrus transmuted from silver into gold.

SOME MORE WRITERS

There are a number of ancient writers whose work as a whole or in part does not easily submit to classification under the headings so far enumerated, but who exerted too potent an influence to be omitted from any estimate. The number is not very small, but we must be content to select three, as perhaps the most significant. They are in chronological order Theophrastus, Pliny and Lucian, whose *True History* has already been noticed. Theophrastus was the friend and to some extent the disciple of Aristotle, and as the author of the first systematic treatise on Botany he is an important figure in the history of science. What concerns us however is not that but a little book, to which he certainly attached much less importance. It is familiar as the *Characters* of Theophrastus, although it would be less misleading to translate the title by *Types of Character*, for the author does not deal with individuals but with types, such as The Superstitious Man, The Talkative Man, The Flatterer and so on. His method is to describe peculiarities of speech and behaviour by which one type may be distinguished from another. This kind of typepsychology is at least as old as Plato, in whose Academy, where he was educated, Theophrastus may have learned to pursue it further. It was a subject in which the generation of Theophrastus was strongly interested. It was the floweringtime of Menander and the new Comedy of Manners, which presented on the stage exactly such types as we find in the *Characters*. Thus he had ready to hand an inexhaustible supply of vivid and amusing material, although we have no reason for supposing that he did not make many observations for himself. The early 'characters' are very short and rather formal and stereotyped, but as Theophrastus proceeded he learned to make his types much more brilliantly distinctive. If he is not given a whole section to himself as the founder of a new literary genre, it is only because it is not a very important genre and its influence was largely restricted, in England at any rate, to the seventeenth century. Within these limits its influence was strong, not merely directly upon imitators like Earle, but indirectly on Restoration Comedy and the early Essayists and even on the Novel.

There were two literary Plinys, uncle and nephew, of whom the nephew was the more accomplished writer, being the author of a large collection of elegant letters, much admired in the eighteenth century. But it is the uncle who is important for this book. He composed (with much else, now lost) a *Natural History* in no less than thirty-seven 'books', none of them very short. It is a sort of encyclopaedia and includes a great deal that we should consider not to be natural history at all, for instance a summary account of ancient art and of what is now called applied science. Pliny was really a learned man, but his erudition is all drawn from books, which he uses quite uncritically, one authority being apparently as good to him as another. He never asks how far earlier scientific information has been superseded by later, and so everything is grist to his mill—the latest discoveries of Greek astronomy and the silliest fables of mendacious or gullible travellers. When Pliny stops compiling and speaks for himself, as he does when the rare opportunity offers, he becomes a not unimpressive writer. It is not that however which has saved him but the circumstance, almost the accident, that he preserved for more ignorant ages a mass of information of the very kind they wanted. A mixture of useful knowledge and marvellous stories was exactly to the taste of the Middle Ages and by no means distasteful to the Renaissance. (We now have the newspapers.) Pliny believed in the divine nature of the universe and was therefore not surprised at anything—an attitude of mind which after all has some advantages over that which condemns everything it does not understand as superstition. He did not affect to any extent the form of literature, but the debt of later writers to him for matter and illustration is almost incalculable. It is true that the Middle Ages mostly used secondary authorities like Isidore of Seville at their beginning and Bartholomew the Englishman towards their end. But Pliny is the father of all these.

The writings which have come down to us under the name of Lucian are very diverse in subject and treatment, but they are nearly all in greater or less degree permeated by the same spirit. It may be called irony, because it has a clear descent from the irony of Plato. But it is a very different irony from the Platonic. The Socrates of the *Dialogues*, being filled with a passion for the truth and believing that the great enemy of the truth is the thinking that we know it when we do not, used irony as the gentlest and yet most effective weapon against this form of self-deception. The successors of Plato in the use of the Dialogue form had neither his moral nor his literary genius and (reverting to the cruder spirit of the Mime) made of irony a species of personal ridicule. The irony of Lucian is not much more, although he has a wit and a distinction of style to which those writers, of whom the chief were Bion and Menippus, had apparently no great pretensions. Such as it is, the irony of Lucian is a delightful thing and his artistry in the use of it is consummate.

During the Middle Ages and indeed long after Lucian was regarded with abhorrence as an enemy of Christianity because he had attacked a Christian called Peregrinus. This has to be considered when we seek to trace his influence, for it was not likely to be avowed where it existed. In fact it hardly manifests itself at all until the Renaissance, when we ought to see it clearly at work in some of the most brilliant writing of Erasmus and Sir Thomas More. Indeed Luther calls Erasmus 'an atheist Lucian'. A good deal of the Greek satirist was actually translated by More and Erasmus, working together. The importance of this for literary history is very great, for these two men, having learned the use of irony as a literary instrument from Lucian, applied it to modern questions. There are of course incidental passages of irony in mediaeval literature, especially in Chaucer, whose irony is as delightful as any in the world. But the systematic use of it was new and this evidently was suggested by Lucian. After Erasmus and More we get the *Epistolae Obscurorum Virorum* and (what is incomparably more important) Rabelais and all that has come from his work. The spirit of irony thus came into the vernacular literatures, and from Rabelais and Cervantes and, much later, from Swift passed into the Novel. It would be absurd to claim the credit for all this for Lucian, but he is an origin and a very important one.

7

Chapter

The Middle Ages

INTRODUCTION

To anyone seeking to trace the influence of the ancient classics upon the mediaeval literature of England, meaning by that the literature of what is called Early and Transition English, it might appear at first as if that influence were negligible. The prestige of Latin is boundless, but it is not the great Latin classics that are read and imitated; the favourite Latin authors of the Middle Ages themselves belong to the Middle Ages. The importance of this cannot be denied, but it can easily be exaggerated. In the first place mediaeval Latin is only classical Latin at a later stage of its development. In the second place a vast amount of the work composed in it is drawn by way of epitome or expansion from the classical writers. We shall find evidence of this as we proceed. Certainly a new spirit which is quite unclassical comes in with the Middle Ages. Yet to a very great and perhaps preponderating extent mediaeval literature is the product of this spirit operating upon classical material, transforming it but using it. Take for instance at the very beginning of the period the *De Consolatione Philosophiae* of Boethius. We see that it is a restatement, though a fine and far from mechanical restatement, of certain opinions held by ancient philosophers, so that it is not so much Boethius who influences the Middle

Ages as the Stoics and NeoPlatonists through Boethius. Or consider another book which towards the end of the period exerted an even greater influence than Boethius, which is written not in Latin but in French, and which is utterly mediaeval in spirit—the original *Roman de la Rose. The form of the poem, which is a dreamallegory, can be traced back to classical literature; the mythology* is classical and many of the allusions; it is Venus half christianised and wholly romanticised. Again we must not forget that permanent bridge between the ancient and the mediaeval world, the Church. Thus the most authoritative of the Latin Fathers, Augustine and Jerome, were classical authors. Clearly we cannot ignore the influence of the classics on mediaeval literature.

To go through the whole of mediaeval latinity tracing its debts to the past and its influence upon the vernacular literature would be an immense task. A running commentary is all that can be offered here. For this it is rather important to prepare our minds by an historical observation. The mediaeval spirit or point of view, although certainly more consistent than the modern, was itself full of change and fluctuation. It is better to follow the changes as well as we can from age to age without indulging in generalisat1ions. That means using the historical, in fact the chronological, method. The reader may be left to draw the broad conclusions for himself.

It seems proper to begin with Bede, for, although he had English predecessors, he assimilated what was best in their work and handed it down, greatly improved, in his own. He was a product of that remarkable 'Northumbrian' culture which was disseminated, so far as scholarship was concerned, from the school founded in York not long after the Christianisation of the English. How high its reputation stood may be judged by the fact that it was from York that Alcuin, in the generation after Bede, was summoned by Charlemagne to superintend the re-establishment of learning in the western Continent. Bede's teacher came from York, and Bede himself became the best scholar and the greatest writer of his time not only in England but in Europe. As his works are all in

Latin, they fall out of our survey except in so far as they were a medium of classical influence upon the vernacular. That they were to some extent such a medium is certain; to what extent it is hard to say. Bede lived in one of the darkest epochs of European history and, although he was an altogether exceptional man and went, whenever he could, direct to classical sources, yet even his mind was clouded by certain preconceptions coming between him and the originals. The very fact that he wrote in Latin was rather a hindrance than a help towards clearly apprehending the differences between their ideas and his own. He had not, and he could not be expected to have, the historical insight necessary for that. Besides, the subject of his greatest achievement, *The Ecclesiastical History of the English People (Historia Ecclesiastica Gentis Anglorum)*, did not require the consultation of classical authorities, at least of the secular kind. He draws to some extent upon them, especially Pliny, but it does not amount to much after all. Nor is his style formed upon classical models. It is mediaeval Latin such as he would use in conversation when speaking with his best care. It is however a good, clear, simple, living, sometimes vivid style, totally different from the barbaric jargon of his predecessors or the deplorable affectations in the style of his older contemporary Aldhelm. Thus Bede, though writing in Latin, set the example to English of a natural, simple and dignified style; and his authority was so great, his eminence for many generations so unquestioned, that we must suppose there was a tendency to reproduce in English as well as Latin the qualities so much admired in him. But, although they are classical qualities, they seem native to him and not acquired by study of the classics.

There is a somewhat abbreviated and not very good translation of the *Ecclesiastical History* attributed, perhaps wrongly, to Alfred. At any rate it belongs to Alfred's time and he was himself the principal translator of his age. In the interval, not far short of two centuries, between him and Bede the history of England had been a series of catastrophes. About the year 787 the 'Danes' began to come, and the

English suffered from them most of what their own ancestors had inflicted on the Britons. In the most habitable parts of the country learning was almost extinguished. Alfred undertook to revive it. If students now require a warning against the assumption that the Middle Ages saw a gradual progress from almost total darkness to the dawn of the Reformation and the New Learning, they may get it from the fact that Alfred looked back to the time of Bede as an era of light and instruction. There was no steady progress at all, but great ebbs and flows then as now and always. We need not however consider the motives which animated Alfred, but merely the books he translated.

He seems to have begun with a handbook (the classical name for which was Enchiridion) consisting in the main of extracts from the Vulgate or Latin Bible and the Latin Fathers, of whom the greatest was Augustine. Both he and Jerome, the guiding spirit and principal translator of the Vulgate, were at work at the turn of the fourth and fifth centuries. Their styles, though not Ciceronian, are still classical, and both were steeped in classical literature. Neither of these statements is true of Gregory, whose *Cura Pastoralis or 'Pastoral Care'* was apparently translated by Alfred himself. It is a typically mediaeval book. Yet the allegorical method of interpreting scripture, largely employed by Gregory, is not a mediaeval invention. It had been applied to the interpretation of Homer as far back as the sixth century before Christ and had been carried to great lengths in later times. It had been used for the interpretation of the Old Testament by learned Jews such as Philo of Alexandria, who was a contemporary of Jesus, and influenced Christian exegesis of the Bible at an early date. The mediaeval passion for allegory is not an inexplicable novelty.

Among other works translated by the king or under his supervision were the *History* of Orosius and the *Consolations of Philosophy* by Boethius. The book of Orosius has for its full title *Historia adversus Paganos, which might be translated "'The Pagans refuted from History'". That at least describes its* purpose. Paulus Orosius was a native of Roman Spain and a disciple of Augustine. He is not important for his literary merits but for the influence of his book. It is a summary of universal history, sacred and profane, with a good deal of geography thrown in. It is quite uncritical, even rather stupid, but its mixture of useful information with controversial piety strongly recommended it to the monasteries. We have only to remark that, in order to make his compilation, Orosius had to consult a number of classical authors. Boethius we cannot dismiss so lightly. The *De Consolatione Philosophiae* must rank among the most influential books ever written, although its influence has not lasted into the modern world. It was composed in prison, where its author, a Roman senator of high public and private character, had been put by Theodoric, the great king of the Goths in Italy. It is composed on a somewhat curious plan, for it consists of sections alternately in verse and prose. In effect however it is a dialogue between Boethius and Philosophy, Philosophy doing most of the speaking. She appears to the writer, as he languishes in prison bewailing the cruelty of Fortune, and gives him reasons for disregarding or even for being grateful to Fortune. This leads to a more general explanation of the moral government of the universe, whereby Boethius is finally comforted. The book deserved much of its prodigious success; the verses (which are in a variety of metres) are often charming, and the prose has considerable distinction. The chief interest of the *De Consolatione* however is this, that it is prophetic of so much that was to follow. For instance Philosophy and Fortune are not merely personified, as they might be in a classical or a modern author, but are allegorical persons such as the Middle Ages delighted in. The matter too profoundly affected mediaeval thought. It was drawn by Boethius from a considerable, but not very critical, reading of the classical philosophers. His philosophy might be described as eclectic and not very distinct. It owes something to Aristotle, a good deal to Plato, more to Plato's interpreters, most of all to Stoicism as he found it in Cicero and Seneca. It is more a profession of faith than a system, and it is such a profession as a Christian could accept so far as it goes. Also the spirit of the book, breathing resignation and trust in the providence of God, must have been comforting to many in their private troubles. Boethius forms a bridge between the classical and the mediaeval world; indeed he is rather the last of the classics than the first mediaeval writer. Unconsciously, he is the herald of a new era; consciously, he looks back—to the Latin classics and, beyond them, to Greek philosophy. Thus Alfred in making him known to his subjects was bringing English literature into one of the main streams of classical influence. The question now was how far, or whether at all, this heritage from the ancient world could be naturalised.

The public misfortunes which followed the death of Alfred seemed to answer this question in the negative. It was about a century later that a fresh effort was made by Aelfric. He had to build from the very foundations. His first business was to instruct the younger clergy in Latin, the knowledge of which had almost disappeared in England. This involved him in teaching the elements of Latin grammar, for which purpose he found it convenient to make a grammar of his own-perhaps the first Latin grammar constructed in England. It is of course almost a pitiable thing by modern standards, but it was a noble achievement for all that and of the greatest importance because it was a way of insisting that people must speak and write grammatically. That was a valuable lesson at a time when there was a real danger of literature dissolving into a formless jargon. Aelfric however did a good deal more than compose this Latin grammar. Among other works it is possible that he translated the *Moralia* or, as they are often called, the *Distichs* of Cato; and, since this was a famous book throughout the Middle Ages, one may linger a moment to give some description of it. The author was neither the elder nor the younger Cato of history, but an anonymous 'grammarian' or literateur. The distichs are a quantity of saws or truisms, normally expressed in elegiac couplets of poorish latinity and attributed to Cato—no doubt the younger Cato, who 'gives laws' to the departed spirits in the sixth book of the *Aeneid* and appears as a sage in Lucan-either by the author or by his readers. Proverbial philosophy has always been popular, but it is odd that ' Cato' should ever have impressed intelligent people. Nevertheless he did and we have to take account of the fact.

The Norman Conquest

The Norman Conquest produced an almost total eclipse of written literature in England, and the eclipse lasted more than a century. Norman French became as a matter of course the language of officialdom. It was not Norman French however, at least to any considerable extent, that became the medium of written literature; it was Latin. English literature had to begin all over again, though of course in the meantime the language had changed and was changing. The Latin too had changed. It was no longer the Latin of Bede or Aelfric, correct enough in its way but somewhat impersonal. The Latin of the brilliant writers about the time of Henry II—men like Geoffrey of Monmouth, Walter Map, Roger Bacon, Giraldus Cambrensis-is full, sometimes almost too full, of their own personality. Largely for this reason it is not classical, nor are these writers much influenced by classical authors even when they have some knowledge of them. They are original men. It is however a fact of general importance that throughout this interregnum we observe an increasing knowledge of Latin idiom and an increasing facility in the use of it. The most accurate scholar of the time was doubtless John of Salisbury, who performed the real service of drawing attention to the great classical authors, especially Cicero. He also expounded Aristotle's logic more clearly and completely than had been done by any one before in England. Thus he did much to open up a more direct route to the genuine treasures of ancient culture.

Aristotelianism

Meanwhile very important changes were taking place at the two Universities. They were mainly due to the new orders of Franciscans and Dominicans, working more in rivalry than in unison. The movement thus initiated affected thought, giving it a more logical and even a partly scientific turn, rather than literature as such; but literature could not fail to reflect the change. Now began the predominance of Aristotle. ' Aristotle' however did not mean to a scholar of that time what it means to a scholar today. The Middle Ages knew the great philosopher very imperfectly. Even the logic which they so earnestly studied was a cast-iron system developed from Aristotle's rather than the Aristotelian method—organon or 'instrument' was his own word for it—in its original form. Still their knowledge of him kept gradually increasing, chiefly through Latin versions of Arabic translations. Indeed the new Aristotelianism was largely imbibed from Arabic sources, particularly Avicenna and Averroes. The great Commentary on Aristotle of the latter had been composed in Moslem Spain, whence it passed readily enough into Christian Europe. There is of course historical reason why Greek philosophy should have reached the west by this roundabout route. The victory of Islam in the seventh century had been over countries, such as Egypt, in which Greek culture had maintained itself for a very long time. The conquered taught their conquerors, who had the sense to profit by the lesson. Thus it came about that the Arabs—to give them that generic name—to a certain extent re-joined the links, which they had so violently snapped, between the Latin-speaking and the Greek-speaking halves of the Roman empire.

But, at least towards the end of this transition period, Arab philosophy and Arab science were not the only links with the Greek world. Greek, although people will call it a dead language, is no more a dead language than English; it has never ceased to be spoken and it has a continuous and continuing literature. Nothing is more easily forgotten by us than the fact that all through the Middle Ages the emperor, that is the Roman emperor, reigned not in Rome but in Constantinople, whose domination, constantly threatened and sometimes reduced almost to nothing, nevertheless with greater or less effectiveness lasted for more than a thousand years. In this eastern half of the old Roman empire the language of culture was of course Greek and its literature was Greek. Moreover there was always some communication, however slight and precarious it may have been, between Constantinople and the West. The Crusades and the conquest of the city by the 'Latins', the carrying of the Venetian arms and commerce to the Aegean, facilitated a better acquaintance. Occasional Greek scholars came to Italy. More of them came, as was only to be expected, when at last Constantinople fell to the Turks in 1453; but to date the revival of learning in western Europe from that event is now seen to be an error. It had begun a century or more before that.

It is against this general background that we must watch the process by which the vernacular literature begins to re-assert itself. As it was not addressing scholars, it did not show signs of direct influence from the classics. But of indirect influence from classical sources it is full. It is not an easy matter to make this clear because of the confusion in the mediaeval mind between the old and the new. We have to deal with that extraordinary amalgam of fact and fancy, of Pagan and Christian, of misunderstood and second-hand information which was all the knowledge of antiquity ever acquired by the average mediaeval man. The result is that the student of mediaeval literature has not only to know the truth about the classical world, he has also to know what the Middle Ages thought was the truth about it. This knowledge is the less easily obtainable because the mediaeval conception of classical antiquity, though in its broad features it did not change much, never was stable, but varied from age to age and from writer to writer. Yet to a certain extent it can be charted. One division thus marked especially claims our attention. It is what is described in a famous phrase (translated from the French) 'the matter of Rome the great'. This 'matter' covers the whole field of classical lore—the story of Troy, the story of Thebes, the story of Alexander the Great and some others.

Dares and Dictys

The Trojan material was conveyed to the Middle Ages chiefly in two compositions attributed, one to Dares the

Phrygian, the other to Dictys the Cretan. They are usually referred to under their Latin designations as Dares Phrygius and Dictys Cretensis. The former, as being pro-Trojan, was regarded as the better authority, at least among the French and English, both of which nations claimed for themselves a Trojan origin. The full title of his book is Daretis Phrygii de Excidio Troiae Historia, 'The History of Dares the Phrygian concerning the Destruction of Troy'. It is evidently a Latin translation or paraphrase or epitome of an earlier work in Greek belonging to a class of books which were not uncommon in later antiquity. They were rather 'rhetorical', that is stylistic, exercises than deliberate forgeries. Thus the Greek man of letters who wrote the 'Epistles of Phalaris', which raised such a controversy at the beginning of the eighteenth century, was merely trying to write the kind of letters that the tyrant Phalaris might be presumed to have written. In the same way the original (Greek) 'Dares' only meant to show what kind of a book a Trojan might be supposed to have written about the Trojan War. The Latin 'Dares' however attempts a little mystification. He introduces his 'History' with a prefatory epistle purporting to be addressed by Cornelius Nepos to the historian Sallust. In this letter 'Nepos' says that he discovered the original manuscript—the actual autograph—of Dares and had translated it literally into Latin. He proceeds to ask whether Dares, who was engaged in the events he describes, is not more to be trusted than Homer, who lived many years afterwards and in any event must have been 'demented', since he represents the gods as fighting with men. Cornelius Nepos was a writer of elegant prose in the Augustan age of Latin literature, while our 'Dares' is a wretched scribbler of perhaps the sixth century. He is a feeble impostor, but he succeeded in imposing upon the mediaeval reverence for antiquity, and his authority was held to supersede Homer's.

'Dares' was translated several times in the Middle Ages and some of the translations had a wide circulation. But all were eclipsed in fame and in merit by the *Roman de Troie*, a metrical romance Of 30,000 lines in Norman French by Benoit de Sainte-More, a trouvère who lived for a time at the court of Henry II. He bases his work on Dares, but expands, embroiders and romanticises to an astonishing extent. The Greek and Trojan heroes become mediaeval knights, the heroines mediaeval ladies. Above all Benoit tells, in detail and so far as we know for the first time, the story of Troilus and Cressida, whom he more correctly calls Briseide. Benoît's poem was used by greater men than himself, namely Boccaccio and Chaucer, whose *Troilus and Crireyde* passed on that story to Henryson and Shakespeare. It is not, so far as can be discovered, a classical story, so we need not go into the question of its origin, in the brain of Benoit or someone else, or the process by which Homer's Briseis became Cressida. But it does concern us to note that the *Roman de Troie* was used (without acknowledgement) by Guido delle Colonne (*de Columna* in Latin), an Italian who was for some time in England and wrote towards the end of the thirteenth century. Guido's book, which is in Latin prose, is entitled simply Historia Troiana. It is written in a style altogether superior to that of Dares Phrygius, who indeed has none at all, and Guido shows a competent knowledge of some classical authors. The Historia Troiana immediately became what might be called the standard account of the Trojan matter and is used as such by Chaucer and others, especially Lydgate.

One of Guido's sources is Dictys Cretensis, and something, though not much, needs to be said about Dictys. As Dares-the Homeric Dares—was a blameless Trojan priest mentioned in the *Iliad*, so Dictys was represented as a comrade of Idomeneus, the Cretan leader in the Trojan war. The one book is just as fictitious as the other, but 'Dictys' is the better writer. He too translates from a Greek original, of which we know something, although it is not enough to tell us how faithful the translation is, or what version our 'Dictys' translated. A close translation it cannot be, for the style is full of echoes and imitations of Sallust, the most popular of the Roman historians with mediaeval authors. The book has got the somewhat odd title of Ephemeris Belli Troiani, 'A

Journal of the Trojan War', doubtless suggested by the Ephemerides or 'Journals' of Alexander the Great. It consists of two unequal parts, the first five 'books' giving a summary account of the entire Trojan war, the sixth and last telling of the home-comings of the Greek heroes. This sixth 'book' is a miserable production and cannot be by the author of the rest, who writes a competent Latin style. These two little books-for both Dares and Dictys are quite short—were the pillars on which the Middle Ages built the astonishing structure of their Trojan matter. It ended in becoming almost entirely unclassical. But the germ was classical and out of that all the rest blossomed. The germ was not exactly Homer; it was the whole saga of the Trojan war as it was known, in epics now lost to us, in antiquity. The contents of these epics, along with Homer, were summarised in prose epitomes; and it was from these epitomes that the Greek 'Dares' and the Greek 'Dictys' cribbed their matter, until they in turn were translated into the existing Latin versions.

Alexander Romance

The Alexander legend, is hardly so important for us. It began immediately after the death of Alexander himself if not before, survived in spite of the historians, and flourished unchecked in the Middle Ages. It is easy to see how it arose. The countries conquered by Alexander, which included Egypt, the Levant, Anatolia, Mesopotamia, Persia, the Punjab, were inhabited by ancient races accustomed to half-deified kings, and credulous of marvels. To them Alexander naturally appeared more than mortal; he must be a god (they thought) or the son of a god or at least of a magician Eke Nectanebus, the sorcerer king of Egypt. So legends originally told of their prehistoric or fabulous heroes tended to cluster about Alexander. Much of this fabulous matter got into a Greek book attributed to Callisthenes, the nephew of Aristotle-Aristotle, all the world knew, had been the 'tutor' of Alexander and a 'wise' man, almost like Merlin—but actually of a later date and, in its final form, for it kept growing, very much later. This is the book usually called by scholars *Pseudo-Callisthenes*. It was translated into Latin early in the fourth century and thereby found readers in the West. This Latin version was the chief, though not the only, channel for the transmission of the Alexander legend, which spread far and wide through Europe. Of its influence upon English literature one example is the metrical romance of *King Alisaunder*. But that is only one example and must not be taken to give a true idea of the extent to which the story took possession of the mediaeval mind. A rather odd indication of that is the popularity, dating from the Middle Ages, of the name Alexander in Scotland, where another common name is Hectorand even Aeneas is not unknown.

Mediaeval Attitude to the Classics

To analyse the sources of mediaeval literature where these are Latin—Greek hardly comes into question—is work for the specialist and must be left to him. For us it is only possible to touch lightly upon the more significant evidences of classical influence upon individual authors. Some broad statements may be hazarded, the truth of which students can test for themselves. (*a*) First, the influence of the classics upon mediaeval literature was indirect rather than direct. (*b*) It came in the main, though by no means exclusively, through French channels. (*c*) It was received without criticism or with such criticism as was worse than none. (*d*) It was transformed by the mediaeval spirit. (*e*) It affected the matter rather than the form of English literature of the Middle Ages. Something may be said under each of these headings.

(*a*) The first point hardly needs further elaboration. The Middle Ages, with rare exceptions, did not drink inspiration from the classics at the fountain head but at such streams as trickled, generally thin and muddy, through the intervening stretches of Low Latin. There was of course always some direct influence and towards the close of the period it became considerable. But there were times when it almost vanished. Generally speaking it varied, as was only natural, with the state of scholarship. There was very little scholarship indeed between Bede and

Henry II and throughout that long space of time it proved difficult to keep alive any knowledge of Latin at all. Perhaps we ought to be glad of this. It was largely ignorance of Latin that protected the growth of English literature, which had to fight for its life against Latin on the one hand and French on the other. If writers in the vernacular had been able to write Latin as well as Joseph of Exeter or even Giraldus Cambrensis, they would almost certainly have written in Latin, since that was the fashion. Our judgement on that point is now so different that we are apt to feel a grudge against men like Geoffrey of Monmouth or Matthew Paris for not writing in English, interesting as they are in Latin. But the vernacular was only biding its time. It did not lose much, perhaps it gained a good deal, by the restriction of classical knowledge within such narrow limits. Mere ignorance was in some ways more salutary than the kind of information that took its place. Dares and Dictys were poor substitutes for Homer and Virgil, Orosiusand Isidore for Livy and Tacitus. To be sure we must not load the dice against the scholars. Their knowledge was not all of this derivative order. They knew their Ovid fairly well, at least the *Metamorphoses*, the *Heroides* and the *Ars Amatoria*, however strangely misunderstood. They knew the *Somnium Scipionis* of Cicero, and in the monasteries at least there was a good knowledge of Augustine and Jerome. They often knew the verses of the Christian poet Prudentius, who was at any rate half a classic. It would be possible to extend this fist, in the case of certain men to extend it greatly. But we are speaking of the average mediaeval writer; and the trouble with him is that very often we cannot be sure whether he really knows at first hand any classical author to whom he refers. It is rather more likely than not that he is borrowing his information or copying his quotation at second or third or fourth hand. For it is one of the notable things about the Middle Ages that there was a common stock of information, ideas, even quotations, from which each writer took what suited him. Originality was not considered a virtue. An original author, such as Geoffrey of Monmouthapparently was, would pretend that he was not original, that he had got his matter out of some ancient, but now perished or hidden, book. This common stock was at first embodied almost wholly in Latin, that is in mediaeval Latin. But as we approach the thirteenth century it begins to be embodied to a notable extent in French, to a smaller extent in Italian.

(*b*) This brings us to our second point. The astonishing quantity, variety and accomplishment of mediaeval French literature gave it an almost unchallenged ascendancy in Europe, not least in England, where after the Norman Conquest most educated persons could read and speak the French language or the Norman variety of it. But it is a great mistake to regard this new influence as anti-classical. On any view of it, it brought a flood of classical reminiscences in its wake. French is in every way nearer to Latin than is English. The point is too obvious to be worth developing. What it is important for us to note is that English was stimulated by French into seeing what it could do along the fines so brilliantly pursued by the French mediaeval masters. One has only to look at Gower or Chaucerfor evidence of that. But their problem was different and harder. After all the French language is itself only Latin in a later stage of its growth. It was therefore naturally susceptible in a high degree to influences from classical Latin and readily lent itself to the reproduction of classical forms and styles. No such easy process was possible for a Teutonic language like English. But what mediaeval French literature did was to make the process easier. France became the interpreter of the classical world to England. And, as France was, if not the creator, the disseminator of the mediaeval spirit in its literary expression, we find English literature in the later Middle Ages accepting the French interpretation of the classical world almost without question.

(*c*) Now this interpretation was itself totally uncritical. Whatever was on record was true—that was the general attitude; it was only interpretation or commentary that was free. The extent to which this acceptance went is on occasion almost incredible. The fictions, even the self-confessed fictions, of the ancients are taken as historical facts. No mediaeval poet —it is somewhat different with the theologians, who had a professional case against classical mythology, although even they are prone to regard the myths as true evidence against the pagan gods—doubted for a moment the literal truth of the loves of Dido and Aeneas, of Troilus and Cressida. The imaginary letters of the heroines in Ovid—Greek heroines of the remote past writing in sophisticated Latin verse of the first Christian century—were taken to be their authentic letters. No doubt it must have been clear enough to Gower or Chaucer, poets themselves, that the real author of the letters was Ovid. But neither doubted that the sentiments described in the letters were really felt by the heroines and that the heroines were just as historical as the Black Prince or John of Gaunt. Practically no one asked what authority lay behind any statement in a Latin book. If the Latin writer said it was So, then so it was. This meant that one authority, however late and bad, was considered as good as another, however early and trustworthy. But we must take account of more than that. The Middle Ages were not merely uncritical in the sense of not applying an adequate standard of criticism; they applied what, to our notions at least, was a false one.

They differed strangely from us in their ideas of what was credible and incredible. Thus of two explanations of an unexplained fact, one natural and the other supernatural, the Middle Ages thought the supernatural explanation much the more likely to be the true one. The eagerness with which they read the *Gesta Romanorum* and *Mandeville* was partly due to this. It is of course the exact opposite of the scientific spirit, and so the Middle Ages were almost totally unscientific so far as the natural sciences go, a solitary genius like Roger Bacon merely proving the rule. On the other hand in other branches of knowledge, sciences too in their way, above all in Logic and Theology, the Middle Ages were eminent. Nothing could be stricter than the method of the great Schoolmen, of whom this country produced some of the ablest. But the logicians and the theologians—they were the same people—had their fundamental assumptions prescribed and limited for them by authority. They were not disposed to extend the boundaries of the natural at the expense of the supernatural, which is what the natural sciences continually tend to do. Since they believed in the possibility of miracles, they were not inhibited from believing in any number of them like the rest of the mediaeval world. Now that went quite against the tendency of educated thought among the ancients, for that was predominantly critical, rationalistic, scientific in the modern sense.

Hence it is that mediaeval writers fasten with especial delight on whatever is marvellous in the classical literature known to them. It is not the history of Alexander the Great that interests them, it is the hotch-potch of oriental fables that we find in the *Pseudo-Callisthenes*. It is not the historical Caesar they care about—which is the more extraordinary when we consider that they had the evidence of Caesar himself for what he had done in Gaul and Britain and Germany —but the Caesar of legend, who was born like Macbeth and had a horse with human feet. They were not content with the sober Life of Virgil which Donatus, a writer well enough known to mediaeval students, had composed out of authentic materials; they turned him into a magician who lived in a brazen tower. It was this love of the marvellous, almost as much as any religious feeling, that led them to delight in the Latin Lives of the Saints with their innumerable miracles and in books like the *Legenda Aurea* of Jacobus a Vóragine or the Gesta Romanorum. Sometimes fragments of genuine antiquity got incorporated in these collections, but not enough to make any difference to their general character. In a word the classics were read for what was wonderful in them, and the wonders were all believed.

(*d*) But this unclassical and unmodern conception of the universe as a theatre of miracles and marvels, although it is what perhaps chiefly differentiates the mediaeval from other ages, is only one of other distinguishing characteristics. There is for example the mediaeval conception of chivalry, in particular the conception of chivalrous or romantic love. It is not for us to consider how far it was conventional, how far it was restricted to a certain class or classes of society. At any rate it existed and permeated a great mass of mediaeval literature. The knights and squires and ladies, to whom the story-tellers and minstrels of the trouvère class addressed themselves, were full of this chivalrous ideal and tried, not too successfully, to live up to it. Consequently the minstrels were full of it too. And through this transforming medium they looked upon the loves of antiquity. The results were often strange enough.

Too much indeed may be made of the difference between the ancient and the mediaeval theory of love. It is quite possible to show that the feeling whose philosophy is 'All for Love and the World well lost' was not a stranger to the ancient heart. Greek mythology in particular is full of the devotion of lovers. But the ancient world had no rules of chivalry, no etiquette of love. It is this that the mediaeval writers cannot understand. They cannot understand why so noble a knight as Aeneas should 'betray' Dido, why Jason should leave Medea, Theseus Ariadne and so on. This is natural enough, and even Ovid was capable of feeling in this way, if he was capable of believing the stories at all, which for the most part he evidently was not. Modern sympathy too is probably here on the side of the Middle Ages. It is important then to realise that the classical feeling—classical in the strict and limited sense, the *Attic* sense —was radically different from the mediaeval on the value of passionate love. The Middle Ages believed that a passionate love, like that of Lancelot for Guinevere or Tristram for Iseult, was something that every knight should desire to have; the Greeks of the fifth century before Christ believed it was something that every wise man should desire to escape. It will of course be recognised that the Greek feeling does not necessarily imply a less propensity to passion than the mediaeval; perhaps it implies more. But it places the whole matter in a new light. And in general it may be said that the blending of the spiritual and the sensual which is characteristic of so much in the mediaeval soul is contrary to all classical teaching and perhaps more than anything else disqualified the Middle Ages from understanding the classical mind, always ready to subject the emotions, even the religious emotions, to the intellect.

Then there was the Christian sentiment. The ancient world had not, until the accession of Constantine in the fourth century, a state theology or orthodoxy. A man might believe what he liked, and was not to be punished for what he believed, unless it led him to attack the security of the state. An Athenian did not think of denouncing an Egyptian or a Syrian for believing in some Egyptian or Syrian divinity and following a different ritual from any known in Athens. On the contrary he was disposed to think that the Egyptian or Syrian divinity was really divine, though not so 'humane' or so respectably connected as his own Athena. Other Greek communities felt in the same way and this spirit of toleration became diffused through the Roman empire. There was however on the outskirts of it one exception to this rule, namely of course the Jewish community. The Jews came to deny the very existence of all gods but their own. The idea of worshipping other 'gods'—mere images of wood or stone—filled them with horror. This sentiment was absorbed by the Christian Church and from the Church absorbed by the Middle Ages. *Lo here, of payens corsed olde rites!* exclaims Chaucer at the end of *Troilus and Criseyde* in a sort of belated apology for a poem he had written with such obvious delight. In the same way Gawain Douglas feels it necessary to express his abhorrence of the false divinities whom he encounters in his translation of the Aeneid. There is no doubt that this feeling, which of course is not confined to the Middle Ages, operated strongly against the influence of the great classical writers, who, at least the poets among them, are nearly all full of their own religion. To the Middle Ages ancient poetry took on the aspect of a siren—the beautiful singer to whom the wise and virtuous man must stop his ears. Some of course, especially in the religious houses, took a more severe view than others; but the general tendency was to feel that there was something illicit in the pleasure found in reading the lovely fictions of the old pagan world. That had been the feeling long ago of Augustine, and no doubt his example helped to protract it. So the monks turned rather to multiplying versions of the Latin Bible and the Latin Fathers, copying Lives of Saints and homilies and missals and books of hours, at the most producing a new manuscript of the Legenda Aureaor the Gesta Romanorum. Some exception might be made in favour of Virgil because he had prophesied the advent of the Divine Child, or of Statius, who had been baptised, they thought, before his death. But even these were viewed not without suspicion.

(*e*) A further cause which militated against the strictly literary influence of the classics was the insensitiveness of the Middle Ages to that beauty of form and style which is after all what gives most of its value to the poetry of Virgil and Horace and Ovid. This insensitiveness was no doubt largely the result of defective scholarship. But that cannot be the whole explanation, for it does not require a great deal of scholarship to feel the charm of an ode of Horace—the beauty of its form is almost visual. Yet the Odes of Horace made no appeal to the Middle Ages, though the Satires did, not at all because of their form but because of their matter. The lack of appreciation of classical form is naturally most apparent in poetry. It was not too difficult to compose an oration somewhat in the manner of Cicero or a history somewhat in the manner of Sallust or a sermon somewhat in the manner of Augustine. But the enjoyment of poetry as poetry depends on a full appreciation of the value of words and, for the classics at least, on a perfect facility in scansion. Mediaeval Latin poetry could be, as in the case of the hymns, both moving and exquisite; but in form it is either not classical at all or, if it attempts to be classical, is incompetent. To be plain, what the Middle Ages valued in ancient literature was the information it conveyed, for while no doubt they took great pleasure in all the lore about the heroes and heroines of ancient love, about miracles and

> monsters, battles and adventures, giants and sorcerers, we must remember that in the first place they were disposed to think it all true and in the second place they continually sought to draw an improving moral from it. Here one may see the influence of the Church. But, however we explain the fact, there it is. The interest of the Middle Ages in the classics was less aesthetic than utilitarian.

The Middle Ages form so vast and varied a period that broad statements about it constantly need qualification. It is broadly true that what they sought from the classics was information, and that of the kind that particularly suited their tastes. But their tastes varied a good deal at different times and in different orders of society. Thus the age and society of Bedewanted edifying information, although even that was oddly mixed up with elements of fable and the miraculous. The age of Alfred was so ignorant that it really needed useful as well as edifying information and tried to get what it could —it was not much—from authorities like Orosius and Isidore of Seville. It must be remembered however that what Alfred, like Dunstan in an equally ignorant age after him, had in mind was the education of the clergy. We cannot therefore infer the tastes of the English people as a whole from the writings of Alfred or Aelfric. It was only after the Norman Conquest, indeed long after it, when education had begun to spread to at least a section of the laity, that we begin to observe what it was that the English people, or at least the privileged classes, delighted in most. It is all summed up in Chaucer, although to get the picture complete we must take into account *Piers Plowman* as expressing at least some part of what was being felt by the unprivileged. Chaucer, to whom may be added Gower, gives a sufficiently representative conspectus of what the Middle Ages liked in the classics. One has only to glance through Chaucer to see how often he is content with mere résumés of love-stories, of 'tragedies' of historical and legendary persons, even with simple lists of names, drawn from antiquity. Consider the Monk's Tale, the *Hous of Fame*, the *Legende of Good Women*. The appetite for the kind of knowledge supplied in these poems is boundless, but no feeling is shown for the beauty of the telling in the original Latin. Yet if the original had been in French, Chaucer would have felt its beauty in every nerve of his being.

Yet all the time, and with increasing force towards their close, the Middle Ages were being penetrated by classical influences. Latin words were coming into the English language, in particular a whole flood of French words derived from Latin, so that the language was becoming more and more capable of reproducing those effects, borrowed from Latin literature, which would have been quite impossible in Early English. The Conquest, the Crusades, the French wars, travels in the Levant and in Italy revealed the Latin countries to the English with an intimacy unknown before—lands whose civilisation had its roots in classical antiquity. Classical scholarship was improving; you can see it improving in the course of Chaucer's own works. Gower could write Latin verse which if nothing else is at least fluent. Gawain Douglas, who, though writing at a time when the Renaissance was in full swing in Italy, is thoroughly mediaeval in temper and outlook, made a translation into Scots of the *Aeneid* which is creditable as an evidence of scholarship and shows some real feeling for the beauty of Virgil's Latin, although it does not prevent him from translating a regrettable thirteenth 'book', the work of a superfluous Mapheus Vegius, who seeks to turn the *Aeneid* into a Christian allegory. In the lifetime of Douglas himself the Renaissance had come to England. But it did not come like a thief in the night. It was the inevitable result of a process that had been going on for a long time in the soul of man, that is the soul of mediaeval man. After long feeling, and at times fumbling, back towards the true classics the Middle Ages came, rather suddenly at last, upon them. In view of that it will not do to dismiss the influence of the classics upon mediaeval English literature as negligible. What produces such a result cannot be negligible. Very often the most decisive influences are not the most visible and measurable.

8
Chapter

The Renaissance

INTRODUCTION

The Renaissance' is a familiar term, not more inadequate than any other, to denote the very remarkable, though in no sense miraculous, change that touched the mind, and through the mind the literature, of Europe at the end of the Middle Ages. It is impossible to say when it began or when it ended. Where it began, we can say; it was in Italy. It stirs there very early. Petrarch, who died in 1374, and Boccaccio, who died in 1375, although they can hardly be said to belong to the Renaissance, have much, or at any rate Petrarch has much, of the Renaissance spirit mingling with their mediaevalism. By the beginning of the fifteenth century the new movement has clearly begun. But no exact date can be given which is not merely arbitrary. The old conception of the Renaissance as a sudden explosion of dawn at the end of a long night of Stygian darkness is probably no longer held by any educated person; but it is still necessary to guard against some of the consequences which have flowed from the original misconception. In particular we must be on our guard against certain generalisations. Indeed generalisations of any kind are especially dangerous here, because people are not even always clear as to what they mean by the Renaissance, sometimes meaning one thing by it, sometimes another.

Fortunately we are concerned with only one aspect of it, that which suggested its name, the 'rebirth' of learning, and with its effect upon English literature. The kind of learning that was 'reborn' was of course classical learning, especially the study of Greek. Though the ignorance of the Middle Ages, even in the matter of Greek, has been exaggerated, the claim implied in the word 'Renaissance' is not more excessive than such claims usually are. For, as we have seen, it was not the classical writers that engaged the attention of mediaeval students so much as the mediaeval continuators and epitomisers of these. Now there was a return to the genuine classics. There was a reorientation of the European mind and, as the Reformation was to show, not of the mind only.

If it is hard to assign a date to the beginning of the Renaissance, it is even harder to date its end. For what began in Italy having spread to other countries, it continued to produce its effects long after these had ceased to operate fully in Italy itself. As our business is with English literature, it is advisable to define the period of Renaissance influence in England as sharply as we can, even at the cost of a certain arbitrariness. The mediaeval element is strong in More, while Nhlton in many respects rebels against the spirit, if not the letter, of the new movement. Yet essentially both are children of the Renaissance. We must not be too narrow in our conception of the spirit it embodied. It tended in fact to differ with the different national characters of the countries it fisited. The Italian Renaissance was not the same as the French nor the French as the English. No doubt they were manifestations of the same spirit, but the manifestations were not identical. As an historical phenomenon however, the English Renaissance cannot be understood without some knowledge of the Italian, which started it. So a little will be said about the Italian Renaissance in its scholarly and literary aspects, with which alone we are concerned.

In Italy scholarship had never so nearly approached extinction as in certain periods in the history of other parts of western Europe. The thread of a continuous tradition from classical times was never quite snapped, in spite of barbarian invasions and clerical hostility. This is perhaps natural when one considers that Italy was the patria of the Roman empire. (Yet it was not at Rome that the tradition of scholarship was best maintained but in north Italy, especially at Verona.) Moreover the clergy were not as in England the sole, or practically the sole, depositories of what scholarship existed. In Italy there was always an educated laity, varying of course in numbers and in extent of knowledge from age to age but towards the end of the Middle Ages—if Italy can be said to have had a Middle Age—rapidly increasing in numbers and learning. It was these men who really made the Renaissance a revival of classical literature. They read for pleasure or instruction, not like a monk for edification. A reading public of this kind is always wanting more books to read, and the old libraries were searched to find them. There was plenty of sacred and devotional literature, but that was not the object of the search. What was looked for was some manuscript, probably long left to moulder in neglect, of some of the pagan classics. Many were found, especially when the search was organised and extended to Greece, Germany and other countries. The new discoveries created intense excitement; it was like entering a new intellectual world. The Church after a time ceased to object, except by fits and starts, and some of the Popes were themselves enthusiastic for the new studies. There was a special ardour to learn Greek, and more and more scholars of Greek birth or speech came to give instruction in that language or expound its literature. A sort of passion for everything classical seized the minds of men.

That was the beginning of the Italian Renaissance. It is not proposed to pursue its course or describe its history even in outline. But certain broad characteristics of it may be mentioned which it is essential for the student of this matter to grasp. First, there was a new appreciation of the beauty and exactness of form in the great classic authors, especially of course but by no means exclusively in the poets. Secondly, there was the revelation of Greek. Thirdly, there was a revival of ancient Greek ideas and ideals, ending in some cases in a sort of cult of Paganism. Fourthly—although this has only in part to do with literature—there was the rise of what has been called Humanism, ending in some cases in the assertion of the individual at the expense of the community. These points may be taken in order.

(*a*) The appreciation of classical form was made possible by a more exact knowledge of the Latin language. (There was no exact knowledge of Greek till towards the end of the period.) The structure of Latin is such that no exact knowledge of it can be had without a correct knowledge of its elaborate grammar. This had been well enough understood in the Middle Ages, but the mediaeval grammars were not very scientific, and above all were not based on the practice of the best authorities only. The Renaissance scholars began quite early to work towards an improved grammar—a grammar of classical as opposed to mediaeval latinity. The great pioneer in this work, Laurentius Valla, who was active about the middle of the fifteenth century, laid it down that the new grammar should be based upon the usage of Cicero. The principle was generally accepted and led to the most important consequences. One of these was the establishment of a standard, at any rate in prose, by which it could be ascertained how far an author's style was correct or not. In the Middle Ages an author wrote such Latin as he could. If he made himself intelligible to his readers that was all they asked. His vocabulary and his syntax he might borrow from any quarter he liked or even, within reason, invent, provided he remained intelligible. When the Renaissance was in full swing he was expected to take both from Cicero. There came to be a cult of the Ciceronian style which was often carried to absurd lengths. There were protests from sensible men like Erasmus, but the style of Erasmus himself is in the main Ciceronian. On one point all the scholars were agreed—there was to be no more 'dog Latin'. They have often been attacked for this. It is suggested that, if the mediaeval fashion of speaking and writing such Latin as one could, without too much regard for syntax or fear of barbarisms, had not been laughed out of existence, there would now be a common speech in Europe which all educated persons could use and which would be a great convenience to scientists. But that cannot be the view of a lover of literature. The Middle Ages had clearly demonstrated that there was no literary future for latin as there was for the vernacular languages. That indeed was not the opinion of the Renaissance scholars. They thought that it was the vernaculars that were doomed, and, while they admitted only too readily that mediaeval Latin had failed to justify itself as a literary medium of a sufficiently high order, they maintained that this was only because the Middle Ages could not write classical Latin. They proposed to write that kind of Latin themselves and no other. But their effort was a *tour de force* and had no permanent success. The fact was that quite early in the Middle Ages Latin became an accomplishment instead of a living speech. It continued to be written and spoken, but only by an educated or semi-educated minority. It drew no sustenance from the native soil, particularly in non-Latin countries like England. Thus it became moribund; and when a language has become moribund it is better for literature that it should become dead.

The scholars however not only despised the old monkish Latin, they despised the vernacular languages. It was generally believed that these could not survive. The time would come, they thought, when men of letters everywhere would write and speak in the purest classical Latin, which was the only language except Greek in which the highest kind of literature could be produced. This notion took a strong hold of men's minds and lasted a long time; it was entertained or at least not repudiated by Dr.

Johnson. That it did a world of harm must be admitted. It is distressing to think of the genius that was diverted to producing Latin (which after all is never in modern times quite of the first quality) when it might have immortalised itself in a living tongue. Nature however pretty soon reasserted itself, and the flood of vernacular literature poured on more irresistibly than ever. Moreover the account is not all credit on one side and debit on the other; very far from it. The scholars failed to destroy the vernaculars, but they reorganised, revivified and almost transformed them. The styles, the forms, the subjects of literature were permeated by the new influences; most of all perhaps the ideas were new. That was the true, though undesigned, service of the scholars. After all their enthusiasm for the great classics was natural. The structure of a Ciceronian period is a beautiful thing, the diction of Cicero is rich and sonorous and (as in the case of Johnson) much more exact and even concise than is commonly supposed. Since many of the Italians learned to reproduce it with great fidelity, it was only to be expected that attempts would be made to reproduce its qualities in the modern languages. The zeal for Cicero was matched by the zeal for Virgil and Ovid. It was natural that the vernacular poets should imitate them. The case of Ovid is particularly instructive. He had been admired all through the Middle Ages, but admired for his subject matter, on which they put their own interpretation. The Renaissance admired him above all for his style and his wit; consequently the poets of that age tried to reproduce these things in their own verses. And so with other favourite writers of ancient Rome from Terence to Tacitus. Two results followed which were perhaps inevitable. There was an influx of classical words into the modern tongues, and. there arose a tendency to adopt or even force classical syntax upon them.

This was a matter of style. But the classical 'kinds' and the classical stanza-forms and even metres were also imitated. The art of the Middle Ages had been shown in the forms and styles they created for themselves. The Renaissance turned its back on these and tried to naturalise in the modern languages the Pindaric and Horatian ode, the Platonic dialogue, the Virgihan pastoral and so on. These experiments, first made in Italy, spread to France and may be studied in the work of the *Pliiade* there, which in turn exercised a strong influence on Spenser and others in England. The results are generally charming, sometimes too artificial, but often magnificent, for the forms themselves are beautiful and only require genius to embody them, and of this there was no lack at the Renaissance. With the classical forms the classical subjects were adopted, for in classical art, as we have seen, form and subject go together. The Middle Ages had above all things loved stories; the classical authors, though liking stories too, had been interested in politics, in art, in science, in criticism, in philosophy in a larger sense than theology. The mind of Europe was now reawakened to problems of that nature, and the change is reflected in Renaissance literature. This does not mean that nobody in the Middle Ages ever thought about them. But the average mediaeval author did not think about them, and the average Renaissance author does.

Then there was the revelation of Greek. That was the most significant discovery of the Renaissance, the spirit of which, at least in its earlier manifestations, is much more Hellenic than Latin. The versatility, the interest in art and science of the Renaissance is Greek and not Roman. This however has misled some modern writers on a point of fact. It is an error to suppose that the Renaissance scholars knew Greek as they knew Latin. For quite a long time few of them had more than a smattering of the older language.

One or two did have more, and these undertook or were induced to translate Greek books into Latin. It was from these translations and from the abundant information about Greek matters and authors in Latin literature that the average Renaissance student got most of his knowledge of ancient Greece. It was enough to awaken an intense curiosity. His instinct told him that a knowledge of Greek literature was the key that would unlock the richest treasures of ancient thought. After that it was only a matter of time before it became the chief ambition of scholars to acquire an adequate knowledge of the Greek language. But it took time. There were none of the modern aids to learning. The student had pretty much to make his own grammar and his own lexicon. And he had to do it not from clearly printed books but from manuscripts which even today can be read with ease only by a trained palaeographer. Still the effort was made, and made successfully. Then it was possible to read Homer in the original and Euripides and Plato and Theocritus and the rest, and the unparalleled revivifying or rejuvenating potency of the best Greek literature could operate to the fullest extent upon the Renaissance mind. Perhaps naturally, its effect, though powerful enough even there, was less in Italy than in France or England, because Italy felt herself to be the heiress and champion of Latin culture. But it was from her that the passion for Greek things spread.

(*c*) With the literature came the ideas. We can say nothing of those which affected the history of science, but such Greek ideas as found expression in the new literatures call for some brief notice. On this account something must be said on the revival of Platonism. One must be careful at the outset to distinguish between what Plato actually said and what later ages supposed that he said. Almost immediately after his death the teaching of Plato began to experience some change as it was developed by his successors, moving especially in the direction of Pythagoreanism, which from being a curious mixture of religion and mathematics had assumed the form of a scientific mysticism, which gradually got less scientific and more theological. This combination or fusion of the later Platonism with the later Pythagoreanism is usually called Neo-Platonism. Its chief representative was Plotinus, who, although perhaps an Egyptian and certainly a Greek-speaker, lectured in Rome. His writings had a marked influence upon Augustine, and through Augustine helped to mould Christian theology. There was little or no word of Aristotle at this time. But after a while the Church came to the conclusion that the study of Plato led to unorthodoxy, if not to heresy; consequently it was condemned. On the other hand there could be nothing unorthodox about logic, and so Aristotle, as the creator of formal logic, was received into favour. The Platonists however were never quite extinguished, and towards the end of the Middle Ages the rivalry between Platonism and Aristotelianism was revived in the Greek Church. It spread to Italy and naturally carried with it a reawakened interest in Plato, especially among the Humanists, who were in rebellion against every form of mediaevahsm. Cardinal Bessarion (1395-1472) was instrumental in bringing to Italy the works of Plato in a much fuller and more correct form than western Europe had hitherto known. They were eagerly studied and a cult of Plato, which almost reached the proportions of a new religion, sprang into existence. Its centre was Florence under the Medici, where an Academy was founded in imitation of Plato's. The head of this institution, Ficinus, did not at first know Greek and his conception of Platonism had been formed under Neo-Platonic influences. These the Florentine Academy never quite shook off. Among others it attracted a young man of genius, called Pico della Mirandola, who elaborated an extraordinary system, in which he tried to reconcile Platonism (as he understood it) with Christianity and Oriental mysticism. For some time he had great influence, which had repercussions in England, where his Life was translated by Sir Thomas More.

With the characteristic ideas of the Renaissance we are only so far concerned as they influenced English literature. It would be easy to show that the Greek ideal of human beauty, of which the Italians were enabled to form some conception from statues, Roman copies from the Greek, still surviving in their country, was a source of inspiration not only to Italian art but to Italian literature. Its effect on English literature however is by comparison inconsiderable. Then the Greek exaltation of reason and intellect has appealed much less to the English than to more logical nations. Even the Greek enthusiasm for liberty, so far as it takes the form of a theoretic republicanism, has never burned very brightly in this country. On the other hand liberty of thought—the right of each man to make up his own mind and speak it—has appealed almost as much to the English as to the Greeks. In the sphere of religion and conscience its consequences have of course been immense, one of them being Protestantism. But Protestantism did not come out of Italy, and it would be paradoxical to say that it came out of ancient Greece. Something else however did, and that was the New Testament. The Greek Testament was first edited by Erasmus, whose text was used by Tyndale in his English translation, which is the basis of the 'Authorized Version'. But there is a convention that the New Testament should not be counted as a classical influence, and that convention will be preserved.

(*d*) The cult of Paganism need not detain us long. We have already mentioned one form which it took—

the enthusiasm for a somewhat misunderstood and sentimentalised Platonism. But it took many forms. In extreme cases it led to the repudiation of Christianity altogether and an actual or pretended belief in the Olympian gods. But in its commoner or milder aspect it was called Humanism. The real ground of Humanism was the old Greek (and Roman) belief in the value of liberty. Only a free man, it was held, was in the complete sense a man at all; a slave was only half a man. The freedom must be intellectual and moral as well as economic and political; in fact, to the Greeks if not the Romans, the latter freedoms were chiefly valued as the necessary conditions of the intellectual and moral. Here education is of the utmost importance. A free man must receive a free or 'liberal' education. There was no subject which more powerfully engaged the attention of the leading spirits of the Renaissance. They wished to make a complete break with the past, which they looked upon as a time of enslavement. In particular they were eager to throw off the restrictions imposed by the mediaeval Church upon their reading. They took, in the famous phrase, all knowledge for their province. Their motto might have been the line of Terence (translated from a Greek original) *Homo sum: humani nil a me alienum puto,* 'I am a man; there is nothing human that I think does not concern me'. They were Humanists. Some of them naturally went further than others. The exulting sense of freedom in thought and speech led to all kinds of exciting speculations. This side of the Renaissance obviously affected Marlowe, who had no caution, and Bacon, who had a great deal, and moreover busied himself mainly with science. But complete freedom of speculation is the inspiration of the one as much as of the other; indeed without that freedom science is impossible. As for Humanism, although it has its ethical side, it is on the whole, at least as far as literature is concerned, an intellectual ideal. The moral ideal rather expressed itself in the cultivation of one's personal faculties, physical and mental. This was Greek enough, but the Greeks had always sought to temper or check the desire for personal distinction by insisting on the danger of excess. The warning however was often disregarded by the men of the Renaissance. Many authenticated stories about them go even beyond anything reported about the Greek 'tyrants'. The end was made to justify the means, as in the *Prince* of Macchiavelli, whose name justly or not became a by-word in England. But the cultivation of personality is not inherently a bad thing, and if it produced unscrupulous ruffians of immense ability, it also produced great gentlemen like Sir Philip Sidney. The textbook of the gentleman was *Il Cortegiano, 'The Courtier', of Castiglione, translated by Sir Thomas Hoby in 1561. It had a considerable effect on the men who were reforming education in England and has helped to produce the Public School* notion of a gentleman, with all that that implies in its expression in English literature. Castiglione's ideal has more in it of mediaeval conceptions like Chivalry and the Courts of. Love than of anything that is really Greek. But the spirit of it is genuinely Humanistic, and so far Greek.

RENAISSANCE IN ENGLAND

We may now return to England and see how these new ways of living and thinking affected our own literature. For many reasons it seems best to begin with the first English author of the new age whose reputation can be said to have crossed the Channel, Sir Thomas More. This ability to obtain an international audience was, at least during the early Renaissance, the test of an author's eminence when he wrote, as More generally did, in Latin, since whoever wrote in Latin was in fact addressing an international audience. More is by no means the author of a single book, but that which has come to be called *Utopia* is so much the most remarkable and celebrated that we may confine the few words we can spare to that. The conception of the book is not new. Plato *Republic* has given a description of an ideal state, and More certainly knew a good deal about the *Republic*. He must also have known the Critias, which describes the lost Atlantis. But it is certain besides that he had long studied and enjoyed what he could get hold of among the works of Lucian, including the *True History*. That he was thinking of Lucian will appear almost certain in the introductory chapters, whatever one may think of the later and more serious parts of the book. The Hythlodaye passage with its mock gravity and 'realism' is full of the Lucianic irony. This is important because it means that More did not intend us to take the *Utopia au pied de la lettre*, as too many of his commentators have done. On the other hand it would be even more stupid to suppose that the book was a mere joke or even that it did not give expression to some very strong convictions of its author. Irony is strong feeling modified by humour.

More was involved in controversy with the early Protestants, among whom Tyndale may be counted, and this provokes the observation that the Renaissance in England was practically from the beginning there complicated by the religious quarrel. This gives it a graver and more serious cast than it originally had in Italy. The fundamental seriousness comes out just as clearly in More, who had a sense of humour, as in that wonderful artist in words, William Tyndale, who seems to have had none. It is observable later in Spenser, and later still in Milton. We must not make too much of this difference between the English and the Italian and even the French Renaissance, for it admitted of many exceptions; but it does exist and it shows the protean character of the new spirit. It has often been suggested that the English Renaissance owes much of its special character to the famous Dutch scholar Erasmus, an older contemporary and intimate friend of More. But the evidence rather points the other way. Erasmus was greatly admired by men like Colet and Fisher, not to mention More; but it was not he who influenced them, it was they who impressed Erasmus. It may be admitted that he gave back what he received in double measure and became, through his incomparable skill in modern Latin, the interpreter to the world and to the English themselves of the characteristically English preference for the *via media*. His most influential writings were no doubt these: the *Adages*, the *Colloquies*, the *Praise of Folly* and his edition of the New Testament with his Latin paraphrase of the Greek. The *Adages* is a collection of witty or proverbial sayings current in antiquity with explanations (often highly entertaining) by Erasmus. The *Colloquies* began as a schoolbook, being imaginary conversations between schoolmaster and pupil, a kind of primer common enough in the Middle Ages. In successive editions the plan of it was vastly extended and changed; it became largely satirical somewhat in the manner of Lucian and ended as something that might almost be counted a forerunner of the realistic romance. (It is used by Lyly, by Scott in *Anne of Geierstein* and notably by Reade in the *Cloister and the Hearth*.) The *Praise of Folly*, dedicated to More, is of course ironical and satirical, and it hit the taste of the day exactly. Although these works are in Latin, they were for a long time the familiar reading of all educated Englishmen. They rivalled in popularity the ancient classics themselves. The Renaissance despised mediaeval Latin, but not its own. Men read their Erasmus and their Politian, their Mantuan and, later, their Buchanan *Psalms* as eagerly as their Horace or their Cicero. This must not be forgotten when we consider the influence of the ancient languages upon our literature. But equally it must not be forgotten that Erasmus and the others were saturated in the classics and imitated them in every word and phrase.

It has never been clearly explained why English classical scholarship made so little progress during the sixteenth century compared with the achievements first of Italy and then of France. Actually the new learning had reached England before it affected France, but when it got established in France it produced a long line of perhaps the most illustrious classical scholars that ever lived. The only scholar produced by this country whose fame in any way rivalled theirs was the Scottish George Buchanan (1506-82), and it was rather for his Latin style that he was admired than for his learning. His metrical version of the Psalms had an immense vogue until at least the nineteenth century, while his polemical works have had no small influence on political theory. Buchanan may be considered an exception and, as he passed a good deal of his life abroad, not a wholly satisfactory one. Whatever the reasons, the primacy in scholarship passed from Italy to France. It powerfully impressed itself on the spirit and form as well as the matter of French literature. That lies outside our province, but no student of English literature can afford to neglect, among other French influences, that of the Pléiade, a name borrowed from the Greek. That company of scholars and authors were enthusiastically, almost fanatically, attached to classical models, and upon certain English poets its influence was not small. There was also a brilliant Renaissance in Spain, the leaven of which worked in our own literature. And on the whole it must be said that, while there was a great increase of classical scholarship in England, particularly at the Universities, and the scholars now went to the genuine classics for the material of their studies, English authors fell into a habit of absorbing classical influences rather through French and Spanish than directly.

Spencer

In writing of an age which ultimately passed into the 'Elizabethan' with its abundant and varied output—an age moreover in which almost every author had a tincture of classical knowledge—it is impossible to do more than make some general remarks. Their detailed application may safely be left to the student. But clearly something must be said about Spenser and Sidney, much more about the drama and Milton. It would not be possible to do even this, if so much had not already been written about them as to make detailed reference unnecessary.

As for Spenser, it is evident that he was a good classical scholar for an Englishman of his time. But, as we have noted, the qualification is not unimportant, for the time, although it produced some men of considerable learning, such as Camden, was not distinguished in pure scholarship. Moreover, while Spenser uses his reading with admirable skill and taste, it is hard for us to distinguish appearance from reality. In other words we cannot tell how much is derived from the originals and how much from secondary sources. But from our point of view that hardly matters; the important thing is that classical influences are strong upon him. They are evident as early as the *Shepheardes Calender*. That very interesting experiment might no doubt be taken as expressing a reaction against the Virgilian type of pastoral; but in order to react against something you have first to be acted upon by it. However it is not impossible that Spenser felt that he was really vindicating Virgil, in whom there are many touches of genuine rusticity, against more conventional successors like Mantuan, an Italian Renaissance author, whose Latin *Eclogues* had an immense contemporary fame. It is however rather more probable that Spenser was following Theocritus, whom he knew, if not in the original Greek, in some version; in Theocritus he would find sufficient precedent for the use of rustic language and the description of rustic fife. In spite of the dream-like element in so much of his work Spenser was a thoroughly English person, and it was an English instinct in him to go for the matter of his pastorals to the countryside he knew. At the same time there is an odd and not disagreeable mixture of rural England and classical divinities and conventions. The characters have often Greek names and seem to know a good deal of classical mythology. There is also what may seem a disproportionate amount of allegory and veiled allusion and anti-papal satire, which had their effect no doubt on *Lycidas*. Perhaps the *Calender* would have been better without the classical elements at all. But there they are and they must be taken into account.

Similar elements run through all Spenser's work, including such parts of it as, like the *Faerie Queene* itself, appear utterly unclassical in conception, structure and metre. This is not the place to track them down; but, as reference is so often made to Spenser's Platonism, as expressed more particularly in the *Foure Hymns*, we are called upon to say a word about that. The present writer finds it difficult to accept some of the views that have been entertained about Spenser's philosophy of Love and Beauty. That it has a Platonic quality or tendency need not be denied. But it is not Platonism; it is a jumble of Platonic doctrine with elements of Aristotelianism and Christianity. It is strange to find not undistinguished persons quoting the stanza that ends For *soule is forme and doth the bodie make as* eminently Platonic; Plato never said anything of the sort. Nor did Aristotle, although he did say *of the soule the bodie forme doth take*. Spenser knew the *Timaeus*—but so did the Middle Ages. He identifies the Creator of the *Timaeus* with Divine Love—but so did Dante. The identification was reached by harmonising Plato with Aristotle's conception of the universe as impelled by love of the Prime Mover, who is God. Spenser had read the Symposium and presumably the *Phaedrus* of Plato, and he has a notion, as clear perhaps as anyone else's, of what Plato meant by the Idea of Beauty. But how to combine that with the inherited mediaeval doctrine he really does not know. The truth is that the Renaissance Platonists were not anything like so clear-headed in their teaching as the mediaeval theologians whom they rather professed to despise. But at least their enthusiasm for what they believed to be Platonism was genuine and led to a better understanding of what Plato actually meant and said. Spenser shared the enthusiasm and found beautiful words for its expression. More than that we have no right to expect from him.

It has often been remarked that Sir Philip Sidney is a typical figure of the Renaissance; say the English Renaissance at its best, and the statement is true. Although his culture was European, he could never be mistaken for anything but an Englishman, and he was a gentleman, which is more than can be said of some distinguished products of the age. He was something of a scholar and he was deeply imbued with classical influences as they came to him modified by the Renaissance temperament and the Renaissance interpretation of antiquity. He thought that Spenser did not follow classical models with sufficient fidelity and would have liked him to use classical metres. He was also an advocate of the Senecan drama in English. Fortunately his advice on these matters was not followed, but his influence must not be underrated. He was immensely admired, and the probability is that his critical advice was disregarded not so much because it was thought to be wrong as because it was impracticable. Dramatists have to give what the public wants, and the public did not want a succession of Gorboducs. And quantitative metre will not work in English. Sidney might have discovered this for himself, for his own lyrical poetry, which is often of a very high quality, was not in quantitative metres or, when it was, was bad. After his death his literary fame was kept alive by the publication of his Arcadia (to give it its shortened name), a long book of a kind already familiar to Sidney—his chief predecessor here was the Spaniard Montemayor—but sufficiently original in Sidney's handling of it. The ancestor of the Arcadia and the others is Xenophon Cyropaedia, complicated by pastorals like Daphnis and Chke and 'novels' like those of Heliodorus and Eumathius (or Eustathius). The result was further complicated by 'courtly' and as we should say romantic ideas. There is little that is truly classical about the Arcadia except the names; but it would be interesting to know how far Sidney realised that. Each generation finds in the classics what it looks for, and Sidney's generation—the Faerie Queene itself is evidence—was looking for chivalry and romance. There is a little of both in Xenophon, and what there was could be spun out indefinitely. As for the style of the book it is distinctly classical in the length and involution of its sentences. And all through there are the classical allusions which no Renaissance book could be without.

The Arcadia had been preceded in publication by the two Euphues novels of Lyly, but does not seem to have been influenced by them. Lyly can be no more than mentioned in spite of his contemporary importance. His style is highly mannered and (as everyone knows) full of *'conceits'. But his* sentences are admirably constructed—much better than

Sidney's—on the general model of the classical period, and his influence in that respect was a wholesome check upon Elizabethan tendencies to formless or broken-backed syntax. He has a very considerable knowledge of classical and postclassical Latin, and he delights, which is at least as much mediaeval as Renaissance, in the sort of information supplied by Pliny *Natural History*, which he must have studied with great devotion. He and Sidney gave a classical colour—it is no more than that—to the Elizabethan novel, or what was trying to be the novel, in its earlier stages.

DRAMA

The native drama of England became in time a thing peculiarly English; but, so far as it has a single origin, it must be sought in certain performances organised by the mediaeval Church, the words of which were Latin. The Latin had ultimately to yield to the vernacular, but it was there first. Nor was the classical drama by any means forgotten in the Middle Ages, though it had not much effect upon English practice. The Renaissance brought a change. The native drama of the time was despised, at any rate among those who could read Latin, in comparison with Seneca for Tragedy and Plautus and Terence for Comedy. There were translations and imitations both in Latin and English. The details of all this and of the history of the classical drama in 'Tudor' and 'Elizabethan' times generally may be found in many scholarly studies of the subject. To some extent the phenomenon explains itself, and, as we know, the end was failure or at best a *succès d'estime*. But the impact of the classical drama upon the kind that did succeed, and above all upon Shakespeare, is too important to be passed over without some comment. Of the plays composed or believed to be by Shakespeare no less than seven, not counting *Cymbeline*, have a classical subject. They are *Titus Andronicus*, *Julius Caesar*, *Timon of Athens*, *Antony and Cleopatra*, *Troilus and Cressida*, *Coriolanus and Pericles Prince of Tyre*, which is classical only in name. Of these *Titus Andronicus* is a typical Senecan tragedy with all its rhetorical emphasis and horrific incidents. Whatever we may think of its merits as a play, it has very great importance for the student of Shakespeare's dramatic development, if we accept it, as we evidently must on the external evidence, as wholly or in great part his work. For it proves that at the beginning of his career he made himself thoroughly acquainted with what went to the making of a Senecan play. With this conception of classical tragedy in his mind he came upon North's translation of Plutarch. Its effect upon him is almost demonstrable. Here he found not only a dramatic vision of history but credible human beings, not the shadowy types that stalk upon the Senecan stage. Plutarch's Brutus and Caesar, his Antony and Cleopatra are credible persons. More than that, Shakespeare's philosophy of history, if that is not too pompous a name for it, is, as we have already observed, also that of Plutarch, for they both are of opinion that events are what they are because the actors in them are what they are. Thus Shakespeare saw at once what could be done with the material he found in Plutarch, and from it he proceeded to create a new kind of classical drama which was just as real, just as alive, just as 'modern' as any of the other kinds he attempted. The contrast with Ben Jonson is instructive. The *Catiline* and *Sejanus* of Jonson are fully documented; the historical and archaeological detail is sufficiently accurate; there is good construction and plenty of action. But they remain dull plays, because the characters are too abstract or not vividly enough realised to make the reader care what happens to them. The Greeks and Romans of Shakespeare are real people, and it is rather beside the point to say that he thinks of them as Elizabethans. It is not altogether true, but even if it were it is of the smallest importance. The essential thing was that they should be alive, and what Plutarch did for Shakespeare was to give him the means of 'seeing' these ancients as they really were. For in general Shakespeare follows Plutarch with great fidelity. In particular every trait of character is seized upon and developed. Thus he read in Plutarch that Antony was a distinguished orator in the Asiatic, and Brutus in the Attic, style. These remarks are made quite by the way, except that Plutarch does dwell a little upon the style of Brutus and makes a few quotations from his letters which exhibit his bare, thin, excessively antithetic manner. Now in Julius Caesar we have the great funeral oration of Antony, entirely the work of Shakespeare, for it is not in Plutarch; and if it is hardly so florid as a speech in the Asiatic style might be expected to be, it sufficiently develops all the resources of rhetoric. Contrast the speech of Brutus, which is also entirely the work of Shakespeare. It is in prose, and the imitation of the Attic style as Roman orators practised it is so perfect that, unless one knew it was Shakespeare's, one might suppose it was a translation. There are other instances of the same careful attention to points of character. In other respects it is notorious that Shakespeare was less careful. Besides, the degree of his care differs from play to play. It is obvious for instance that he took far more trouble with Julius Caesar and Antony and Cleopatra than with Coriolanus or Timon of Athens.

These four dramas were based on Plutarch. Titus Andronicus, Troilus and Cressida, and Pericles Prince of Tyre were not, and they call for less comment from us because in fact they were less classical. Titus we have discussed. Troilus and Cressida is something of a problem. It deals with the old mediaeval story as it was developed by Chaucer, and is therefore only by courtesy a classical drama at all. The same may be said of Pericles, so far as it is or may be Shakespeare's. The story on which it is founded has a strange and complicated history which takes it out of antiquity into the Middle Ages, to which it really belongs. So we need not trouble about it. Nor about the Roman passages in Cymbeline, because there we are really dealing with the medieval 'matter of Britain'.

The influence of classical Comedy upon Shakespeare is comparatively slight. If he wrote the Comedy of Errors, as there is no good reason to disbelieve, he was following Plautus in his Menaechmi. The Menaechmi in turn was translated from a Greek play of the Middle Comedy. It is funny in Plautus and it must have been funny in the original. The joke lay in the misunderstandings that arose when two brothers, identical twins, were mistaken for each other, one of the twins being a good young man and the other not. Shakespeare gives the two indistinguishable brothers two indistinguishable servants-an idea evidently borrowed from another comedy of Plautus, the Amphitryo-which makes the whole thing incredible and so ruins the fun. It was an unfortunate beginning for him, but he did not repeat the mistake. He proceeded to create his own form of Comedy. We may well believe that a closer following of Latin comedy would have been less helpful than harmful to him. For that was a Comedy of Manners with stock characters, and stock characters were abhorrent or impossible to Shakespeare.

Critics, considering Shakespeare in relation to the 'University Wits' in the earlier part of his career and to Jonson, with his double following of Latin models in Tragedy and Comedy, in the later, are disposed to think of him as resisting or transforming classical influence rather than accepting or yielding to it. On the whole that judgement is sound, but it requires some modification, if not in Comedy at least in the historical dramas. The reconstruction of ancient Rome in Julius Caesar and of ancient Alexandria in Antony and Cleopatra can only be described as a triumphant s' ccess. There are of course blunders and anachronisms, but the essential truth of the contrasting pictures astonishes the historian. No doubt the materials were provided by Plutarch, but they were there for the other dramatists to use if they could. Compared with these plays Jonson's Roman dramas are archaeological confections. The classical plays of the University Wits have not even Jonson's scholarship. The fact is that both they and Jonson fell into the error of trying to be classical first and human second. Shakespeare went straight to human nature, saw his characters in their natural setting, and thereby actually got nearer in spirit if not in letter to the Roman scene than did the scholars. This is surely rather accepting classical influence than fighting against it. The adaptability of Shakespeare's genius is of course one of the most astonishing things about it. Compared with Chapman for example he has almost no classical learning. But

Chapman, even in translating Homer, is strangely unclassical both in temper and in style.

Attempts have indeed been made at various times to vindicate for Shakespeare a not inconsiderable, if scrappy, acquaintance with Latin itself. But there is nothing either in the plays or in the poems that justifies this claim to first hand knowledge. Doubtless he knew a little Latin, but it is greatly to be doubted if he made much or any direct use of it. There was in his day a common stock of classical knowledge from which he took what suited him. But, although Shakespeare made no pretensions to learning himself, many of his contemporaries did. This learning, despite a growing interest in history and antiquities which accompanied the growth of nationalism, was predominantly classical. It was not, as we have already had occasion to remark, exact or critical; but it was often wide and varied, and naturally it had its influence on the mind and taste of its possessors. It made them reluctant to give up classical metres and Senecan drama and other obsolete things. Thus Fulke Greville and his Scottish successor Alexander went on writing tragedies on the Senecan model, but with a preponderance of the sententious over the sensational. The effect is often impressive and in the case of Greville even striking, but it did not last. The English genius remained incurably English. But this ought not to blind us to the depth and extent of the classical background. Even if it did not affect their own writing or not to any extent, their learning helped to make Jonson and Chapman, Donne and Campion, Bacon and Hooker the writers they are. Nor were they by any means alone. And they were succeeded by men even more learned, such as Burton, Taylor, Milton, Browne. The classical background was then in immense force.

So far we have been speaking of the Drama; but this seems, the natural place in which to say something of those poems of Shakespeare which have a classical subject, namely Venus and Adonis and the Rape of Lucrece. Both stories were excessively familiar to the Renaissance public, and it is not very likely that Shakespeare went to the classical sources for his matter, although he may have refreshed his memory of

Ovid, for he had some Latin if not much. But if the stories are classical the treatment is not. The style is rhetorical and 'conceited'; much of the description not essential to the story but purely decorative. Now these are characteristically Ovidian defects; but it must be admitted that Ovid not only tells his stories better, but compared with Venus and Lucrece he is a model of succinctness. Both in fact are typically Renaissance poems and are only so far Ovidian as the Renaissance itself, in one chief aspect of it, was markedly Ovidian. It would therefore be an error to suppose that Shakespeare was directly influenced by Ovid, although the indirect influence is unmistakable. His immediate models, so far as he had any, were Spenser and Marlowe. The Hero and Leander of Marlowe is a magnificent poem, but it too has very little of the true classical spirit. It is an elaboration in highly ornate and impassioned verse of a post-classical Greek poem of some, but not comparable, beauty. Marlowe, who had been at Cambridge, was more of a scholar than Shakespeare, and his work, what survives of it, is full of classical allusions. But he is even more 'romantic' than Shakespeare. In his way he is as typical a figure of the Renaissance as Sidney, but one cannot say that he represents like Sidney the best side of it. He is full of intellectual and moral arrogance, although we must admit that as what Matthew Arnold called a 'poetical force' he is almost of the first order. He is the complement of Sidney, and anyone who understands both of them will have a good idea of the English Renaissance.

PROSE

It is perhaps not necessary to say much about the prose of the period. In spite of the genius of individuals it never acquired a settled or standard form. The 'Authorized Version' of the Bible is not, as is rather commonly supposed, a masterpiece of Jacobean prose; it is a masterpiece of Tudor prose, preserved with some modification from the time of Tyndale. In any case it is not affected by any classical model. The only Elizabethan prose of the finest quality is Shakespeare's. It would be quite easy to show that some of it, and by no means the least effective, such as the speech of Hamlet beginning *What a piece of work is a man!* or the oration of Brutus in Julius Caesar, is quite remarkably classical in structure. But in general Shakespeare's prose is too personal to be called classical or anything but Shakespearean. The others experiment with greater or less success. It can however be said that there is a broad movement towards what may for the sake of brevity and convenience be called a Ciceronian style. Hooker very nearly attains it. Later, Donne, Milton, Browne and others elaborate it, sometimes too much; and all latinise heavily. But the euphuistic style was in its way classical too. The sentences are balanced in the careful, antithetic style of ancient rhetoric; they do not keep the looser, more colloquial structure, which seems natural to English. Some time after Lyly there was a new fashion of aphoristic prose, exemplified in Bacon *Essays* and Jonson *Timber;* and that too could be paralleled, if it was not derived, from ancient models, for a great deal of classical prose is studious of what the Greeks called gnomai and the Romans *sententiae.* But Elizabethan and even Jacobean and Caroline prose never fully escaped the danger of formlessness, and until prose has done that it cannot be regarded as securely classical.

We have been speaking of prose style. If we go beyond that and ask how far the fashion of our prose writers' thinking was classical, the answer is far from easy. It is much less easy in the case of English authors than of Italian or even French, partly because the English did not fall so readily into schools devoted to the cultivation of some aspect of ancient fife or literature, and partly because there did not exist a standard English prose. In such conditions no prudent critic will permit himself to indulge in generalisations. Every author calls for a separate discussion. It is of course obvious to inspection that the thoughts of Jonson and of Milton were constantly engaged with the great authors of antiquity. But others as widely if not as accurately versed in classical literature as they seem only so far affected by it as to make constant quotations from and references to it. They think their own thoughts, and very unclassical thoughts they often are. A writer like Clarendon, dealing with contemporary history, or Hobbes, evolving a modern system of political thought, can hardly be expected to draw their materials from the past. Yet in fact both these writers have more affinity to classical thought and even style than Donne or Taylor or Burton. But from all this one fact emerges, which after all is the important fact for us. All these men were steeped in the classics.

TRANSLATIONS

Nothing better shows the general interest of the age in the literatures of antiquity than the number and popularity of the translations from them. It is not necessary to make out a list of these because, while they vary greatly in merit, they have a more or less uniform character. The translator makes the best he can of the original or, as very often happened, of a French version of the original, and then thinks only of how he shall put the sense into the most vigorous and eloquent English he can. The natural consequence is that the translation acquires an Elizabethan, which is as much as to say a distinctly unclassical, quality in the process. But, whatever objections there may be to this from the point of view of scholarship, there is none from the point of view of literature. In fact all the most famous translations have been made more or less on this principle. And so we find that many of the Tudor and Elizabethan translations have fine qualities of their own. It would seem like an act of ingratitude not to mention here the name of Philemon Holland, who translated so much and so well from the classics that he holds no mean station even among the authors of that great age. We have seen what North's translation of Plutarch (made from the French) meant to Shakespeare. Both North and Holland write admirable, vivid and energetic prose, which owes nothing but its matter to their originals. The translators in verse are in the mass not nearly so good, although even among them we must count Marlowe and Chapman. Marlowe might have been among the greatest of translators, if he had cared to translate; but Hero and Leander is at best a paraphrase, while his youthful versions of Ovid *Amores* and of some other things are more spirited than accurate. Chapman's Homer is a fine achievement. But Phaer's Virgil and Golding's Ovid are scarcely readable now. They were however found eminently readable in their own day, and it is that which lends a special importance to them and to the other translators. For it was they who more than anyone else supplied the 'general reader' of the time with his classical knowledge. That the classics became to some extent transformed in the process, so that the ancient heroes were seen as so many Elizabethan gentlemen, is true enough. But every age sees the classics in the light of its own taste and education. No doubt Pope thought that he was giving the true Homer, which Chapman had travestied. Pope seems to us as far from the true Homer as Chapman. A later generation may think us as far wrong as either.

MILTON

In John Milton, so far as England is concerned, the classical Renaissance culminates. For that very reason it may not be necessary to deal with him at such length as would be necessary if a case had to be argued. But the case is not always presented in its full force. It is of course true that there were other influences than the classical at work at all times, and with increasing power as he grew older, upon Milton; that even his diction is often sturdily English; that he never gives the impression of living in antiquity like many scholars, his contemporaries and predecessors. But merely to call him a scholarly poet is quite inadequate. His poetry is not just scholarly poetry, it is scholarship distilled into poetry. In this he resembles Virgil and, among our own poets, Gray. It is something of a reproach to English scholarship that there does not exist an adequate commentary upon this side of Milton's work as distinct from what has been written about his life and his text. Consequently the most that can be done here is to offer a preliminary remark. Classical scholarship was not with Milton an end in itself. From his youth he had dedicated himself to poetry and for this mission he deliberately set to prepare his mind. He had two things to master—the technique and the material of poetry. As a true though belated child of the Renaissance he felt that these things must be studied in Latin and in Greek. It was not that he was ill acquainted with English literature; he knew it well from Chaucer to Donne, being particularly drawn to the Puritan Spenser; and he learned a great deal from that. But Milton can hardly be blamed for thinking, like every other educated man of his time, that the classics were still the unapproached models of style and, in their mythology and philosophy, the great sources of poetical material. He therefore flung himself with ardour into the study of the ancient languages. The direction which his studies took was on the whole more typical of the Italian revival of learning than of the contemporary English or French. His ambition was to excel in the composition of Latin verse and prose. It was for his Latin, not his English, verses that he was so much admired in Italy when he travelled there. Later, his skill in Latin prose marked him out as the man to defend the Commonwealth against criticism from abroad. His controversy with Salmasius made, as he says himself, *all Europe ring from side to side*. Milton's genius, his power of expressing himself in the Latin language, his youthful vigour gave him a real or apparent victory over Salmasius, who was old and sick. But it was a literary victory. In mere extent of learning Salmasius was at that time beyond comparison superior. Even for that age his erudition was prodigious. But he never learned to write clear or fluent Latin prose. It is one of the differences between the early Italian Renaissance and the later, mainly French, one that, while the Frenchmen were by far the more learned and critical scholars, the Italians were in general the better composers; and it is this which links Milton with them rather than with men like Salmasius. This is not to deny that in time he came to be as learned perhaps as any of his English contemporaries. But we must explain him from his first essays in writing Latin. It was this that taught him to appreciate, as no Englishman except perhaps Jonson had done before, the classical qualities of style. But it goes much beyond that. It taught him his own style.

It is necessary however to be clear as to the meaning of this. Milton never at any time of his life submitted passively to anything. So when we speak of classical influences upon him let it be remembered that he did not think of himself as following the classics so much as continuing them. His ambition was hardly less than to refashion the English language so that it might compete on equal terms with Greek and Latin. What Virgil had done for Latin he aspired to do for English. He forgot that Greek and Latin have a natural affinity; which does not exist between them and English, so that while Virgil might impose all the artifices of Greek poetry and even many Greek idioms on Latin without doing it violence, it was impossible to thrust Latin syntax and the Latin order of words on English without subjecting it to a much more noticeable strain. That Milton nearly succeeds in achieving the impossible is no more than a proof of his personal genius. His aim was wrong and his example did harm. Yet a poet must be allowed to write poetry in his own way and not in that of somebody else, and one cannot imagine Milton producing the effects he did in any style but that which he made for himself by his study-and how profound and subtle it is!—of the poetic art of the ancients. One can see the process of its creation from L'Allegro or even earlier to Paradise Lost. These earlier poems largely explain themselves. The most important of them no doubt is the masque we call *Comus*. It is naturally full of classical reminiscence, and it already shows the kind of scholarship described before with its unequalled sensitiveness to every exquisite turn and phrase of ancient poetic style. However the playor poem is by no means wholly inspired by classical influences nor does it follow any particular model. Even its theme, though intensely characteristic of Milton, is not equally characteristic of pagan antiquity. Yet there is one Greek play, the *Hippolytus* of Euripides, of which the hero is a young man who is a devotee of the goddess of chastity. Of this play, as appears from many evidences, Milton had made a special study. Among the ancient dramatists Euripides was his favourite; there are no traces of any enthusiasm for Seneca. That shows how far Milton was in advance of his age in literary scholarship. Perhaps he was the first Englishman who felt the full poetic value of a Greek tragedy or indeed of Greek poetry in general. At least he was the first who succeeded—and *Comus* and the *Arcades* are proofs of it—in transfusing into English in any great measure the special virtues of Greek as distinct from Latin poetry. True, *Lycidas* draws its inspiration from Virgil more than from Theocritus, but it is a highly original poem in spite of its obedience to the conventions of the classical Pastoral. The imitations in it of ancient poetry, which are both numerous and close, do not affect its essential originality.

When we come to Paradise Lost we find the Miltonic style in its full development. It is of course a highly personal thing, but many classical elements have gone to its making and above all the epic style of Virgil. It has three eminently Virgilian characteristics: the verse paragraph, *enjambement*, an exquisite manipulation of the musical values of words. The first two of these characteristics have been discussed already in connexion with Virgil himself, and little need be added here. Milton equals Virgil in the architecture of the verse-paragraph. He bad shown his power in this at least as early as *Lycidas*, but it is perhaps most notable in Paradise Lost because that has to get this effect without the aid of rhyme with its internal responsions and answering echoes. Then in his love of making one line overflow into another Milton resembles Virgil. Thirdly he resembles him in his exploitation of all the resources of verbal music. If it was not Virgil alone, it was surely Virgil chiefly who was his teacher in these three arts. But beside these three points on which one can lay a definite finger, there is an important affinity between the Miltonic and Virgilian style. They are both personal in contrast with the impersonal style of Homer. That is a real distinction, much more significant than any label—of doubtful validity at the best—between the natural and the artificial or literary epic. The personality of Milton however is not only expressed in his style but asserted, openly or indirectly, in Paradise Lost itself in a manner foreign to the diffident Virgil. This is especially evident at the beginning of certain books—the first, the third and the seventh-where the poet speaks of himself. Whether these passages are in accordance with the principles of classical art, which forbids irrelevant digressions however splendid, may be doubted. But only a pedant would wish them away because they are perhaps the noblest passages in all Milton, just as the passages of personal reminiscence or self-defence are the noblest parts of his prose. But even these passages the author would probably not have allowed himself unless he had classical authority for them, as in Lucretius and the Georgics.

With respect to the structure of Paradise Lost it is of course designed on the classical model, as may be seen by analysing it. No doubt here again Virgil was the chief master. Besides that, Milton—and here again is a point of resemblance with the Roman poet—was eminently a *doctus poeta*. He has levied contributions from all quarters—English, modern and mediaeval European languages, and Renaissance latinists as well as from the classics. Among ancient poets, apart from Homer and Virgil whom he naturally and almost necessarily most studied and followed, he was perhaps chiefly attracted to Ovid and to Euripides. But the extent and variety of his indebtedness—if a poet is indebted for that which he improves in borrowing—are beyond reckoning. Thus his scholarship is transmuted into poetry. To anyone who may think that implies a lack of individuality the answer is sufficiently crushing: there is no writer in any language who gives a stronger impression of intense individuality than John Milton. At all events his poetry is utterly and intentionally traditional. Thus, following the epic tradition, he is led to employ 'epic machinery' and the Homeric type of simile. In a poem with the subject of Paradise Lost divine intervention is perhaps inevitable, for it is the mainspring of the action in the Bible narrative itself. But the use of the Homeric simile was not necessary.

It is a concession to tradition, beautifully justified by the result. Here again we see the man's poetical scholarship.

The qualities of Paradise Lost reappear in Paradise Regained with a certain loss of colour and increase of argumentativeness. Milton is getting older, more censorious, even turning against the classics he had adored in his youth.

He has adopted an absurd theory, put forward by certain Jewish scholars in Hellenistic times and taken up by the Christian apologists in antiquity, that Greek poetry is a plagiarism and perversion of Hebrew poetry, as contained in the Old Testament. There is something ironical in the fact that, when Paradise Regained is taken in hand by the reader, he finds that the finest passages of it are exactly those which owe their inspiration to the classical writers and not to the Bible.

Samson Agonistes, 'Samson at the Games'—a title on the model of those invented by ancient scholars for the Greek plays—is best explained by the introductory 'Epistle' entitled Of that sort of Dramatic Poem which is call'd Tragedy. It deserves close study for the critical theories stated or implied in it. It may seem strange to find Milton, who in his younger days had read Shakespeare with delight, reverting to Tragedy of the Greek type in concurrence with Aristotle, who was merely describing the only kind of Tragedy he knew, not necessarily condemning every other kind. We must however bear in mind that in the year 1671, when Samson Agonistes was published, Tragedy of the Elizabethan sort had fallen into a somewhat deplorable condition, from which Milton evidently hoped to rescue it. It is also a little strange that so consummate a master of verbal music should have preferred the irregular metre of his lyrical passages to the balanced strophes of the ancient chorus, which are a chief part of the beauty and impressiveness of Greek drama. It may further be objected to Samson that Milton has not used the method of tragic irony, which a familiar story like that of Samson would seem to demand. Consequently the play is devoid of dramatic tension and interest. But as dramatic *poetry* it is magnificent. It is the only English tragedy of the classical type sufficiently in 'the grand style' to be put on a level as mere writing with the Greek masterpieces. In spite of its Hebraic, and even more English, spirit it is one of the most classical poems of considerable length in our literature. In poems of smaller compass it is much easier to attain the severe beauty and undecorated grace of Attic style. Jonson had achieved it in some of his lyrics and so, but still with an Elizabethan quality, had Campion. The songs in the *Arcades* and *Comus* have got the 'Dorique delicacy' of which Wotton speaks; so have some of the sonnets, as for example that beginning LAWRENCE *of vertuous Father vertuous Son* or that which begins CYRIACK, *whose Grandsire on the Royal Bench.*

Of Milton's prose it need only be said that the attempt to cast the English language into a classical mould proved much more difficult than in his verse—proved so difficult indeed that he failed completely to accomplish it. It is almost incredible that so fine a scholar could have tolerated such sentences. They have indeed magnificent phrases, but they trail their length along like wounded serpents. It is however at least permissible to think that Milton was seeking to produce in prose certain effects of organ-like music, which had not been attempted before except by Sir Thomas Browne in his Religio Medici. But Browne succeeded much better and his sentences, though not succinct, are never formless. At their best both Milton and Browne, with Donne every now and again in his Sermons and *Devotions,* have attained harmonies of modulated eloquence such as no other English writer has reached, for Ruskin has not their intellectual and imaginative subtlety. This statement is quite compatible with another: that Milton's prose style is the worst possible model for other and weaker men. So far as it had a model it was probably Cicero. It is at least Ciceronian.

SOME STUDIES IN THE ENGLISH RENAISSANCE

Renaissance Studies in this year of the twenty-first century has moved toward its historically central topics: New World discovery, the Reformation, bibliography, classical influence. The study of these topics, however, is now imbued with a very sophisticated mastery of the work done in the last two theoretical decades of the twentieth century. The study of subjectivity is no longer so purely a psychoanalytic project; it is also revisiting religious discourse and the spiritual practices endemic to the Reformation. At the same time, however, study of the classics and of New World discoveries is most usefully inflected with an understanding of psychoanalysis. Bibliography as the "histoire des livres," or study of the "material book," is distinctly the most vital of the more traditional topoi. Clearly the revolution in editing practices that seeks to render as fully as possible the book as a historical object has revivified the study of the material book— taking perhaps even greater force now from the accessibility granted by the Early English Books Online database. Now completely embedded in the most detailed and thickest of cultural descriptions, study of the book as physical object has produced a number of weighty volumes packed with information. It has even captured the interest of historians—two books in an established history series from a British publisher take the material book as their focus. Perhaps the most traditional of Renaissance topics is the legacy of the classics, and this too is well represented with a number of studies—and here, especially in the case of Ovid, psychoanalytic theories have enabled new readings and connections.

Some of the new issues that were first opened by late-twentieth-century criticism, such as the place of women's writing in Renaissance culture, carry on with renewed force. While only one new edition of women's writing appeared this year, a generous number of studies digest what has already been published. The remapping of political influence around the globe is the focus of a number of books. And the importance of material bookmaking has had its effect on the study of global connections—specifically, on a fairly large group of books directly devoted to map making. The New World, however, has found its place within the Old, the New World having been first considered by Columbus to be the Old World. Such globalization of Renaissance studies means that we need to take into account Islam and India as well as America; this new-old fold in the history of the European empires is also now represented by a number of compelling monographs. Allied to this field is a continuing concern for national identity—a number of studies concern the construction of "Englishness." These identity studies verge on, as they borrow from, the theory of "postcolonial" studies, especially in the context of the Elizabethan (re)conquest of Ireland.

That said, it is important to stress that one of the most significant books published in 2001 is Valerie Traub's Renaissance of Lesbianism in Early Modern England, based on a series of articles she has been publishing for the last decade. Combining a powerful intervention into the history of sexuality, the history of the family, and "queer theory," Traub's study builds on the twentieth-century achievements of feminist criticism and scholarship into alternative sexualities. We first thought to call this a "groundbreaking" book which "opens" up a whole new field (the study of female same-sex erotic desire), formerly understood, in Traub's own formulation, to be of relative "(in)significance". Second thoughts, however, present the book more as a capstone to the queering of the Renaissance insofar as it finally supplies a crucial missing term (female-female eroticism)—which thus makes it possible now to integrate queer theory into the history of sexuality as a whole. Traub's book not only brilliant ly locates a lost history of female-female eroticism, it also narrates a history that almost entirely changes our sense of the development of heterosexuality during the seventeenth century.

The study of power politics has offered up mature work that focuses on court cultures. But such sites are now more fully integrated into the study of a broader reach of social activities, including press censorship, manuscript circulation of the news, and even pornography. Fairly new to the field is what might be termed ecological criticism: this is represented by a study of animals, Erica Fudge's Perceiving Animals: Humans and Beasts in Early Modern English Culture, which focuses on the problematic line drawn between the human and the nonhuman, as well as by a few essays that aim to investigate the beginnings of ecological consciousness in some Renaissance poets, and two collections of essays, some of which deal with the Renaissance. Timothy Sweet's American Georgics: Economy and Environment in

Early American Literature attempts a truly transatlantic project; it does not fulfill that goal, but it does open up a far more historically responsible kind of ecocriticsm. So new is this field that its terms seem al most comical; that it is clearly a critique we need to understand as quickly as we can only adds to one's sense of its at-present somewhat juvenile procedures.

Argument about Empire

Possibly the two most important books on New World topics in 2001 are Shankar Raman's Framing "India": The Colonial Imaginary in Early Modern Culture, and Barbara Fuchs's Mimesis and Empire: The New World, Islam, and European Identities. Raman paints a massive canvas to outline what colonialism means in the Renaissance, beginning with the changes to medieval Aristotelian philosophy wrought by Renaissance cartography and Baconian science and locating the origins of Freudian and Lacanian psychoanalysis in the subjectivity created to handle European colonial adventuring. The temporal spread is matched by the geographical, as Raman tracks the Portuguese mercantile empire in India, Francis Drake's incursions into that empire in the Spice Islands, and John Dryden's celebration of the British conquest of the Dutch in the Near East. Breathtaking in its reach, this study brilliantly illuminates small textual details in the exemplary works of literature which Raman reads with a powerful and precise Marxist critique.

Beginning with the centrality of cartography to the Portuguese voyages to India, Raman articulates how space became redefined in such a way as to throw into question the stabilities of the medieval cosmos. Simply by measuring space differently—not cadastrally (that is, concretely locating humanity within divine creation), but geographically (that is, abstractly ordering standardized measurements)—Renaissance maps allowed a fundamentally instrumental relationship between man and the natural environment to develop, a relationship that radically changed man's experience of his own subjectivity. Contrasting the Portuguese empire with the subsequent Spanish one, Raman argues that the abstract grid the Spanish laid over the New World by constructing uniformly designed colonial towns, which required the eradication of native habitations, was similar to the Portuguese attempts to master the trading networks of the Indian Ocean which did not require eradication, but simply total control over pre-existing networks. " India," in such a project, names not so much a real "place" of culturally valuable objects as a desire for domination over newly articulated abstract spaces.

Raman turns from Luiz Camoens's epic, the proof text of the Portuguese empires, to theater to outline Britain's belated but exemplary entry into the colonial arena. Reading John Fletcher's The Island Princess, Raman understands that a major problem for the English was a class distinction between gentry and mercantile attitudes toward an empire either of conquest and colonization or of trading and maritime power. While the gentry tended to support the Virginia Company (forty-seven percent of its financing came from this class) and territorial (read "aristocratic") ventures, the merchants of the East India Company (only fourteen percent of the capital for which came from the gentry) jealously guarded their class rights against aristocrats. Both companies were founded within a few year s of each other, but the differing class agendas needed to be made coherent: the play brilliantly solves the problem by casting the heroes—gentleman adventurers (knights)—as merchants in disguise; thus "mercantile imperialism" is born and the European ships plying the surface of Renaissance maps can carry both "factors and guns".

Perhaps the most remarkable insight of this book, suggestive in so many ways, is the argument launched in relation to the Indian boy in Shakespeare's A Midsummer Night's Dream. Asking why the boy is Indian, Raman builds on Louis Montrose's seminal reading of the gender asymmetries of the play to understand that the patriarchal politics of the play reads the colonization effort as a version of its oedipal problems. In contesting ownership of the Indian boy, Oberon and Titania are contesting control over colonial merchandise. "By restoring the Indian Boy to his proper place, Oberon establishes the nuclear family and mercantile exchange as normative forms of social life". As Indian and as boy the changeling reveals how "the politics of trade and colonialism are ... directed to a single end, that of producing the phantasmal trace of the other through which the Western male subject constructs itself as Western and male".

Taking a more narrowly focused view of the Spanish imperial project, Fuchs makes a persuasively literary investigation, suggesting how crucial the restriction on the circulation of books of romance was to Spain's New World undertaking. Because they feared that Native American readers would learn to disbelieve the Bible if they were also to read untrue things in books, the Spanish denied to the Indians the specific kind of literature so fundamental to the mentality of the conquistadors themselves. Spanish experience in the New World, already complicated by their conflict with the intimate peninsular others, the Moors, "altered European attitudes toward truth in literature". Fuchs locates this most interesting anxiety in Torquato Tasso's problems with the marvelous in his epic: "What seems on the face of it a purely European discussion about the ideological implications of romance comes into sharper focus when juxtaposed with anxieties about the marvelous worlds that Europe was attempting to digest while Tasso wrote".

Moving to a consideration of epic in America, Fuchs argues that Alonso de Ercilla's La Araucana and Gines Perez de Hita's Guerras civiles de Granada, simultaneous bestsellers in 1590s Spain, both demonstrate how valorous military enemies such as the Moors and the Incas cannot be so easily othered. Both texts end by revealing "fractures of sympathy" that undermine the Spanish imperial program. Tracing the complications of subject positions in two other texts, the mestizo writer Sebastian Gardilaso de la Vega's Commentarios reales de los Incas, and another by the native Peruvian Felipe Guaman Poma de Ayala, Fuchs notes that Louis Althusser's standard sense of interpellation "fails to account for how Garcilaso and Poma talk back to Spain" by managing to manipulate Spain's racialized religious ideology for their own purposes. Analyzing petitions against the 1567 decrees prohibiting Moorish cultural practices and the fabricated Moorish histories of the fall of Spain to Islam, Fuchs argues that "the se ostracized others imitated the Spanish self so well and addressed its religious needs so completely, they could never be completely disentangled from the sell".

Reading plays such as John Heywood's Fair Maid of the West and William Rowley's Fortune by Land and by Sea, Fuchs not only qualifies to be in this review, she also traces the disappointments the English faced when they discovered their exploits would never be like the conquistadors; "the vanishing banquet that tantalizes the starving Europeans in The Tempest serves well as a metaphor for the expected abundance that vanished when the English arrived in the New World". A final chapter returns to Spanish concerns with a study of La Dragoneta, an epic about Drake, the quintessential English pirate. Equating English depredations on the Spanish New World empire with the attacks of the Ottoman Turks against Europe, this poem reanimates the parallel between the Reconquista and the Conquista. Fuchs points out that this is a fundamentally imitative concept; the equation of Islamic Barbary corsairs with English pirates demonstrates the pervasive cultural function of mimesis, which can often allow the imitator to destabilize the original.

To take the concept of mimesis as a cultural tool is a very powerful move and one Fuchs does with real elegance in this book. This is a new and indeed widely applicable set of tools, and her call for further comparisons—between, for example, the English experience in Ireland and the Spanish with the Moriscos— does most suggestively instruct us that "the manipulation of sameness and difference appears as a constant preoccupation" of the period. Such a book demonstrates how leaving Spain out of English Renaissance studies has cost us a great deal indeed. Mimesis and Empire does a lot more than recuperate that loss.

Discourse in Early Modern England

A Cultural Study of Landscape and Legitimacy, Kari Boyd McBride analyzes a new (and very long lived) locus for legitimacy in England. For centuries after the dissolution of the monasteries, whose lands, wealth, and furnishings were made available to gentry landlords in the Great Rebuilding of the sixteenth and seventeenth centuries, the country house remained a site of aristocratic power. Celebrated in a special kind of poem and also in paintings, these country houses offered an authority different from the royalty centered in urban London, and depended upon the performance of hospitality that required a specialized architecture still to be seen at Longleat, Hardwick Hall, Penshurst Place, and Knole (the names of the houses are themselves famous). McBride persuasively argues that there is a shared and occluding discourse about social structures symbolized by the house, as newly minted aristocrats learned to make money out of an increasingly capitalist ration alization of agriculture. McBride's most interesting point is that women were strangely empowered by this legacy, even though their power was still "domesticated". Within the great houses, however, domesticity packed a real punch: heiresses and widows such as Ann Clifford and Elizabeth Shrewsbury could amass immense cultural capital in their inhabitation—and construction—of some of the greatest "prodigy houses" in the land. The locus classicus for the country-house poem is Jonson's "Penshurst," and read in relation to the other texts in this very long discourse (which goes back deep into the sixteenth century), Jonson's poem does more than render invisible the labor required to sustain the economics of the place. We find in the country-house poem one answer to the problematic tension between mercantile and gentry wealth which Raman outlined, as well as testimony to the growing significance of home (as Helgerson noted) within the globally expansive realm of England. The country house becomes the space for the construction of a centrally important imperial ideal, white womanhood, domesticated, attended by African servants, and utterly powerful as an icon if not in herself. McBride locates the end of the discourse in Blenheim Palace, a pile in which the land is buried beneath the massive structure, a monument not to a private nobleman, but to royal—actually—national power. It is an architectural manifestation of the legitimacy in which Parliament authorized a distant claimant to the Stuart throne along with her consort, the ruler of another country and scion of another quite foreign "house."

The Material Book

In Graffiti and the Writing Arts of Early Modem England, Juliet Fleming boldly argues that England, suffering a paper shortage in the sixteenth century, saw a proliferation of writing practices upon a remarkably wide range of physical materials which themselves demonstrate a far greater range for the social practices of literacy than we ordinarily allow. Beginning with graffiti, or writing on walls—which was, according to Fleming, socially sanctioned in the Renaissance in ways quite foreign to us now—the argument moves on to embrace "whitewash" which could either erase writing already on the wall (while simultaneously preserving it, as in a memory system) or prepare the surface for new writing. Providing numerous pictures that persuasively illustrate the ordinariness of the act of writing on walls, Fleming deftly finds that "language does not seem to be aspiring to full transparency, and is still tending to accord full ... presence to its own material supports", a fact which testifies to an underlyi ng resistance to a Reformation concern for idolatry.

In portrayals of early modern tattooing—or writing on the body—Fleming finds evidence of a discourse that made the New World native over into a version of the European barbarian; she reads, for example, John White's picture of a Pictish warrior tattooed with the image of a flower found in Peru. Both Pict and Native Americans painted and tattooed themselves; tattoo thus serves as one of the first demonstrations of the ethnographic noncontemporaneity of early modern European and New World others. Such a practice is particularly apt, Fleming points out, because it "stands as a ready figure for the border skirmishing that defines conceptual relations between the inside and the outside of social groups", because, of course, a tattoo relies on inserting a foreign substance into the skin, the outer surface of the body itself.

A final chapter on "Pots" marshals some very elegant theory (Jacques Lacan, Sigmund Freud, Jacques Derrida) to make an argument that seems, on its face, to work against theory itself. In surveying the various means by which crockery of all sorts (pots, jugs, urns, cups, pitchers, dishes) seek to "speak," Fleming argues that the vessels "underline the role played by brute, somatic and intellectual matter in the generation of meaning". Such a meditation allows Fleming to propose that early modern knowledge is a mode which does not rely solely on representation or reference, but rather simultaneously "thinks through matter and accords it a sensibility of its own". Such an argument proposes a profound change in the way we should think about the early modem objects of our literary criticism.

A Collection of Essays on Popular Literacy

Studies in Cultural Practices and Poetics, edited by John Trimbur, publishes a couple of essays concerned with the Renaissance, one of which concerns materials similar to Fleming's pots. Pamela H. Smith, in "Giving Voice to Hands: The Articulation of Material Literacy in the Sixteenth Century," studies the works of Bernard Palissy, a Huguenot potter, who produced signed objects and three printed texts about the materials of his craft. Catherine de Medicis, Queen Regent of France, employed Palissy to decorate the halls and gardens of the Tuileries. What interests Smith is that Palissy claimed to be able to read nature without an intermediary—which she finds analogous to the Protestant claim to read scripture without the mediation of the Church. His public lectures in Paris were attended by noblemen as well as craftsmen; his argument was in part that the knowledge of nature was sacred and that his manual labor was worship. Such a study puts the work of an artisan suc h as Benvenuto Cellini in a new light, and Fleming's pot makers might also be said to be literate in the same way as the far more famous Cellini.

Allied to the history of the material book but not of it, Joseph Loewenstein's The Author's Due: Printing and the Prehistory of Copyright functions, like Fleming's book, to destablize our assumptions about material writing practices, but he achieves his ends by very different means from hers. If Fleming comes at bizarre and new objects armed with elegant twentieth-century theory, Loewenstein rewrites the history of copyright by patiently, painstakingly, and with great narrative detail, rehearsing the way technological changes in the making of books ushered in a whole new way of thinking about them and their very various producers.

Loewenstein argues that modern notions of copyright and authorial rights to intellectual property did not, as Michel Foucault has suggested, derive from the historical practices of censorship, but from the dissolution of the medieval guild system enshrined in the Stationers' Company, which regulated printing practices from the middle of the sixteenth century to the encroaching Civil War. Breaking down the confluence of historical developments that allowed for the creation of copyright, Loewenstein focuses on specific conceptual nodal points. Of central importance is the change wrought by the impact of print on the handmaking of books, not by fixing the page, as many have urged, but by changing the means of production and dissemination. The manuscript book, he points out, "comes into being at the demand of the purchaser"; the printed book, in contrast, "anticipates an uncertain desire". It is this uncertainty and the transformation of commercial relations (including the greater capital investment neces sary in machinery) that transformed the book culture into the "book trade." Although the Stationers' Company was chartered by Mary Tudor to control the traffic in heretical books, the actual company worked to stabilize as much as possible the volatile mercantile nature of printing, publishing, and bookselling for its own members. It was this company's monopolistic nature, whereby certain printers were, granted rights to certain titles, rather than royal (or ecclesiastical) censorship, Loewenstein argues, which provided the regulatory practices that ultimately evolve into copyright.

Loewenstein refuses to see even so late an author as Milton arguing for individual authors' ownership of their intellectual property. His reading of Areopagitica beautifully unravels the ideological contradictions of that tract and the quite wonderful way Milton erases the entire printing, publishing, and bookselling industry when he turns books into living things, the oral echo of their authors. It is Milton's intervention not into the history of print, but into the historiography of print, which, Loewenstein argues, makes the "struggle Within the book trade to redistribute the fruits of monopoly" into "a struggle for ideological freedom of publication". In thus repressing the history of the industry by recasting it as the history of censorship, Milton changes the terms and provides the ground for so many modern misunderstandings of the history of copyright. Its magisterial scope matched only by the precision of its local details and its charitable and humane disagreements with an earlier scholarshi p on which it monumentally builds, The Author's Due is exemplary literary history. It is also fun to read.

Two large—and largely statistical—studies, one of English printing and another of the Scottish book trade, aim to account for the sheer amount of printing done at the time and the various social activities—censorship, wealth building, and copywriting—which attended upon this explosion of human activity. In Print and Protestantism in Early Modern England, Ian Green gives a thorough accounting of what the best- and steady-selling religious books of 1500 to 1729 can tell us about their owners and readers. Most writers of such books were full-time clergymen; their output is broken down into various categories, including treatises, sermons, prayers, devotional tracts, and "mixture," which means a book that includes verses, observations, applications, etc. Green begins with bibles, surveying such things as the changes in typeface, the introduction of visual aids, patterns of ownership, ownership among scholars, among moderately well-educated laity, and what he calls "the lower orders"—although, as Green argues , bibles remained prohibitively expensive in relation to the penny or twopenny "godly ballad" affordable by a craftsman earning eight pence a day—a full bible would have cost him a week's pay. It is nice to note that Paradise Lost makes this bestseller list (thirteen editions before 1729), but was clearly outsold by Andrew Jones's "Black Book of Conscience" (fifty-four editions between 1658 and 1700).

Alastair J. Mann gives a slightly less statistically-driven view of printing in The Scottish Book Trade, 1500-1720: Print Commerce and Print Control in Early Modern Scotland, but he does provide some hard facts about the economics of the book trade, especially in terms of the wealth various categories of book traders accrued. He also compares the value of this trade to other groups such as apothecaries and surgeons. More book traders lived at the poorer end of the scale, but prosperous traders could make as much as other venders of staple goods. Wealth peaked in the 1620s; a much larger spike of prosperity appeared for three decades after 1700. Scotland had its own very viable industry—its growth indeed cut into the numbers Green studies in England. Mann concludes that the Scottish trade was larger than has previously been assumed and did have its own nature: censorship was less aggressively physical than in England, for example, but the number of banned books marks it as typical of other book publishing countries. Mann gives lists of banned books in an appendix and also provides copyright dates.

Associated with the history of the book is the history of reading, of which there are a number of studies. Jennifer Andersen and Elizabeth Sauer offer a collection of essays on Books and Readers in Early Modem England: Material Studies. Notable among the essays is Peter Stallybrass's fascinating argument about the physical effect of the codex on discontinuous reading practices, especially associated with the typological organization of the Bible into two testaments, one old and one new, which needed to be read discontinuously and simultaneously—a thing not possible when the book is organized as a scroll where it is impossible to flip back and forth easily between different parts of the text. Stallybrass suggests that the development of aids to reading the Bible ("alphabets," verse numbers) increases the ease of discontinuous reading, or searching the scriptures, and empowers individual readers to check their own texts against the preacher's arguments. Michael Mendle surveys the mass printing of cheap pamphlets which exploded on the scene in the 1640s. Mendle's emphasis is not on the pamphlets themselves but on the ways in which they were collected together, at the time by George Thomason (forming the basis of the British Library collection), George Clarke (Worcester College, Oxford), and the earls of Bridgewater (Huntington Library). Uncategorizeable according to traditional distinctions among printed volumes, the pamphlets were sewn together in bundles and sold as such. Of the few extant collections, Mendle singles out Thomason's as the most heroic (in size) and points to its principle of organization—strict chronology—a thing which has made the collection of enduring use to scholars, Thomas Carlyle once asserting that "the whole secret of the seventeenth century" was contained in the mass of rubbish.

Queer Theory

Making visible what is "behind the seen", Traub reads a vast amount of cultural material with great historicizing power (including an increasingly explicit series of portraits of Queen Elizabeth I) to reveal that the Renaissance was fully aware of the erotic, self-pleasuring female body. Reading early modern medical manuals, Traub argues how earlier in the period anatomical bodies and erotic behaviors were mapped onto each other, so that the threateningly visible tribade was made to look very different from the chaste female friend. Otherwise, feminine friendship was imagined in a pastoral elegiac (Ovidian) mode, Traub argues, so as to render it essentially insignificant to the reproduction of patriarchy. As the seventeenth century progressed, however, these two figures coalesced and by the final years of the seventeenth century, the chaste friend began to absorb into her figure the behaviors previously attributed to the "unnatural" tribade. Traub's arguments with current feminist theory are instructive, but it is with the history of sexuality per se and the history of marriage and the family—two projects which, Traub argues, have all too happily proceeded without awareness of each other— that Traub makes her most important interventions. From the vantage point of tracing representations of female homoeroticism, Traub understands there to have been a true "crisis" in the patriarchal system that organized sexuality in the seventeenth century. It was resolved only by the creation of a new construct which she calls "domestic heterosexuality". Against this new construct, chaste femme love becomes more and more threatening, visible, and in need of control. And it is in this context that some women finally write about female sexual desire for other women, a story which Traub finds in the work of Margaret Cavendish, Aphra Behn, and Katherine Philips. A tour de force of theoretically informed inquiry, this is cultural history at its most powerful and elegant—completely rewriting the history of sexuality in the seventeenth century.

Stephen Guy-Bray's Homoerotic Space: The Poetics of Loss in Renaissance Literature is a more straightforward study than Traub's, in that it locates a "space" for thinking about male homoerotic love and loss in very traditional Renaissance imitations of classical texts. First articulating an elegiac homoeroticism in Theocritus and Vergil, Guy-Bray then reads some Renaissance Latin elegies by Baldassare Castiglione, the earl of Surrey, and Milton, and finds there destabilizing effects similar to Traub's. According to Guy-Bray, Surrey's elegy for the duke of Richmond, his childhood playmate, and Milton's for Charles Diodati, both elegize the impossibility of male homoeroticism, which can thus articulate itself only as irreparable loss. Reading more overtly expressive texts by William Browne, Marlowe, and Richard Barnfield, Guy-Bray traces the screen provided by imitations of Vergil but ends by arguing that even in such texts we can see how the homoerotic space of classical pastoral finally disappears, leaving on ly the grief that itself is unable to speak its name. Unlike Traub's powerful historical argument, Guy-Bray courts his own anachronism; his unapologetic modernity, however, does not really compromise the local pleasures of his humanist readings of densely layered texts.

Women's Writing

Five collections of essays devoted to understanding women's writing in relationship to their very various domestic activities attest to the manifold ways by which women gave shape to their experience in a number of different expressive forms. Taken as a group they represent the remarkably broad spectrum on which women's studies continues to work in the Renaissance—and perhaps in their overlapping paragraphs, contributors, and objects of focus, they also represent how collaborative scholarship has become.

In Women's Writing and the Circulation of Ideas: Manuscript Publication in England, 1550-1800, editors George L. Justice and Nathan Tinker have assembled a collection of essays that speak to a tendency of women writers to seek publication not in print but in manuscript, even after print culture has been well established. What Justice calls "scribal publication" held on even into the late eighteenth century; he traces the choice of Frances Burney to publish (like Alexander Pope) in the "dirtied" marketplace of the day but only in the novel form, taking as a singular case the nonperformance of one of Burney's plays in which she critiques the self-indulgence of coterie publication. That she ultimately "suppressed" this play after a vigorous manuscript circulation suggests how vulnerable women writers remained to the potential for scandalous publicity.

Mary Sidney Wroth was one of the first women to suffer the opprobrium of scandal with the publication of her huge romance, The Countess of Mountgomerie's Urania (1621). Michael Brennan takes up the creation of Wroth's authorship on the part of two people, Jonson and Wroth herself. In a series of manuscript poems that were ultimately collected in Jonson's Works, Jonson announced Wroth as the inheritrix of the Sidney family's patronage and as a writer in her own fight. The Sidney family bulks large in the collection, as two other essays devoted to the countess of Pembroke study the effects of her decision not to print the translation of the Psalms she completed, but to circulate it only in manuscript. Such a decision, the essays agree, had less to do with the "stigma" of print especially problematic for a female writer, than with the countess's concerns over the theologically idiosyncratic nature of the translation which she expected would be controversial. She therefore elected scribal publication because it w ould be easier to control. Other women throughout the seventeenth century and into the eighteenth century chose to publish, like the countess, both in print and in manuscript coterie circulation.

In Maternal Measures: Figuring Caregiving in the Early Modern Period, edited by Naomi J. Miller and Naomi Yavneh, Susan Frye's discussion of "Maternal Textualities" is of special interest. She argues that needlework was not the silencing mechanism we have been told it is from masculinist discourse. It was not opposed to writing, but a literate activity through which girls learned the alphabet and by which women congregated in communities of great power within the domestic space. Her proof texts are the wall hangings created by Elizabeth Talbot (and her professional needlemen and women) at Hardwick Hall and Elizabeth Tudor's teenage embroidery of book covers. Like Fleming's argument about wall painting, Frye's understanding that embroidery is also a writing practice allows us to move beyond our usual assumptions about what letters are. Two essays on music in this same collection, one by Linda Austern concerning the music and pictorial representations of women music makers and another by Claire Fontijn on repre sentations of Mary in seventeenth-century Italian song, demonstrate the real "interdisciplinary" reach of the volume. McBride's piece on native-American mothers, including Pocahontas and Sacajawea, as well as articles on Spain,

Germany, and France, demonstrate the geographical range. Copiously illustrated, the volume moves scholarship in the right direction—transatlantically and toward the undiscovered continents of motherhood and women's communities.

As editor of another collection of essays, Domestic Arrangements in Early Modern England, McBride borrows from some of her work in the book on country-house discourse and makes it the foundation for her understanding that domesticity, whatever the scale of the domus, is an important site of study. With essays on writings by Cavendish and Behn, the collection sees domesticity from the point of view of women, but juxtaposes it to revisionary work on more canonical texts. A clear and lucid account of Cordelia's predicament in King Lear by Stephanie Chamberlain shows how an understanding of actual inheritance laws as they apply to women illuminates the great transgressions Lear contemplates in the opening scene of the play, not only coming close to incest, but clearly abrogating traditional rules of equal portions for daughters.

A collection edited by Barbara Smith and Ursula Appelt, Write or Be Written: Early Modern Women Poets and Cultural Constraints, rehearses older assumptions that women were embattled when they turned to writing (not assuming, as the other collections seem to, that women wrote in a number of different ways). Margaret Hannay, at least, finds it no surprise that Mary Sidney Herbert should translate the Psalms, as psalmic discourse saturated the lives of men and women in the sixteenth and seventeenth centuries. Women thus turned to them, in paraphrase and in private devotions, as an immediately accessible form for expressing their interior experiences; Hannay notes the importance of Thomas Bentley's huge compendium of these paraphrases as an expression of women's truly copious writing in this vein. Shannon Miller reads very carefully the poems Mary Herbert appended to her translation of the Psalms and finds in them subtle negotiations of a personal relationship with Elizabeth I as well as arguments for the queen's renewed commitment to the national project of the Protestant cause. Claire Kinney reads Mary Wroth's sonnet cycle, Pamphilia to Amphilanthus, with exquisite tact and a keen eye for punning poetic detail.

A Companion to Early Modem Women's Writing, edited by Anita Pacheco, collects further essays on what is beginning to look like a canon of women writers in the Renaissance, Isabella Whitney, Mary Sidney, Aemilia Lanyer, Elizabeth Cary, Wroth, Cavendish, Anna Trapnel, Philips, Behn, and Mary Astell. Essays on these individual writers read the texts with an eye toward the quite specific individual situations of each. Patricia Brace understands that Whitney's lower-class position allows her an acute angle of vision on the functioning of an urban economic system, and the very structuring of her poetic stance speaks to the mercantile realities of print markets. Debra Reinstra makes a very interesting argument for Mary Sidney's Psalms, taking their formal experimentations quite seriously as a means for responding to the historically eclectic nature of the biblical book they were translating. Unlike a sonnet cycle, the Psalms respond to the entire history of Israel. An early editor of Lanyer, Susanne Woods gives an o verview of her poet's work and life, while Elaine Beilin speaks to Cary's play about Herod's wife Mariam as a Roman history play specific to the change in England from the rule of Elizabeth to James. Shannon Miller pursues an interesting argument about the central importance of female affinity and friendship in Mary Wroth's Urania for enabling female agency, while Gweno Williams notices how Cavendish creates her own authority first by framing it with the status of her male relations, father, brothers, and husband.

Almost as if in direct demonstration that the best scholarship is completely collaborative, the new edition of Juan Luis Vives's Instruction of a Christen Woman is the work of no fewer than nine women listed on the title page, and a larger number of other workers acknowledged in the introduction. The introductory material is fascinating and capacious—not only do we get a full accounting (and generous illustration) of the many different sixteenth-century reissues of the text, but also we are instructed about the personal anxieties under which Juan Luis Vives worked while he wrote the tract. A conversos from Spain, Vives suffered much torment because his family was under constant scrutiny from the Inquisition (which Vives called "Fortuna"), suspected for relapsing to their former Judaism. During the time Vives wrote the Instruction his father was under arrest, so his orphaned sisters were helpless. Subsequently, his mother's body which had been buried for twenty years was exhumed and publicly burnt. Such a sit uation, Virginia Beauchamp argues (informed by the work of five other scholars), might well have contributed to Vives's sense of extreme vulnerability for females and his concomitant misogynist rage. One also learns as much about Sir Thomas More's humanist circle as about the text itself. The editors argue that they decided to edit the text when, in collaborative work during the last century, they discovered that there was no reliable modern edition of the whole text. This edition does far more than supply that lack; it reestablishes the importance of Spain and Spain's own complicated experience of racial differences, for an understanding of humanist ideas about the reformable nature of man.

The letters of Dorothy Osborne to her future husband Sir William Temple (later, Jonathan Swift's employer) have been collected and edited by Kenneth Parker for the Early Modern Englishwoman editions; Parker sees Osborne not so much a radical as a woman who, while accepting the limitations placed on her gender, managed to work her own will on her world and marry the man to whom she had proposed marriage. The letters are charming, and because they tell the story of a courtship—this time from the woman's experience—they anticipate the pleasures of the novel. The introductory comments are a little scattered but earnest—a handy summary of each letter beforehand locates the reader in the saga of will-they or won't-they marry.

A single essay in R. Andrew McDonald's collection, History, Literature, and Music in Scotland, 700-1560, quite brilliantly, in my view, addresses the problem of Margaret Tudor's rule in Scotland during James V's minority. Sister to Henry VIII, Margaret has been overlooked by historians. In an essay on 'Tudor Family Politics in Early Sixteenth-Century Scotland," Margaret McIntyre argues that Margaret exercised her power far more subtly than anyone has so far cared to notice, and that it required a balancing act between the demands of her natal and her marital families. This might seem to state the obvious, but as a signal instance of the "bond" between men, Margaret shows how her remaining ties to her brother, however tyrannical, endowed her with a great deal of agency.

Religion and The Discourses of the Self

The Theology of Figure from Augustine to the Sonnets, Lisa Freinkel brilliantly reorganizes our understanding of "modern" subjectivity as expressed in Shakespeare's supposedly Petrarchan poetry by analyzing it as a stage in a developing history of the figural understanding of theological time. Tracing the idea of a figural understanding of time, whereby Old Testament types foreshadow New Testament antitypes—or, in Erich Auerbach's terms, "fulfillments" of the earlier "figura"—Freinkel explains the difference between Augustine and Petrarch as one between a peculiar kind of reader (Augustine) and a quite specific sort of author. Temporally, the Augustinian reader reads in a present moment which is the future of the text when it was written in the past. The text is addressed to the reader in that future and only in that future can the figura be fully understood, in its fulfillment. Petrarch takes the gap between past and future/present, and instead of locating it between the text as written and the reader's reading, he installs that gap within himself as secular author. As Freinkel argues, Petrarch's lyric "I" of the rime sparse is related to the "ego" of the Psalms; "the Psalms help explain the transition from a psalmic, confessional, and Latin first person to the restless 'io' of Petrarch's Italian lyrics". It is not so much that the content of desire is secularized—a switch of Laura for the Blessed Virgin Mary—but that discourse itself becomes secularized.

The poetic structure no longer points to a transcendent meaning (as it does in Dante), but instead meaning itself becomes that which structures poetry.

Martin Luther's own change in the use of figuralism prepares it for Shakespeare's Reformation poetics. Particularly in his insistence on the real presence, Luther makes figura into a catachresis (where it had been a chiasmus over time for Augustine). Flesh and Spirit do not follow one another in time; instead they are simultaneously and impossibly present.

According to Freinkel, the book called Shakespeare's Sonnets, which original title she takes seriously, as a material book critic should, "deploys a theology of catachresis in order to establish a poetics of collapsed ideals in place of Petrarch's poetics of deferred meaning". She most pertinently finds the collapse of figure in the multiple pun on the name of "will," which attains a kind of "zero-degree of maximum density: low and high, false and true, flesh and spirit"—which is indistinguishably both flesh (slang for penis) and spirit. Such an argument directly challenges Joel Fineman's reading of will as "chiasmus." Reading in particular the "young man" or "procreation" sonnets, Freinkel shows that time is no means for renewal but "only ripens on the path to rotting". Beauty can be no ideal then, but is a fault itself, which the poet is forced to love. As being both canker and rose, beauty (which the poetic "will" loves) itself is catachrestic. Again true to the demands of the m aterial book, Freinkel also reads "The Lover's Complaint" and finds there an apt demonstration of the catachrestic poetics she has tracked through the sonnets. With a final chapter on The Merchant of Venice, Freinkel's discussion continues to take seriously all the complications of flesh and spirit, seeing the play as another instance of the central importance to Shakespeare's culture of the theology figure, that is, the continuing importance of the relations between old and new laws as worked out in all the complications of Shylock's bond.

What this book accomplishes is a major shift in our understanding of Renaissance lyric as a fundamentally theological, rather than psychological, activity. Fineman's Lacanian understanding—as well as many other nuanced and intelligent probings of the sonnets for psychological evidence of an early modem subjectivity—are not so much corrected as incorporated into what seems the far more capacious history of theological discourse.

Cynthia Marshall's Shattering of the Self: Violence, Subjectivity, and Early Modern Texts makes a profound psychoanalytic argument about the early modern period's pleasure in experiences of the "shattering" of the self. In reading Petrarchan sonnets, Shakespeare's Titus Andronicus, and John Ford's The Broken Heart, Marshall pursues the question in resolutely psychoanalytic terms. For instance, when reading John Foxe's Acts and Monuments of the Martyrs, she confronts the "jouissance" of the martyrs' detailed tortures and later recognizes that "[a]lthough today we situate discussions of subjectivity and personhood in the domains of psychology and philosophy, in the early modem period these were primarily issues for theology". The early modern period in its historic specificity anticipated the discourses of psychoanalysis, which is why they can be used, she argues, to such effect.

In specific counterargument to Stephen Greenblatt's notion of "self-fashioning," Marshall pursues a Lacanian line of inquiry that focuses on the subject's pleasure in contemplating pain. Taking Lacan's seminal interpretation of Freud's fort/da narrative, Marshall understands the pain experienced by the child in repeating the loss of the object to be a moment when language displaces reality—securing a crucial link between language and masochism. Such masochism is at the heart of Petrarchan sonnet cycles. As in the fort/da game, "the symbolic rendering of a lost object negates its loss", and such may help to account for the exquisite tortures of the Petrarchan poet. She also notes that the trope of calling the beloved a "goddess" may, in fact, draw on the conjunction between sexual and erotic jouissance.

The violence in her title is a profoundly embodied force, however, and as in the pictures she presents of dismembered saints, body parts lying askew, Marshall seems not quite to realize that her fundamental concern is the body. She relies on Gail Paster and Elaine Scarry in quite central ways—and notes that Ford is peculiar in the "significance he grants to the language of the body". While she spends an immense amount of time explicating her psychoanalytic tools, her real interests seem to lie in finding those moments when the "shattering of the self" has a theological resonance. Thus Thomas Cranmer thrusts his hand into the flames to burn it for signing a recantation of Protestant faith; and George Herbert's sense of a shattering is "then was my heart broken as was my verse". It may simply be that reading Marshall's book in the context of Freinkel's powerful argument made me pay more attention to the theology than we might otherwise, but Shattering of the Self seems less finally an argument for psychoanalysis against new historicism than an argument that theology is not just a discursive cover for power politics, but also itself a language that anticipates psychoanalysis.

David Hawkes makes a curiously parallel argument to Marshall's, that theology offered alanguage for talking about psychological subjectivity. For Hawkes, the theological idea of idolatry is a concept through which early modern people voiced their fear and anger about the changes early capitalism was making in their everyday lives. Abstracting the experience of life, capitalism turned things into commodity fetishes; a way to critique this was to inveigh against idolatry, that is, the turning of some object into an idol. It is a fascinating thesis, and as part of the new "economic criticism" the argument is informed and au courant with the latest developments. It is, of course, nothing new to point out the language of alchemy in John Donne, but to understand that alchemy itself was perverted in this period into a purely material practice of turning base metals into gold arid had lost its idealist foundations in the a nalogous relations of micro- to macrocosm, is to understand how Donne's lament for its degradation is also a lament for the loss of a correspondent cosmos and the arrival of a world created artificially, out of man-made customary modes of representation—like the abstraction of money itself. With chapters on Milton and Thomas Traherne, Hawkes's argument changes how we perceive problems we have always noticed. His discussion of Bunyan does more, we think, and helps to explain Bunyan's strange mode of mixing allegory with realistic novel techniques. "Christian's elect status is indicated by the fact that he conceives of the world as peopled by [personifications of virtues and vices], whereas Badman's reprobation is conveyed through his delusion that he is not an abstraction but an independent, autonomous agent". Avery provocative argument, freshly conceived, and powerfully made.

Religion and Literature

An older manner of dealing with literature and theology can be found in the anthology Wrestling with God: Literature and Theology in the English Renaissance, edited by Mary Ellen Henley and W. Speed Hill. A festschrift for Paul Grant Stanwood, the volume collects essays by many from the generation of what used to be called "new" critics as well as a leavening of younger folk; Donne is the poet of choice, being the focus of essays by Louis Martz, Ted-Larry Pebworth, William Blisset, Wyman H. Herenden, Diana Benet, G. Richmond Bridge, and Bryan Gooch. Some of the essays are by churchmen, perhaps fitting for Donne. There are also some essays on Milton and Jonson scattered throughout. The editors speak of "theology begetting literature ... and literature siring further" theological discussion and here—although there are women contributors to be sure—the workings of the spirit are quite relentlessly male and canonical.

Equally "old style" is a collection entitled The Bible in the Renaissance: Essays on Biblical Commentary and Translation in the Fifteenth and Sixteenth Centuries, edited by Richard Griffiths for the St. Andrews Studies in Reformation History. Girolamo Savonarola, Erasmus, Luther, William Tyndale, Cardinal Cajetan, and Gil Vicente (a

Portuguese dramatist), the Homilies of the Church of England, and interestingly, "The Welsh Bible and Renaissance Learning," are the focus of learned and for the most part lucidly descriptive pieces.

Catholic Literature and the Rise of Anglicanism by John R. Yamamoto-Wilson asks a useful question: what use did Protestants make of Roman Catholic literature during the Reformation? Tracking the publication in English editions of a number of notable Catholic writers, Yamamoto-Wilson demonstrates that even in the face of a lot of polemic there were Protestants reading Catholic writing. It is quite strange to see Martz's Poetry of Meditation missing from the bibliography.

Single-Author Studies

Donne—Clayton G. MacKenzie in Emblem and Icon in John Donne's Poetry and Prose tracks five different topoi to be found in both emblem books and church icons that have a particular pertinence for Donne's use of imagery. MacKenzie is not interested in translating Donne's paradoxes into visual images, but in understanding the quotidian understandings of the age as evidenced in the possibility of everyday exposure to images in books and on church walls. Donne's use of death, for instance, is utterly unsurprising given the ubiquity of the skull in wall paintings and emblem books. The juxtaposition of emblem-book images with church-wall paintings has the most salutary effect of taking the emblem images out of their heretofore recondite and "secretive" coterie context and making them far more readable within their wider culture; they were a fad, after all, and spoke with the same voice as the paintings on church walls which had been around for centuries. The author offers up his amateur photographs of, for example, a charmingly seductive female skeleton offering a rose to her unaware lover—a piquant image equal to Donne's humor in "The Apparition" (although MacKenzie does not adduce the connection). This is not to say that the secrets of alchemical language do not play a role, but such secrets are clearly displayed in the emblems MacKenzie provides. A particularly apt image is of two naked lovers with winged souls hovering above them, recalling (as MacKenzie does argue) "The Ecstasie" and representing the union of male and female principles in alchemical purification.

Donne and the Resources of Kind, edited by A. D. Cousins and Damian Grace, collects together a number of essays devoted to generic investigations of Donne's oeuvre. Indeed, the issue of emblems makes its appearance here, as Eugene D. Hill argues in the wonderfully titled essay "Donne the Snake Handler" that a sermon on St. Paul's handling of a viper in Acts 28:1-6 might well have been a reference to the Donne family's ancestral emblem, a sheaf of snakes. Heather Dubrow remarks upon Donne's elegies to women as part of the "ugly beauty tradition" surprisingly without reference to Nancy Vickers's germinal argument about Petrarchan blazon and anti-blazon as a means to enact male poetic rivalry. N. H. Keeble talks about the stresses and strains of Donne's sonnets as part and parcel of their negotiation with the other genres in which Donne clearly delighted—epigrams (with their paradoxical wit), satires, and elegies.

Spenser—Judith Owens offer some interesting adjustments to Loewenstein and Montrose on Spenser's position vis a vis the print market and patronage systems in Enabling Engagements: Edmund Spenser and the Poetics of Patronage. Reading the dedicatory and commendatory sonnets appended to various early volumes of verse and The Faerie Queene, Owens argues that Spenser used the print market as a means for standing apart from court-centered Petrarchan supplication, in order to speak to the baronial and belligerent radical Protestant wing against Elizabeth's pacific policies. She makes a very subtle and persuasive argument from the insertion of seven extra dedicatory poems to The Faerie Queene during John Wolfe's print run, pointing out that the poems are grouped in specific ways that insist on ever more martial engagements, specifically in Ireland. We have all known that the epic has far more than the normal amount of dedicatory materials; Owens tells us why and in the process recalibrates our sense of Spenser's neg otiation of print and patronage. Three of the added seven sonnets were addressed to licensers of the press. She also finds Spenser to be especially critical of Sir Walter Raleigh in the dedicatory poem and especially in the Timias episode, chastising him for his Petrarchan passivity. This is a short but pertinent contribution to material book studies which fits the first part of The Faerie Queene into a nationalist-imperial agenda.

The Classics-Ovid Rules

As even so fashionable a study as Guy-Bray's book would agree, "The classics were the raw material of the English Renaissance." This pronouncement is Madeleine Forey's at the outset of her new edition of Arthur Golding's translation of the Metamorphoses. Indeed Ovid takes pride of place among the ancients in the twenty-first century, with one monograph and one collection devoted to his impact on Renaissance poets. But Pindar and Plato (as filtered through Marsilio Ficino) are the focus of two books which contain lifetimes of learning by Jon A. Quitslund and Stella P. Revard. In this group we can include Holofernes' Mantuan, Lee Piepho's study of the impact of the Italian humanist who was deemed by Erasmus to be an acceptable model for the appropriation of Greek and Roman learning and who became a standard text for English schoolboys.

As the title suggests, Ovid's Changing Worlds: English 'Metamorphoses," 1567-1632 by Raphael Lyne is itself a historical study of the different ways Ovid was handled in Arthur Golding's (1567) and George Sandys's (1632) translations and in the intertextual densities of Spenser's imitation in The Faerie Queene (1596) and Michael Drayton's reorganization of Spenser's imitation in PolyOlbion (1612). Lyne sees the front matter of Golding's translation, for example, as an important key to understanding Renaissance notions of intertextuality, and he takes seriously the signals the book as made thing can tell us about its contents. If he less able to leverage the dense text of The Faerie Queene than he is able to understand the geographical particularity PolyOlbion shares with Ovid's epic, that is perhaps because, as Lyne acknowledges, Ovid is only one among many of Spenser's intertexts,

Taking up Sandys's translation as a further extension of Drayton's concerns for geography, Lyne asks what significance there is to the fact that Sandys wrote his translation while living in Virginia. Invisible in Sandys's pre-Milton Latinate elegance, the translator's Virginia site only shows up in the commentaries (added in 1632) which continually announce that the world has expanded far beyond Ovid's reckonings: Sandys "puts Ovid's world-picture in its place, encompassed geographically, but also physically within the book, by his own".

Lyne has an essay in a collection devoted to Ovid and the Renaissance Body, edited by Goran V. Stanivukovic. Far more theoretically ambitious than Lyne's monograph, the collection aims, in its editor's terms, to see the Renaissance use of Ovid as a distinctive "constitutive history of the body" which vies with medical and theological discourse and which, in its fascination with sexual and physical transformations, is a "proleptic psychoanalysis". Many of the essays in the collection sustain this claim, beginning with Carla Freccero's Lacan-inflected study of the difference between male and female subjectivity as voiced in the rewrite of the Actaeon myth by Petrarch and Louise Labe, and including Mark Dooley's study of same-sex desire in Ovid and John Lyly, Morgan Holmes's investigation of the disruption of an emergent heteronormative sex gender system in Andrew Marvell's "A Nymph Complaining for the Death of Her Fawn," and Traub's afterword, which reads the volume as a means for revitalizing the study of Ovid to make it "more troubling, provocative, dangerous, sexy, and, in all senses of the word, queer". Not all of the essays find their strengths in psychoanalysis, however: many of them take their power from considerations of the embodiment of literature in the material text. Ian Moulton's study of Sir John Harington's translation of Ariosto, for example, understands the importance of the work from its physical, large-format printing and puts it into dialogue with Golding's and Sandys's translations of the Metamorphoses as well as very differently organized Continental editions of Ovid. Other essays in the volume deal with problems of masculine identity and desire: Jim Ellis traces the installation of heterosexual male mastery in the epyllia; Mario de Gangi follows Jonson's satirical portrait of narcissistic courtiers in Cynthia's Revels to shore up a besieged aristocratic male elite; Bruce Boehrer analyzes the sexual unease of the cuckold's dilemma inherited from the A mores in two plays by Jonson and Thomas Middleton, concluding that any male identity predicated on female constancy is always beyond successful management. Two essays focus on a very interesting interstice in Ovid's mythology for female voicings—the figure of Echo. Gina Bloom tracks Sandys's subtle changes in Ovid's language to reveal how the voice disarticulated from the body may take on female authority, much like the female "voice over" theorized by film scholar Kaja Silverman. This same figure becomes, for Judith Deitch, a means by which Spenser is able to master Ovid in the echoing refrain of his Epithalamion.

In a learned and beautifully crafted work that has clearly taken a lifetime of empassioned study, Stella P. Revard's Pindar and the Renaissance Hymn-Ode, 1450-1700 offers the purest sort of humanist literary history in outlining why Pindar was of unique and sublime importance to so many Renaissance poets for two and a half centuries. Covering Italian and French imitations as well as English, and tracing the changing notions of Pindar, from the vatic sublime bard of the earlier period fifteenth, and sixteenth centuries) to a wayward genius (in the seventeenth century), Revard gives a fascinating tour of Pindar's oeuvres. She explains why a poet who celebrated athletes should be of such crucial concern to so many different Renaissance poets. One of the most fascinating elements of Revard's study is the comparison not between Pindar and any Renaissance Italian,

French, or English poet, but Horace. Revard argues that when Horace reverses the order of address in Pindar's sacred Olympian ode from god-hero-man to man-hero-god, he delivers "a message to Augustus Caesar quite different from that which Pindar delivered to Theron". Such detailed display of various Roman poets' negotiations with Pindar—and the impact these negotiations had on Renaissance poets' understanding of their own imitations of Pindar—adds impressive subtlety to her peeling back multiple layers of intertextuality in the poems she reads. Revard's study puts true flesh on the assumption that without the recovery of Greek there would have been no "Renaissance."

Jon A. Quitslund's Spenser's Supreme Fiction: Platonic Natural Philosophy and "The Faerie Queene," reverses Revard's focus on the influence of a single classical poet on multiple Renaissance followers and studies the multiple Greek and neo-Latin confluences that help to make Spenser's Platonism the idiosyncratic thing it is. While he capaciously surveys the range of Renaissance Platonisms in their great variety, he plumps for a specific trio whose effect on Spenser's "mind" he finds especially important to two key passages that interest him most. In the Garden of Adonis and the "Mutabilitie Cantos," Spenser is most indebted, according to Quitslund, to Ficino, Leon Ebreo, and the French translation of Louis le Roy. One of the things Quitslund is most concerned to reorient in Spenser studies is the rift he sees has opened between male and female experience where ceding power to one or the other gender as authoritative interpreter of the experience at hand is a zero sum game. Quitslund argues for complementarity rather than separate masculine and feminine domains.

A great virtue of this study is Quitslund's generous regard for other critics whose views find their way into his readings; he is not afraid, of course, to disagree as he does most pointedly with Harry Berger or with Lauren Silberman, but he does so with the greatest possible tact and intelligent understanding of their actual arguments. By placing an argument about gender into the context of what has been a strong focus of traditional Spenser studies—the Italian neoplatonist "background"—he pulls the one to the foreground and puts the other into a resonant philosophical context. The treatment enriches both critical projects.

Formal Studies of Lyric Poetry

George T. Wright, writes about what it is like to hear, rather than read, poetry. The essays selected range across genres and periods, from Thomas Wyatt to Robert Lowell, with a number of essays on Shakespeare, Donne, and Jacobean dramatic blank verse. In "Hendiadys and Hamlet," for example, Wright argues that the rhetorical figure (one in two) is fundamental to the play's concerns about the divided nature of the self (he has counted sixty-six appearances of the figure in the text). In "Wyatt's Decasyllabic Line" Wright locates Wyatt's irregular meters within the complex context of the prosodic system he inherited and the Italian one that influenced him. It is not meter but stanzaic form that is important in Donne—but Wright strangely neglects to consider the source for the intermixture of shorter lines with pentameter lines in the Sidneys' (Philip and Mary) translation of the Psalms (though he does credit Philip Sidney for doing so in some poems). A strange oversight, but it does not, however, derail his analysis of how the varying line lengths work in any given poem.

Mark David Rasmussen, the editor of Renaissance Literature and Its Formal Engagements, polemically hopes, in his introduction, to bring the study of Renaissance literature back to formalist considerations and away from its current cultural studies bent. Loewenstein finds himself conscripted into the project, but uses it to argue that the study of prosody as a somatic practice—a cultural poetics of the throat—might well be a way to understand play speech materially, as he takes the question of censorship to be tied to material and cultural conditions of printing and bookselling. Mark Womack embraces Shakespeare's plays on words, even and especially when they do not serve an overarching interpretation. Paul Alpers generously rehearses what specific New Critics had to say about Shakespeare's sonnets, arguing that one needs to work with their readings, not simply to work in antagonistic battle against them.

Jonathan F. S. Post has had a charming idea for an anthology—to ask contemporary poets to write something about the Renaissance poets they most admire. Thus in Green Thoughts, Green Shades: Essays by Contemporary Poets on the Early Modern Lyric, we have Anthony Hecht on Philip Sidney's sestina "Ye Goteheard Gods": "one of the greatest achievements of Renaissance poetry"; Calvin Bedient on Donne: "Pace T. S. Eliot, he can't be read solemnly", and William Logan on Milton's invention of modern poetic personality in the everyday language of his sonnets (so very different from Paradise Lost). Eavan Boland makes most clear that the poets of the present must remake the poets of the past: not surprisingly, she is a woman poet writing About Ann Bradstreet, another woman poet. It would have been nice to have a poem from the contributors—perhaps the one most influenced by the author under question.

Court Culture

Peter C. Herman's excellent collection of essays plus selections of verse explicates and exemplifies the work of four rulers, two kings and two queens, in Reading Monarch's Writing: The Poetry of Henry VIII, Mary Stuart, Elizabeth I, and James VI/I. Leah Marcus, one of the editors of the recent collected works of Elizabeth I, writes about that new edition; Constance Jordan reads Elizabeth's French poems; Herman and Lisa Hopkins address Mary Stuart's French poetry; Sandra Bell and Appelbaum address James's work when king of Scotland. Herman and Ray Siemens see Henry VIII's poetry as expressions of political as well as poetic authority. The poetry selections printed in the second part of the book exemplify the kinds of issues broached by the scholars. What is surprising is how much better a poet Henry VIII is than the others, possibly because he kept to a shorter line (John Skelton was his teacher); both Elizabeth and James used the unfortunate fourteener and the casket sonnets are so problematic in their histo rical context that it is hard to appreciate them as poetry—as if all Henry's songs were written to Ann Boleyn or another whom he had beheaded. Henry's poems are songs to anonymous persons—and still sing.

Another collection of essays beautifully printed on glossy paper from the British Library and edited by Marie Axton and James P. Carley, "Triumphs of English": The Life and Writings of Henry Parker, Lord Morley, Translator to the Tudor Court, considers the figure of Morley from a number of different perspectives. Morley translated Plutarch, Boccaccio, and Thomas Aquinas for Henry VIII, but also presented to Mary Tudor translations of Cicero, Erasmus, Richard Rolle's Latin psalter, and Seneca's epistles. A tactful aristocratic survivor of the perilous changes in Henry's court who remained a friend to Mary Tudor and a proponent of Elizabeth's succession, and who seems to have supported his own daughter's execution for treasonous complicity with Catherine Howard, Morley is best remembered for having recommended that Thomas Cromwell read Machiavelli. Does one read Morley for comments on current courtly scandals—as James Simpson reads his presentation to Henry of a translation of Boccaccio's On Famous Women a mer e year after his daughter's death? Or does one read his remarks, as Jeremy Maule does, as exemplary humanist treatises that might apply to the court in the future, should the king have wit to apply the lessons?

Richard C. McCoy's Alterations of State: Sacred Kingship in the English Reformation stakes out a new argument about the secularization of society; much like Malcolm Mackenzie Ross five decades ago, McCoy demonstrates that the Reformation controversy about the real presence of Christ in the Eucharist helped to aggrandize Tudor and Stuart assumptions about the sacred nature of kingship itself—and that, as McCoy's opening chapter title has it, the movement was from "Real Presence to Royal Presence." Studying the reigns of three Tudor monarchs and three more Stuart kings, McCoy juxtaposes the work of a key author in each period with funerary monuments and other iconographical images to trace the development from reign to reign of the changing fortunes of the king's assumed sacrality. Ironically, Henry VIII, although head of the Church, never had a tomb of his own—chantry chapels having been abolished during his son's reign. With the suppression of Corpus Christi feasts under Elizabeth, her Accession Day celebra tions had little ecclesiastical competition and so her cult became a virtual national religion. McCoy reads Shakespeare's Hamlet as a meditation on the waning of Elizabeth's reign—where everyone frets about the impossibility of getting a decent burial. James I removed Elizabeth's tomb and built another far more lavish for his mother, putting himself in line with Henry VII as the originator of another dynasty. John Milton and his struggle with the divine-right kingship of Charles I wittily turns, McCoy points out, on the monumental power of Charles's Eilcon Basilike: "Milton's own reverence toward books returns to haunt him". The sacrality of royal authority, especially in death, dies hard, McCoy points out. Courting bathos, but finally making his point, McCoy briefly ends by referring to the civil (and global) idolatry exhibited at Lady Di's funeral. This is a gracious book, shifting gears among iconography, close reading, and church history with a smoothness that belies the speed of the argument. A longer and clunkier book might have been more persuasive, but not so much of a pleasure to read.

John Huntington, in Ambition, Rank, and Poetry in 1590s England, usefully reminds us that there was a group of poets who were not fixated on success within the patronage system. Similar to Owens's revising our notion of Spenser's position within the patronage and print systems, Huntington traces the early careers of a group of specifically disaffected poets, George Chapman, Marlowe, Jonson, Thomas Lodge, and Spenser, particularly of Cohn Clout's Come Home Again—as well as the most interesting addition of Lanyer. Huntington begins by assuming that wherever the authorities expressed hostility there must have been a real threat, even though the poems may seem boring and beside the point to us.

Huntington thus finds a wonderful contrast to Shakespeare's aristocracy-pleasing Rape of Lucrece in Willobie His Avisa, the story of a middle-class woman who defends herself against five suitors. Condemned by contemporaries, the work clearly offended against rank. Huntington traces through Chapman's earlier poems—especia lly his continuation of Marlowe's Hero and Leander—what he calls the "sociak anger" which is registered more explicitly in the drama, Bussy d'Ambois. Using the subtle notions of practice borrowed from Pierre Bourdieu, Huntington hunts for sociological rather than directly political critique; Lanyer's lament that she has been spurned by her aristocratic friends now that they have all left Cookeham is placed in its class context. It is time someone said it.

In Solomonic Iconography in Early Stuart England: Solomon's Wisdom, Solomon's Folly, William Tate traces the use of the figure of Solomon for representing James I and Charles I's royal authority. Reading masques, plays, sermons, and particularly Marlowe's, Jonson's, and Bacon's various works dedicated to James I, Tate explains how the iconography of Solomon allowed the Stuarts to figure various projects as biblically inspired: the building of the Temple becomes the expansion of the Jacobean empire, his "sloth" according to Lucy Hutchinson becomes "Gospell meekenesse and peaceableness", James's learning replicates Solomon's wisdom. With Charles, however, the iconography goes through a sea change, emphasizing the Song of Solomon and the erotic romance between Charles and Henrietta Maria. occasioning Milton's criticism of his "uxoriousness" but more importantly, allowing Milton to criticize the lack of chastity in the court in Comus. A subtle and far-ranging argument which compellingly persuad es the reader that the figure of Solomon was far more important for James than the figure of Deborah was for Elizabeth, for example, the book is quite harmed by a lack of any plates illustrating the various pictorial images it discusses. One would have hoped that inexpensive plates, downloaded from the Early English Books Online for example, could have been used. They would not have been beautiful, but they would have been most helpfully illustrative.

Alastair James Bellany has written the only book-length history of the Overbury scandal in The Politics of Court Scandal in Early Modern England: News Culture and the Overbury Affair 1603-1660. As the title suggests, he sees a very long aftereffect not so much from the affair itself but in the circulation of the materials and images created around the murder and trial as they continued to be recycled in pamphlet and play. Working to expand on Lawrence Stone's early suggestion that court scandal was one of the causes of the English Revolution, Bellany demonstrates that the nexus of these events lies in the news culture that grew up in early-seventeenth-century England: that the "Staple of News"—as Jonson called it—became a powerful shaper of public opinion as manuscript news reports (called "separates") circulated widely throughout the realm and then continued to do so on into the century. Bellany does something different from traditional historiography, aiming instead to write an "ethnography" of early Stua rt political culture. Less interested in what actually happened, he is more concerned to trace what people thought happened and how they transmitted to others their feelings about the events. His work has the understandable narrative drive of the scandal itself; although he says he is not interested in it but in what the common understanding of it was, he gives the clearest exposition of the sequence of events we have seen. But he beautifully sketches in just how the court communicated with the country and powerfully evokes the multiple means of private and more commercialized communication at work in spreading news of—and thereby shaping—the scandal. A brief excursus on the semiotics of poison demonstrating how Jacobeans felt about murder by poison makes the drama of the period far more easy to understand, and a little less comically over-the-top.

N. H. Keeble's Cambridge Companion to Writing of the English Revolution collects essays by various hands about the writing done during the Revolution: Thomas N. Corns,

David Lowenstein, and Annabel Patterson talk about "Radical Voices"; Susan Wiseman, Helen Wilcos and Sheila Ottweay, and Elaine Hobby discuss "Female Voices"; while Alan Rudrum, Isabel Rivers, and Paul A. Salzman discuss "Conservative Voices." Two other sections provide essays elucidating contexts, such as the press, religious thought, and the aftermath of war, with pieces by David Norbrook on English historiography, Nigel Smith on Paradise Lost, and Richard Greaves on Bunyan. These pieces are introductory in tone; they presume no prior knowledge and would therefore be fine for use by interested undergraduates. A handy chronology helps students to locate individual texts throughout the century and another chronologically organized list gives the birth and death dates of all the significant writers in sequence.

Henrietta Maria: Charles I's Indomitable Queen by Alison Plowden grants the reader an inside and strikingly familial view of the events leading up to the English Civil War. Seen from the point of view of the woman who made John Milton call Charles "uxorious," the English Civil War reads far more like the French Revolution, where feckless royals are overrun by events, than it has ever seemed before. Because Henrietta is only practicing her own religion as allowed by her marriage contract and then trying to bring up her children in her own faith, as any mother might, Plowden makes Henrietta's plight deeply sympathetic, and Parliament becomes a wonderful villain. A very different view of English history from a distinctly idiosyncratic standpoint, Henrietta Maria also allows something like an insider's view of the Glorious Revolution and the relations between Charles II and his brother James.

James Grantham Turner understands Henrietta Maria to have been a major problem for Charles in Libertines and Radicals in Early Modern London: Sexuality, Politics, and Literary Culture, 1630-1685. Descended from a long line of authoritative Medici women, Henrietta was only one of a number of women whose increased agency became problematic during the Civil War and its aftermath. In response to this increased agency, Turner sees the rise of what he calls "political pornography", that is, an attack on illicit female sexuality such as prostitution as a means for making political critique. Such "pornography" was useful in attacking royal women such as Henrietta Maria—and later Charles II's infamous mistresses—but it was also deployed for attacking women who had participated in sieges during the war and in petitioning Parliament for their own—and their husbands'—rights. "These waves of 'tumultuous petitioning' contributed greatly to the extension of women's activity. Apart from the composition and public ation of the document itself, they had to gather signatures, adopt and distribute the marching colours ... and move coherent masses of women by water arid land. Under the guise of traditional defence, they articulated not only alternative policies but forthright justifications of their independent action".

The libertinism of Restoration culture, however, was alternatively a means to legitimize the new regime by contrast with the repressive Interregnum, although such a posture could become problematic. When, in the bawdy-house riots of 1668, the court became alarmed at what it perceived to be more than ordinary licentious tumult, it chose to punish four rioters for high treason because they had criticized the king's mistress, Lady Castlemaine. One of the more interesting parts of Turner's argument is the response to this libertinism of such female writers as Cavendish, Behn, and Jane Baker, who use it to their own purposes of enabling female agency. Turner ends by saying that the world-changing idea of feminist politics reverses Karl Marx's famous dictum: apparently feminism made its first appearance in the seventeenth century as farce. Whether or not the libertinism of the Restoration is an attempt to contain the female agency unleashed by radical factions during the Civil War, or whether female agency is simpl y a cover for what is ultimately going to resolve itself in the Glorious Revolution, is not something Turner ever makes clear. It may be a modern (feminist) mistake to perceive a difference between a collective political action on the part of a group of petitioning women and the power wielded by a highly placed courtesan, and therefore to question the legitimacy of arguing that pornographic satire can police both. But clearly that misogynist age saw no difference between them, and so Turner may be quite right to do so as well. Learned and lubricious, the book is witty, exceedingly well informed, and a little bit obscene.

9
Chapter

The Eighteenth Century

INTRODUCTION

The term ' eighteenth century' is used here according to the usual convention to denote a period of our literature with a more or less uniform character of its own. Thus it includes Dryden, who was born in 1631, if not Waller, who was born in 1606, while it excludes Wordsworth, who was born in 1770. The writers of this period believed themselves to have achieved the classical virtues of form and style in a degree beyond their predecessors, and they were inclined to believe that they understood the classical authors better. Seeing that every generation since the Renaissance has believed that it has best understood the classics, the eighteenth century need not be blamed for sharing that opinion; while the other part of their claim—that they reproduced the special qualities of classical style in a superior manner—has in it considerable truth, though less than they supposed. It appears best to begin our consideration of the matter with a note upon the classical scholarship of the time, because that is something one needs to know in order to judge the truth of the eighteenth century claim.

The writers of the seventeenth century are distinguished for their learning. Jonson, Chapman, Donne, Bacon, Milton,

Browne, Burton, Taylor, Butler, Hobbes and many others were men of wide and varied reading. At that time it may be said that literature and scholarship went together. But the learning was discursive rather than exact, comprehensive rather than critical. Milton was perhaps alone among his English contemporaries for his nice observation of stylistic refinements in ancient poetry, but he never thought of applying the methods of historical criticism which had been discovered or used by Scaliger and others in France.

For some reason the generation of Dryden had less extensive learning than its immediate predecessor; indeed so far as its men of letters were concerned it was comparatively ignorant, although Dryden himself was a man of rather wide if unsystematic reading, while a minor figure like Creech had genuine scholarship. But the generation after Dryden produced Richard Bentley, whose importance may be greater than is generally recognised in the many histories of English literature, which represent him merely as a great scholar with a command of racy English. They also observe that he was engaged in the Phalaris controversy and drew upon himself the satire of Swift and Pope. But what the classical student knows is that Bentley initiated a new era of critical scholarship. His knowledge was so great, his acumen so penetrating, his felicity in emendation so extraordinary that he achieved an unrivalled position both as a Grecian and a Latinist not only in England but in Europe. But if he brought the supremacy in classical scholarship to England he also divorced it from literature, not because he was himself devoid of literary gifts—for he wrote very well-but because he set the standard too high for the ordinary man of letters. Henceforward we have the professional scholar on the one hand and the professional author on the other. Such a result was no doubt inevitable sooner or later, but it was Bentley more than anyone else, especially by his handling of the defenders of the Phalaris letters, who made it come sooner than otherwise would have happened.

But even in Dryden's time classical learning from being an essential part in the equipment of any author who aimed at distinction was becoming not much more than a desideratum. It was however at least that, and the Restoration, while seeming to make fight of erudition as something rather beneath the notice of a Cavalier and a gentleman, considered that even a gentleman should know his Horace and perhaps his Virgil. Authors assumed this knowledge in their readers. An educated man was a man who knew Latin—that was what it amounted to. A man who would be ashamed to say he had not read Horace or Tibullus would not be ashamed to say that he had not read Chaucer or Spenser. That is a state of things which continued much longer than might be supposed, and it must be kept steadily in mind by anyone who wishes to understand why the literature of the eighteenth century pursued the course it did, for literature naturally follows the taste of its patrons. Dryden was always very sensitive to public taste—which Milton despised—and his writings did not so much form it as were formed by it. He is therefore more representative of his age than almost any other of our major poets. His education had fitted him for this. As a scholar he is of course not to be mentioned in the same breath with Milton, but he had what is called a good working knowledge of Latin and had read fairly widely in that language. He had also read a good deal of French poetry, drama and criticism—all three at that time very classical in tone—and was influenced in this way like other writers, his contemporaries. Of general literature, native and foreign, he had a very competent knowledge, so that compared with him Pope, for example, is little better than an ignoramus. For a man who was to interpret the classics anew to a generation that wanted a fresh—what people go on calling a 'modern'—interpretation of them he had exactly the right equipment.

In some respects the new attitude to the classics was not a characteristically English thing, which perhaps accounts for the comparative lack of original inspiration in eighteenth century poetry. Dryden himself never whole-heartedly adopted it. It was primarily French. During the first half of the seventeenth century the supremacy of France in classical scholarship had its effect on French literature, The *Pléiade* under its leader Ronsard sought to accommodate the French language to the graces of classical style. They particularly affected 'odes' in the manner of Horace and in what was supposed to be the manner of Pindar; but they sought to acclimatise many other forms as well. The work thus produced was often exquisite or at least charming, but the *Pléiade* was addicted to prettinesses and conceits, which are not in the best Attic taste. The somewhat artificial prettiness enraged Malherbe, who thought that poetry should be the flower of common sense. His opinion prevailed and was later defended by Boïleau, whose critical pronouncements were received with reverence not only in France but in England. He maintained that his view—that poetry was a sort of distillation of common sense—was the true lesson taught us by the classics. To live in accordance with nature is the great maxim of the ancient sages, who added that this is the same thing as to live in accordance with reason. The ancient poets, Boileau considered, believed this and acted upon their belief. *To copy nature is to copy them*, says Pope, and they are, models of good sense as well as of noble inspiration. With this view there was another combined, largely if not exclusively adopted from Horace. The good poet must be 'correct', that is permit himself no licences of diction or metre. Such was the doctrine that came to England.

Dryden was not the first to put it into practice, and he was too good a critic and too thorough an Englishman to think it entirely adequate. But it suited his talents and his temperament, and it suited the spirit of the age; so he took it up with characteristic energy. He always looked on Waller as his precursor in this, a circumstance which gives that poet more importance than he would otherwise possess. What he chiefly learned from Waller was the use of that formally correct heroic couplet in which his own and Pope's greatest triumphs were to be achieved. Dr. Johnson has been a good deal sneered at for thinking the Dryden-Pope couplet more musical than *Lycidas*, but it is evident that Dryden and Pope thought so too. We cannot explain what looks to us like an insensitiveness of ear, but we have to accept it as a fact. We must know what the age admired if we are to understand its approach to antiquity. What it admired then was good sense, pointedly expressed, and an almost geometrical regularity of form with a corresponding regularity of metre. It must be allowed that these things are to be found in classical literature and the eighteenth century view is not so much wrong as inadequate. It is a view that had the right to be expressed, and if the results were disappointing or even bad in poetry they were almost wholly splendid and salutary in prose.

Dryden's most eminent achievement was in satire, and it will suit our purpose to consider him as a satirist along with Pope. There had been a good deal of satire composed in the sixteenth and seventeenth centuries, but it had not, even in the hands of Donne, attained a steady level of excellence. One reason was undoubtedly this, that it was composed under the impression that satire ought to be rugged, if not uncouth. Dryden saw—and here the new doctrine of 'correctness' was entirely helpful—that, to be effective, satire cannot be too highly polished. The special malicious pleasure which it generally aims at giving is strongly intensified by the intellectual and artistic pleasure one derives from exquisite workmanship. Dryden then did not take much from his English precursors, but went direct to the Latin models, above all to Juvenal, who suited him better than Horace. It is true that Dryden attacks living contemporaries, which Juvenal did not do, and is therefore more personal in his attack, at least in appearance, for Juvenal can be personal enough in his censures of the dead. But Dryden has got the invective force of Juvenal; his inexhaustible variety and resource, his moral superiority, real or assumed, to the men he assails. Pope has not this superiority; he is jealous and spiteful. But he assumes the air of having it, and professes himself a follower of Horace in satire. That he studied Horace is proved by his incomparably brilliant *Imitations*. But his real master is neither Horace nor Juvenal, it is Dryden. He takes Dryden's weapon of personal satire, polishes it still further and (some would say) envenoms it. But of course it all goes back in the long run to the ancient satirists.

It is also inevitable that Dryden and Pope should be considered together as translators. Dryden translated a vast amount of classical verse, but all we need take into account is his version of the *Aeneid,* which is entirely typical of his method. He saw that (to use his own words) 'it is almost impossible to translate verbally, and well, at the same time', and so he did not try. But he endeavoured to make up for the deficiencies of his version, when he had to render the more inimitable parts of his author, by adding when opportunity offered 'new beauties' of his own. Dryden's beauties however are not at all like those of Virgil, at least as we now feel them, and it is perhaps not unfair to say that Dryden *Aeneid,* while retaining or even adding to the vigour of the original, loses all its subtle and almost evanescent beauty. Pope *Homer* is more carefully written and is really a masterly attempt to turn Homer into an eighteenth century poet. Only 'you must not call it Homer'. Whether Bentley said this or not, it is a just criticism. Yet it is a splendid production, especially the *Iliad;* it is with all its faults of taste and scholarship the most impressive version of Homer in the language; and it must be read in order to see how the eighteenth century looked at the ancient epic. Pope has the same theory of translation as Dryden, from whom no doubt he derived it, and of course it encouraged him in the work of adding new beauties. The concentrated, self-conscious, antithetic style of Pope is quite unsuited to reproduce the large, undeviating movement of Homer's verse; but at least he gives us a highly wrought work of art, which is the first essential if you are to translate another. Pope was not greatly hampered by his lack of scholarship. It is true that he could not make much or anything of the Greek and that, to put it bluntly, he worked with cribs. But these gave the meaning satisfactorily enough, and all that Pope pretended or even wished to do was to express the meaning in Popian couplets. His contemporaries did not feel this to be presumptuous.

What they wanted was to see what their best poet made of the best Greek poet.

The best of the modern poets in all languages', wrote Garth to Pope at the beginning of the latter's career, 'are those that have the nearest copied the ancients.' The young author accepted and maintained this opinion throughout his life, and it may be called on the whole the orthodox view of the eighteenth century. No one therefore can hope to understand that century unless he understands something of what the classics meant to it. The depth of its perception, the soundness of its interpretation of ancient literature are different matters. It would be altogether unfair to suggest that the century failed to recognise in that literature the presence of what, for want of better words, we call genius and inspiration; but the tendency was to identify genius with a supreme capacity for saying the right thing in the right way—meaning by that the generally accepted thing in the 'correct' way. The danger inherent in the cult of 'correctness' is that the correctness is apt to be pursued for its own sake. This is never the case with Dryden or even perhaps with Pope, at any rate in his maturer work. They had always or almost always if not a 'message' at least an object, though it might only be an object of attack. But their followers and imitators had in general little to say, and then the inadequacy of the doctrine was revealed. This exposure had already been made in France, and French example no doubt had its effect on English practice. The result is conveniently described as 'classicism'. It is somewhat the habit to treat classicism as if it were the same thing as the pseudo-classical But this is hardly fair. It is quite likely that our best attempts to be classical have something 'pseudo' about them for the simple reason that they are modern. The classicists were not pretending to be classical, they thought they were. If they failed, as no doubt they did, it was in taste, and this failure of taste was largely due to ignorance of Greek, an ignorance of course not total but comparative. They looked to Latin for their models, just as the Latin writers had looked to Greek. This prevented them from seeing where the Latin writers had fallen short of the artistic standard set up by the Greeks. So long as they followed Virgil and Horace they were reasonably safe, although it is quite easy even in following them to reproduce their form without their spirit—to be turgid in epic and emptily decorative in lyric. But the danger is greatly heightened if one admires—and the eighteenth century vastly admired them—Ovid and Statius and Claudian. For these poets are themselves rather classicist than classical. Ovid is largely saved by his wit and his picturesqueness, but he has almost no passion and his art too often degenerates into virtuosity. Claudian has exactly that kind of plaster-cast beauty which we now dislike so much. The classicism of the eighteenth century is therefore for the most part a bad inheritance passed on to us by France which had gone even further in that direction. But it remains a style and fine work can be and has been done in it. Thus an architect may consider the baroque a bad style, but he will scarcely deny that very fine work has been done in the baroque.

CLASSICISM

There is a good deal of classicism even in Pope, though he got rid of it as his art matured. But it is his school that shows it most completely. The emptiness of it began pretty soon to make itself felt, and this enabled Thomson even in Pope's lifetime to make a success with his *Seasons*. That poem or series of poems had a great influence, abroad as well as at home, and must be given the credit of directing poetical thought into a new or at any rate a disused channel. (Thomson had been to some extent anticipated by his fellow-countryman Gawain Douglas, whose *Aeneid* he not improbably knew.) But the classical influence on Thomson is stronger than is always recognised. The style, which is obviously affected by, if not formed upon, that of Milton is more Latin than anything in Pope. Beyond Milton he evidently looked to Virgil, for he could not have written the *Seasons* without thinking of the *Georgics*. Thomson then, while he may have started a 'return to nature', was not heading a rebellion against the classics. What he did rebel against was the tyranny of the heroic couplet. On the whole the revolt proved abortive, at least after a time and till it was carried to success by Cowper and Wordsworth. It certainly did not find a recruit in Samuel Johnson, who was from the first and remained to the end a champion of the Dryden-Pope tradition. But he understood it better than their more conventional followers. He saw that Pope and Dryden, however formal their style, were always driving at things and people, at least in their most characteristic work; they did not just embroider familiar themes with traditional graces. His own two satires, *London* and *The Vanity of Human Wishes,* continue the work of Dryden and Pope in their manner but with sufficient independence. This is none the less true because his professed model was Juvenal. *London* is an 'imitation'-in Pope's use of the word—of the third satire of Juvenal, *The Vanity of Human Wishes* a like imitation of the tenth. They are not so brilliant as their originals or as the work of Dryden and Pope; but they have, especially the *Vanity,* a greater moral dignity than any of the three, and to express this dignity was a real contribution to English satire.

Johnson was widely read in Latin literature both ancient and modern (but not mediaeval), and his own style both in verse and prose, though more obviously in prose, is somewhat heavily charged with a Latin vocabulary. This is almost too well known, especially to those who have not read Johnson. That he was deeply indebted to his Latin reading—he was not much of a Greek scholar—can never be denied. But he was far from being enslaved to it. When allowance is made for his point of view with its classical or rather perhaps its anti- romantic bias, you will find in his *Lives of the Poets* that he is prepared to back Shakespeare and Milton, Dryden and Pope against any poets of any age or country. He is full of a not really reasonable contempt for bards who carry their admiration of the ancients so far as to adorn their verses with the classical mythology. He was in agreement with Crabbe about the absurdity of the eighteenth century Pastoral with its picture of an Arcadian existence led by shepherds and shepherdesses with Greek names. He made a distinction between what was permanently valuable in the classics and what was antiquated, and would have the modern poet reject all but the permanent. With that reservation he had no doubt of the value of the ancient classics both intrinsically and as models. That perhaps is why he attached so much importance to translation from them and not only regarded Pope *Homer* as his greatest work but gave what seems to us altogether excessive praise to versions like Rowe *Lucan* and Creech *Lucretius* and the *Horace* of Francis. Yet this is less the attitude of an admirer of Latin than the attitude of an admirer of eighteenth century English poetry.

It must be allowed that both in extent and in accuracy of classical learning, at least in Greek, Johnson was excelled by his younger contemporary Gray. In spite of this Gray is usually represented as turning his back upon the classical tradition and looking towards, if not actually attaining, the romantic world as it was finally conquered by *Lyrical Ballads*. It is true that Gray discards the Popian couplet; it is not true that he has ceased to be classical. His style is more steeped in classical reminiscence than that of any other poet since Milton. The inversions and personifications of which he is so fond are merely external evidences of a classical cast of thought which could only be the result of living daily and intensely with the Latin poets. He knew the Greek poets too, but he is not penetrated by them as he is by the Latin. This comes out in the Odes. It would be interesting to know how far Gray himself thought they reproduced the manner of Pindar. So good a scholar must have known that the kind of 'Pindarick' ode borrowed by Cowley from France and taken up by Dryden was born of a misunderstanding. Because these French and English poets could not scan Pindar they considered that he had no regular scansion, but wrote lines of any length that happened to suit him or in no particular metre at all. In this view they were encouraged by Horace, who uses language about Pindar that might be taken to imply it. It was Horace who gave the Renaissance and later poets the ideas they adopted about Pindar, which came to this, that Pindar was the type of the inspired bard, the child of genius without art. Gray knew better than that, but he has chosen to follow Dryden rather than Pindar himself in the construction of his odes. The resulting effect, in Gray as in Dryden, is on the whole rather rhetorical than lyrical, which is not far from saying more Latin than Greek. This criticism does not apply to the *Elegy* with its unforgettable picture of the English country side. But if the setting is English the sentiments and their expression remember the classics at every turn. The debt of Gray to them cannot be estimated in detail, for it is nearly omnipresent. Nor is its extent always fully realised. The *Hymn to Adversity,* which has a special interest as having suggested Wordsworth *Ode to Duty,* was itself pretty clearly suggested by some fines to Nemesis by Mesomedes, a Greek poet of the second century.

Thus Gray, and we must say the same of Collins, did not really divert the stream of classical influence. Classical subjects became perhaps less common, but classicism—the pursuit of the form without the spirit of the classical tradition—was if anything intensified, and there arose poets like Mason and Erasmus Darwin. Those who revolted against it—and these were the best poets, Blake and Burns, Cowper and Crabbe-were men who had none of them, except Cowper, any classical background at all. Cowper, who had much of the scholar's temper, translated Homer from the Greek, which was more than Pope could do. The translation was in blank verse and was made partly for Cowper's own satisfaction and partly in rivalry with Pope. It is, when one remembers the author, unexpectedly heavy and dull—the very last adjectives that could be applied to Homer. Pope, however unhomeric he may be in other respects, is never heavy or dull, and for that reason his version, though less accurate, is superior to Cowper's. Although Cowper had received a better education in the classics than Pope and had read more widely in them, he is not nearly so much under the influence of classical models and authority. In this respect he may be said to anticipate Wordsworth and Coleridge. Crabbe, so far as metre and even style goes, reverts to the Popian tradition; but in him even more than in Cowper we see the fading of the classical impulse. One says 'classical', but in fact Greek literature had never much effect upon the age. The eighteenth was a Latin century. It was rhetorical in its taste and never quite understood the reticence of the Attic style. Collins, though he could be rhetorical enough as in his ode on the Passions, came nearest to understanding it. But throughout the century it is the Latin manner that prevails in its poetry, even in that of Collins.

Something has been said about the excellence of the eighteenth century in satire. It is worth noting as significant that it excelled also in the mock-heroic. The mock-heroic may of course be combined with satire or be a form of satire as in *MacFlecknoe* and the *Dunciad*. But it may stand by itself as in *The Rape of the Lock*. These are three masterpieces, and they do not stand alone. Swift and Fielding adapted the form to prose, as in the *Battle of the Books and Jonathan Wild*. The mock-heroic epic is, rather surprisingly, of very great antiquity, the first we hear of, the *Battle of the Frogs and Mice*, being attributed to Homer himself. If it were asked why the English eighteenth century did so much better in the mockepic than in the epic itself, which it nevertheless kept attempting with equal industry and ill success, the answer might suggest itself that this was just because the century was thoroughly English at heart and in secret rebellion against the Latin influence. But it must be remembered that in general people parody what they like rather than what they dislike. The mockheroic is the tribute that satire pays to the heroic. The century remained faithful to the classical tradition. Even Blake and Burns do not attack it; they are merely outside it.

DRAMA

A good deal might be said of classical influence upon the Drama from Dryden to Sheridan, but perhaps it is not necessary to say much, because the facts are unusually simple. Here French influence is very important. There is no doubt that, whatever deductions and qualifications may have to be made, French classical Drama comes from Latin—Tragedy from Seneca, Comedy from Plautus and Terence. The French dramatists improved upon their models, partly by learning like Racine from Euripides, partly in ways of their own, but they never cast them away. They have of course much greater merits, but they succeed along the same fines. In Tragedy they have the careful construction, the rhetorical style, the heroic types of good and evil that we find in Seneca, joined with a truth to nature and a poetic splendour which we miss in him. In Comedy we have the stock situations, the stock characters of Plautus and Terence treated by Molière with a literary genius to which they could make no pretensions. Not only this but there was a marked tendency to choose subjects from ancient myth or history or romance. This was the kind of drama that came to England with the Restoration, and so far its origins are classical. Yet except in scholarly productions like Addison *Cato* and Johnson *Irene* it must be confessed that the new Drama has not a very classical look to us. No age, not even the mediaeval, which accepted its own ignorance on the subject, has had so false a notion of ancient Greek fife as that which produced Le Grand Cyrus. This is reflected in much of French Tragedy and of English Tragedy which followed that model. The 'heroic' sentiments expressed by the characters are quite unlike anything we find in classical Greek literature. It is quite likely that Dryden knew this well enough, but heroic sentiments were the fashion, and so his tragedies are full of them. It is much the same with Otway and others, although Otway at least has something else to give and his people speak more like men of this world. In its influence upon Comedy the Gallicised Latin tradition was much less damaging; it was almost beneficial; for Comedy must almost of necessity be steeped in contemporary fashion and sentiment. Hence Restoration and eighteenth century Comedy is infinitely superior to its Tragedy. It is not to be supposed that it was very conscious of any classical background. Yet the background, perceived or not, was there. For eighteenth century Comedy even in Goldsmith, even in Sheridan, to say nothing of Congreve and their other predecessors, is the old Comedy of Manners, adjusted to English life and English society.

PROSE

An age like an individual often values itself most on what is not its strongest point. The eighteenth century, while it boasted of 'reforming our numbers', was far more successful in reforming our prose. It is obvious that prose like that of Milton or Browne could only be written by men of similar genius. What was needed was a standard prose, and this the century provided thanks in the main to Dryden. It was much more plain, unaffected and even conversational than theirs, but it was just as carefully written. If it has not so many Latin words and constructions it has in a higher degree the classical virtues of definition and lucidity. It is probable that Dryden learned something from French models, but it was the native bent of his mind to be plain and perspicuous. He had great powers of rhetorical elaboration—what the ancients called amplification—but he had little taste and perhaps little talent for musical and pictorial decoration such as one finds in Spenser or in Keats and among prose writers in Jeremy Taylor and Ruskin. This very defect saved him from the somewhat gothic structure of later Renaissance prose. How far he had any classical writer in mind is doubtful; most probably he had none. Yet consciously or not he was leading English into what is the main tradition of classical prose, which condemns anything like prose-poetry and makes a sharp division between poetry and what Dryden himself calls 'the other harmony of prose'. Whether the division ought to be so sharp—whether it is not a genuine modern discovery that it need not be—is another question. The ancients made it and Dryden follows the ancients. So for the most part did his successors. Swift indeed, although he knew his classics very well, prided himself on being influenced by nobody. Yet his prose with its strong sense of form, its purity and conciseness, its disdain of 'flowers of speech' is more influenced by classical example than he thought. Addison made a style of his own, of exquisite grace and urbanity; but Addison, who was an excellent Latin scholar, knew very well that these were Horatian qualities, and it is not at all improbable that Horace was in fact his chief inspiration. For the *Satires* and *Epistles* are much more akin to prose than to what we consider poetry, and the 'mission' of Horace in these, which was to cure people of their offences against good taste and good manners by gentle ridicule, was exactly the mission of Addison.

A plain style like his or Swift's requires a flavour of irony, or some special interest of subject, if it is to keep an exclusive hold on public taste. Without either it has to compete with the desire for something of greater complexity and richer texture. This desire found expression in the prose of Johnson and somewhat later, and partly no doubt under his influence, in that of Robertson, of Gibbon, of Burke and others. As a result this more elaborate and polyphonic prose may be said to have conquered the field from the plainer style of Swift and Addison. But it was not a mere reversion to the seventeenth century, strongly as Johnson at least was influenced by Sir Thomas Browne and the pulpit orators of that time. Dryden and his successors had at least seen to it that the kind of ramshackle sentences which astonish us in scholars like Milton and Donne could no longer be tolerated. The grammatical structure of Johnson's or Burke's prose is impeccable. This regard for grammar is one of the virtues of the eighteenth century. It is a realisation of the fact that, if a man does not express his meaning grammatically, his meaning may and often will be misunderstood, whereas to make one's meaning understood is the primary virtue of any prose style. That these writers of the later eighteenth century learned a great deal from the classics is certain. Johnson's head was full of Latin words and turns of phrase; Gibbon's 'classical background' is the great fact of his life; Burke was steeped in Ciceronian oratory. In fact this elaborated prose, of which the period is the characteristic sentence, is essentially a thing of classical origin.

ESSAY

There were certain kinds of prose literature which the eighteenth century practised with special assiduity and success. Such were the Essay, the Dialogue, Oratory, History and above all the Novel. Classical influences were at work, though with varying energy, upon all of them. As the number of authors and their productions increases with time, our treatment of them must be increasingly general. We must deal less with individual writers and more with tendencies. If we begin with the Essay, we may say that, while the word comes from Montaigne, the thing is hardly of his invention. The *Moralia* of Plutarch are to all intents and purposes essays, and Montaigne owes so much to Plutarch that in a man of less originality of mind it might almost be called plagiarism. It is the point of view of Montaigne that is unique, not the form of his work. Bacon *Essays* are full of classical quotation and allusion, while their aphoristic style recalls that of ancient authors like Seneca and Tacitus. When we come to Addison the Essay has a new stream of classical influence playing upon it, that of the Theophrastian *Character*. There had been a development of this genre in the seventeenth century in the hands of men like Hall and Earle, and its association with the Essay was natural. But Steele, and still more Addison, carry it an important stage farther. Sir Roger de Coverley is not merely a type, he is an individual. He is as distinctly, if not as fully, drawn as any character in a novel, and he converses like one. No doubt Addison owes much to Restoration Comedy, which he softens and humarises. But that Comedy in turn developed, as we saw, from Latin Comedy, while Theophrastus drew upon Attic Comedy. We are in the stream of the classical tradition all the time. Later essayists like Johnson and Goldsmith extended the range, but did not materially change the character, of the form, although this cannot be said so definitely of Hume. The prose of Addison is perhaps the most Attic in the language. Yet it would be an error to assume that he gave it this quality as a result of studying the Greek masters. He got it rather from Sir William Temple and Dryden, and both he and they gained very much from their French studies. For French literature, at least in its prose, has more of an Attic quality than that of any other modern nation. For all that Addison must be counted among those English writers who have a prevailingly classical or rather Latin background. There is not much of exaggeration or epigram in calling him a classical don who took to writing English essays.

DIALOGUE

The Dialogue was a favourite form throughout the century. Its history is so clear that it may be said to explain itself. It is convenient to divide the Dialogue into two varieties, the Platonic and the Lucianic, although the latter is only a development of the former. The chief master of the Platonic Dialogue in the eighteenth century is Berkeley, the chief master of the Lucianic (unless one counts Swift) is perhaps Fielding. Neither Fielding nor Berkeley was ignorant of Greek, but, as the fashion of writing Dialogues in both varieties had long prevailed in France, the impulse to write them in English probably came from there. It is certain nevertheless that Berkeley had made a serious study of Plato; no doubt with the aid of the Latin version which was then normally printed in parallel columns with the original Greek. Although he disagrees with Plato in much, he is perhaps the most Platonic of English philosophers in the quality of his thought, certainly in the quality of his style. Fielding *A Journey from this World to the Next*, unhappily never finished, is written in very successful imitation of Lucian. It is quite easy to underestimate the extent of Fielding's classical knowledge, because he makes so fight of it himself.

ORATION

That Oratory is a branch of literature is a dogma of ancient rather than of modern criticism, which has almost ceased to think of the public speaker's art as a mode of literary expression at all. The eighteenth century however agreed on this point with the ancients. We too may agree that Burke at least must be included among the masters of English prose. He is clearly in the succession of Demosthenes and Cicero, and is familiar with all the resources of ancient eloquence. But, although his style is in the Ciceronian tradition, it probably owes a good deal to his study of English and even French oratory, so far as that itself is not merely Ciceronian. More important, it is strongly stamped with his own personality. He is not the slave of the period, but constantly varies the form of his sentences, which are sometimes long and involved, sometimes short and almost abrupt. His figures of speech are numerous, vivid and original; his vocabulary enormous and drawn from a wide range of reading. Occasionally he goes outside his reading and takes words from the market-place, if not the gutter. In virtue of these qualities he may be regarded as not only the continuator of the classical, but a herald of the romantic, style.

HISTORICAL WRITING

It is a matter of some surprise that this country had to wait so long for a true historian. There had indeed been a vast amount of historical or quasi-historical writing in the Middle Ages and later, but it had been mostly in Latin. What was in English came to little more than chronicles or memoirs or brochures like More's history of Richard III or Bacon's history of Henry VII. Even Clarendon *History of the Rebellion* is not quite a true history; it is the personal reminiscences of Edward Hyde worked up into a continuous and reasoned narrative. Moreover, it is the work of a partisan, though considering what he had suffered an unusually fair-minded one. No doubt Clarendon had read the Roman historians, but he is more amenable to French than Latin influences. His prose is seventeenth century work of the complex Ciceronian type. It is more plausible to date the beginnings of true historical writing in English with Hume *History of England*. Hume was a very great critic of thought and possessed an excellent if slightly artificial style; he had as a philosopher trained himself to impartiality, and he had a shrewd, though somewhat abstract, understanding of human nature. Yet these qualities did not make him a great historian. He never troubled to go beyond the printed evidence, out of which he was content to make a clear and continuous narrative, sometimes doubting but never investigating his authorities. That is no way of ascertaining the truth, which is the first and almost the last duty of the historian. Hume was followed by another Scotchman, William Robertson, who wrote histories of Scotland, of Charles V, and of America.

It is certain that Robertson spent more time upon his authorities than Hume and he has more of the historical imagination. But essentially he belongs to the same school of historians—elegant authors who got their materials from books rather than original documents. The style of both Hume and Robertson is classical eighteenth century prose. How far their background was classical might be difficult to say. Doubtless they read the Latin historians, but it is not clear that they got very much from them. Hume in particular, though a Tory and no lover of innovations either in fife or in literature, is the most acute critic the modern world has seen of that belief in reason which runs through ancient philosophy. This strongly differentiates him from Gibbon, who believed in reason and might be said to five in a world of Latin and Greek. For this very reason it is unnecessary to discuss the background of the *Decline and Fall*. It is worth reminding ourselves however that Gibbon's main subject is not classical antiquity but the Middle Ages, so that his authorities tend to be post-classical. His style is as Roman as his subject except for a dash of irony, which is not characteristically Roman.

NOVEL

In the older histories of English literature it was accepted without question that the Novel was invented by Samuel Richardson. It is now seen that this will hardly do. Unless we are to restrict the Novel within certain rather narrow limits, we must admit that it existed before *Pamela* or did not come fully into existence till after it. So far as we are concerned all that need be said is that Richardson had no classical background; indeed he had very little literary background of any kind. It is true that when he was a boy people still read with avidity, in the original or in translations, the seventeenth century French romances, which created a pseudo-classical world of their own. Richardson had no doubt read some of them himself, but he reveals no sign of knowing or even being interested in ancient literature. It is very different with Fielding.

He was a man of considerable scholarship and extensive, if rather unorganised, reading. He certainly knew, for he has imitated, Lucian; it is obvious that he has read Petronius. But he seems to have a good knowledge of many ancient authors, some of them Greek. And it is not a journalistic knowledge; the classical student recognises in Fielding a fellow student. But more important than any number of references and allusions is his conception of the novel as a comic epic in prose. The eighteenth century indulged an ill-rewarded passion for epic poetry of the most classical kind. Fielding thought of taking the heroics out of the epic, bringing it down to the level of ordinary fife and, so to speak, humanising it. He was always satirising the heroic pose, in Jonathan Wild or another. But it would be quite wrong to suppose he meant his satire to apply to Homer or Virgil. His real object was rather to be a sort of prose Homer, saving himself from the absurdity or presumption of this by the use of irony and humour. He knew the famous criticism of the *Odyssey* by an ancient writer, quoted by Aristotle, that it was 'a mirror of human life'. Fielding saw that the novel should be a mirror of human life and not merely (as Richardson had thought) the history of a human soul.

Both Smollett and Steme were bookish men as novelists go, and their books, as was inevitable in their time, were largely the Latin authors. Smollett was the better scholar. The Roman dinner in *Peregrine Pickle* comes from the author's own reading, not from a dictionary of antiquities; nor can his brutality conceal the fact that he is a man of good education. Steme is less honest. He is capable of giving us the impression of personal learning when he is merely plundering Burton or Rabelais. But at least he has literary tastes. Even Goldsmith, it will be remembered, brings a little Greek into *The Vicar of Wakefield*. When one considers that from the first the chief readers of novels were women, who in the eighteenth century were with very few exceptions destitute of even the rudiments of classical knowledge, it is a surprising testimony to the force of tradition to find the novelists still so conscious of the classical background.

SUMMARY

The general inference would seem to be that the eighteenth century whole-heartedly accepted the classical tradition so far as it understood it. The qualification no doubt is important, but does not affect the broad conclusion. Of all the centuries of our literature it is the most Latin in temper and outlook. If we were to name the Latin author who most strongly appealed to it, we could hardly avoid naming Horace. The 'correctness' of that poet, his humorous common sense, his interest in man rather than in nature, his distrust of fanaticism all have their reflection in what is on the whole the most successful and characteristic work of the century. At the same time the seeds of something else were beginning to mature. The respect for the ancient classics was genuine, but it was fast becoming part of an orthodoxy rather than a living creed. It was not fed by sufficient reading. There were indeed great professional scholars from Bentley downwards, and there were individual authors like Gray and Gibbon whose learning would have made them eminent in any age. But the average man of letters was no longer learned nor did his public expect learning from him. There was a certain modicum of classical knowledge diffused from the public schools and universities, more widely in Scotland than in England, but that was about all. To make up for the deficiency there were many translations from the classics ranging in merit from Pope's Homer in verse and Melmoth's translation of Pliny's Letters in prose. The eighteenth century indeed was almost as much a century of translations as the seventeenth. They were more read no doubt than the originals. Their interest for us is historical as well as literary. Almort better than anything eke they show us the classics through eighteenth century eyes. One has only to look at the illustrations in early editions of Pope's Homer to see what kind of figure an Homeric hero presented to the imagination of the artist and perhaps of Pope himself. The actor who took the part of Cato in Addison's play wore a wig. But this only means that eighteenth century men saw themselves in the ancients, and this is what every century does, whatever the degree of its archaeological knowledge. Such knowledge helps us to realise the past and to understand better certain passages, otherwise unintelligible, in ancient authors. The exciting discoveries of Schliemann at Troy and of Sir Arthur Evans in Crete stirred the imagination of more than scholars and threw all kinds of surprising fights upon the history of ancient culture. We ought therefore to be in a position to form a sounder estimate than the eighteenth century was able to do of classical antiquity. But literature is a question of the human spirit, and it is perfectly possible to know more of a literary age and to move further away from it in spirit. And on the whole it would appear that this is what has happened. The eighteenth century did not know so much about the Greeks or even about the Romans as we do, but classical literature appealed more directly to it.

10
Chapter

The Nineteenth Century

INTRODUCTION

For the historian of literature the nineteenth century may be taken as beginning with the publication of *Lyrical Ballads* in 1798 and continuing well into the twentieth century. The reaction against the Popian school of poetry and the Swift-Addison school of prose had of course begun long before 1798. Indeed Johnson himself was half-conscious of fighting a rearguard action against the taste for Gray and the 'Gothic', while his own prose is the opposite of Addisonian. But now there was a reaction against Johnson in turn. It was not always consciously directed against him, at least at first. Thus Blake and Burns were not thinking of him at all. But Blake was hardly known to his contemporaries and Burns was looked upon as a gifted ploughman who might, if he had been better educated, have written very creditable English verses. No one however could doubt the significance of the *Lyrical Ballads*. They make a clean break with the past, which for them was the eighteenth century. It had been a century which felt a deep admiration for classical literature, which again meant for them chiefly the Augustan period of Latin literature, whose standards of taste and criticism it accepted and sought to apply, though with decreasing enthusiasm or conviction. It was therefore inevitable that the new movement initiated by *Lyrical Ballads* should have or appear to have an anti-classical, at least an anti-Latin, tendency.

Coleridge

This was not due to ignorance or a want of sympathy with the classics on the part either of Wordsworth or of Coleridge. Both had received a classical education. Wordsworth, though an undistinguished student at Cambridge and never much of a reading man, taught himself a respectable amount of both the ancient languages. Neither is it irrelevant to remark—for after all it makes part of his background—that his brother Christopher and his nephew were Greek scholars of high distinction. Coleridge was a somewhat brilliant undergraduate and even from his school days read very widely in a discursive sort of way both in Greek and in Latin. The learning of Coleridge is not in question, but it cannot be said that he had a scholarly mind. He was the victim of his own genius, putting his own interpretation on what he read or remembered, or thought he remembered, and attributing that to his author. But if he cannot be ranked very high as a technical scholar, as an interpreter he ranks with the highest. Perhaps no poet since Gray was so deeply versed in ancient literature. The strange thing is that there is almost no trace of this classical lore in his poetry—when it is fully inspired. That he got much from ancient literature is certain, but what he took was all transformed in that original mind into something rich and strange.

What befell between say Cowper *Task and Lyrical Ballads* has been described and discussed almost more than any other period of our literary history. There is the less need for going over it again here. In any case the origins of the so-called Romantic movement are not within our province. It has however long been recognised that there is a danger in pressing the contrast between romantic and classical. The art of literature does not change in its essentials, but only in the subjects it adopts and the feelings it seeks to express. Towards the end of the eighteenth century there came a wide-spread longing for new subjects and the expression of new feelings. That century had thought of nature as something that was only good or at any rate was only at its best when fashioned by art. The new age loved nature for its own sake and felt almost a repugnance to art for interfering, as it seemed, with nature. This prejudice—for that is what it is— was encouraged by books like Macpherson *Ossian* and Percy *Reliques of Ancient English Poetry*, which seemed to prove that poetry could, nay that it did, originate in an artless age. This led to the exaltation in Germany, where the theory most flourished, of what was called *Volkspoesie*, poetry produced by tribes living in 'natural' conditions, 'natural' meaning primitive or uncivilised. The Ballads appeared to be just such poetry, and they suggested the notion that literature began with ballads. This suited the temper of the time, which was inclined to attribute its evils to civilisation, and to envy the happy simplicity and admire the picturesqueness of less sophisticated races and eras. Now it is true that in classical literature the poets occasionally celebrate, with how much sincerity we need not enquire, the felicity of a mythical golden age; but in general the whole tone of it is dead against any tendency to prefer the fife of the savage to that of the civilised man. It had cost the ancients too much to civilise themselves to permit them to cast discredit upon civilisation. This is reflected in their literature with its insistence on the virtues of self-discipline in character, and of precision and propriety of form in art. That undeniable fact troubled the new school of critics a good deal, since, if they were right, it was to be expected that Greek poetry, being the oldest we have, would show more signs of its origin in 'folk-poetry'. They got over the difficulty in two ways, partly by saying, quite truly, that civilisation is not a matter of dates, and partly by saying that as a matter of fact the Homeric Poems are ballads or 'lays' which were skilfully combined into epic poems in historical times. Into the merits of that theory we cannot go, but it had this effect that Homer was now exalted at the expense of Virgil, who was considered to be a mere court-poet and the *Aeneid* a 'literary epic'. In general Greek literature was preferred to Latin as more original and spontaneous in its inspiration. Both in Greek and in Latin those authors were most admired who showed most of this spontaneity. Thus many now preferred Catullus to Horace and Lucretius to Virgil. The classics were not less read—indeed Greek was read more-but critics and authors turned with eagerness to the vernacular literatures, to the Middle Ages, to natural scenery, to magic and diablerie—all things that the eighteenth century had cared little or nothing for, although individual authors had cared.

Scott

Now it would be possible to say a good deal about the classical background of Wordsworth and Coleridge and even Scott, whom we may take as the three leaders of the Romantic movement. But the really important fact for us is that it scarcely entered into their most characteristic work. They felt the classical influence, but were not penetrated by it. Wordsworth's conviction, which is the source of nearly all his best poetry, that natural objects have a fife and almost a personality of their own, has an odd resemblance to the feelings which must have inspired Greek mythology, but never found clear expression in Greek or in any other literature known to him before he gave it that expression in English. Again there is nothing in classical literature at all like *The Ancient Mariner* or *Christabel or Kubla Khan*. The case of Scott is almost more remarkable. He never knew any Greek worth mentioning and soon forgot what he knew; but he contrived to read a surprising amount of Latin, chiefly mediaeval or modern, because it was there that he found the kind of stories in which he delighted most. He never lost his taste for eighteenth century literature, as Wordsworth and Coleridge seem to have done. His novels are starred with Latin quotations, not always accurately remembered, but always apt and delightful. There is even something Homeric about his genius. But his spiritual home is in the Middle Ages, or the Middle Ages as he imagined them, and as a source of inspiration the classics mean nothing to him. Much the same may be said of Byron. For although Byron admired the Dryden-Pope school of poetry beyond all others, and professed to champion the 'classical' against the 'romantic' in literature, the instinct of all Europe in hailing him as the very coryphaeus of romanticism was not mistaken. He has indeed plenty of classical quotations and allusions, drawn from a not inconsiderable reading, but they are purely accessory. To be sure the impersonal character of classical art makes it the antithesis of everything that people like or dislike in Byron.

Wordsworth, Coleridge and Scott were however in a special degree pioneers, and while they set the tone for others, and indeed for the century as a whole, they were not the sole arbiters of taste. The traditions of the eighteenth century were still strong, and the historian must not disregard their strength because they suffered defeat. The poetry which Scott himself really liked best, although his own was so different, was that of Dryden and Johnson and Crabbe. There is much of the eighteenth century even in Wordsworth. It might be claimed that the *Ode to Duty* is as fine an example of the classical style as we shall easily find in the language-pure, unadorned, lucid, alive with concentrated emotion. It is certainly more truly classical than the odes of Gray. *Laodamia*, greatly inferior in poetic intensity, has a noble simplicity of style that may fairly be called classical. One might make a fist of such exceptions, but they do not alter the fact that what pre-eminently distinguishes Wordsworth from all the poets before him, his interpretation of nature, is something new. He does not any more than Coleridge or Scott or Byron draw inspiration from the classics. But there were others who did, and these, though now appearing minor figures by comparison, cannot simply be neglected. It may however be sufficient to deal with one, the most accomplished, Walter Savage Landor.

Landor

Taking his work as a whole, we may call Landor the most classical author in the language. He is indeed less classical than he thought himself, for in temper he is almost extravagantly romantic, but to everything he writes he seeks to give the qualities which he admired in classical art. His weakness is that the matter he has to communicate is too often unworthy of the manner in which it is expressed. He wrote too much, had too many whims and too little intellectual power to live up, as it were, to the undeniable beauty and dignity of his style. He is too apt to give us a succession of golden platitudes. But the mere form of what he says, whether in prose or verse, is always nearly impeccable. And its virtues, so far as they go, are classical virtues. His prose—and the quality of his verse is so like that of his prose that it need hardly be discussed separately—is more like the best Greek prose than anything produced in the eighteenth century. So far as it had an English model, Landor's style was evidently formed, upon ornate seventeenth century prose, chastened and clarified by a very close study of the ancient masters. By a very similar process his verse recalls that of the seventeenth century purified of its tendency to extravagance, so that his lyrics are more like those of Jonson and Campion than anything in between. But it is Landor's prose that is his great achievement. It was made possible by his knowledge of Greek. It was this which enabled him to produce a less, or at least a more subtly, rhetorical type of sentence than the periods, fundamentally of Roman construction, of Johnson and Gibbon and Burke. Landor had not the genius of these men, but he lived at a time more favourable for doing just what he did.

This was because it had now become possible for men, not professional scholars, to read Greek literature easily enough to perceive and enjoy its qualities. But it was the professional scholars who had created the possibility. Bentley had been as great in Greek as he was in Latin, and although none of his successors equalled him in genius they inherited from him the lesson that Greek must be studied with the same thoroughness as the other language. Indeed the Latin scholars themselves discovered that their own studies could not be carried beyond a certain point unless they learned

Greek. The Renaissance had rather divined than revealed the beauty and interest of Greek literature. A really competent knowledge of Greek was and remained for long a rare acquirement. But the labours of those who did know it gradually bore fruit, and towards the end of the eighteenth century Greek was as much studied among scholars as Latin itself, if not more so. The most famous of these Grecians was Richard Porson, who joined a considerable literary talent to a methodical exactness of research that has never been excelled. He and a number of other scholars, trained in his method and only less eminent than himself, produced such an effect upon the teaching of Greek in the Universities that it could now be learned there as easily as Latin. That being so, the superior power and range of its literature made itself felt upon the minds of all who were naturally attracted to poetry and philosophy. There arose an enthusiasm for Greek studies, not indeed to be compared in intensity with that felt or expressed at the Renaissance in Italy, but more according to knowledge. Landor shared in that enthusiasm, was faithful to it all his life, and was rewarded by a style of singular distinction. His favourite medium was the Dialogue, which he extended in directions never dreamed of by his predecessors in English. He may have been influenced by Fontenelle and Voltaire, but he does not seem to have read much in French. It is more probable that he got some suggestions from Lucian. The greatest probability of all is that it simply occurred to him that there was no reason in the world why the form should be monopolised by philosophers and humorists. Since people in real life talk about everything under the sun, surely they may do the same in dialogue. At any rate they do so in the *Imaginary Conversations*. A large proportion of them have classical subjects, but even when they have not they are redolent of classical sentiment and constantly recall classical turns of phrase.

At this point a general observation may be made. Expressed somewhat paradoxically, it is this. The eighteenth century is less, and the nineteenth is more, classical than it seems. By this is not meant that the eighteenth century paid only lipservice to classical canons of taste and rules of composition. On the contrary it whole-heartedly adopted them and to the best of its ability applied them. But who does not feel that the eighteenth century is, of all periods of English history, the most thoroughly and typically English? On the other hand the nineteenth century, while ostentatiously breaking the fetters of classicism, does not really repudiate the genuine classics. It rather looks in them for things the eighteenth century had passed over, uncared for or unobserved. It discovers the *romantic* charm of the *Odyssey*, of Sappho, even of Virgil. But it is above all in Greek literature that it makes its discoveries. If the eighteenth is our Latin, the nineteenth is our Greek, century; so far of course as it is classical at all. Latin suffers an undue neglect. This is clear when we consider the men we have mentioned (except Scott) and their contemporaries, such as Peacock, who was soaked in Greek literature, Moore, who translated and imitated Anacreon, Campbell, who made a spirited version of the song of Hybrias the Cretan; it is even more clear when we consider the next generation: Shelley, Keats, De Quincey and others. Greek meant a great deal to these men, Latin very little. It is impossible to deal with them all; it is equally impossible to pass over Byron, Shelley and Keats.

Byron, Shelley, Keats

Byron died for Greece. It may seem therefore an unnecessary and even an insulting question to ask what exactly Greece meant to him. Yet it is a question that is bound to present itself to any reader of his works. For what he finds there is that, while Byron has a real and sometimes a passionate interest in Modern Greece and its history, he does not seem to know very well or care very much about classical Greek literature. It is doubtful how much of the ancient language he actually knew; it is certain he forgot what he had learned of the modern language. It was the scenery of Greece that impressed him, as well it might, the picturesque contrast of Turk and Giaour, the bandits, the bearded priests, the black-eyed virgins. The Greece of Sophocles and Plato, which meant so much to Shelley, seems to mean very little to Byron. The old mythology, which was so dear to Keats, makes no appeal to him. There is however something that does—the passion for political liberty; and this Byron knows very well was handed down from ancient to modern Greece. Nor did he deny in any way the intellectual and artistic superiority of the ancient classics. He even recognised more than most of his contemporaries their right to tell us the difference between good and bad writing. He went so far as to compose those *Hints from Horace* which nobody can now bear to read. But the character of Byron's genius made it impossible for him to mould his poetry on classical lines. He could not be impersonal in his art. He gets his effects by expansion, not concentration. However much he may have admired Pope, he would never take the trouble that Pope took to express himself. And so we must say that his inspiration was not classical.

It is very different with Shelley. He read Greek eagerly as soon as he could read it at all, and it was a permanent source of inspiration to him. It may even be suggested that its influence upon the development of his genius has been a little obscured by the attention bestowed upon the political theories of Godwin. No doubt these greatly excited him and appeared to him as novel as they were sublime. Even today commentators are apt to regard them as typically modern. Yet they are not quite that. Godwin must have the credit of elaborating his idea with plausible eloquence. But the idea or ideal—for that is rather what it is—of a golden age which would return if men would only abolish war and its causes, and follow their natural instincts—crops up quite often in ancient literature. The sect of the Cynics advocated the simple fife. The still more influential sect of the Stoics maintained that all men were citizens of one city—the City of the World or even the City of God—and urged them to live 'according to nature'. Thus even if Godwin had never written a word Shelley was able to find in the classics material to feed the flame of his enthusiasm. That this sometimes vitiated his literary judgement can hardly be denied. Thus he thinks

Lucan a better poet than Virgil because he was a republican, while Virgil accepted the rule of Augustus. Even in Greek literature (which, and not Latin, was his true love) his tastes led him in somewhat unusual directions. That he felt to the full the sheer poetry of the great Greek dramatists and lyrists is beyond all doubt. If he chose to translate the *Cyclops* of Euripides and the Homeric *Hymn to Hermes* instead of something better than either, he obviously did it for his own amusement, not because he specially admired them. Yet on the whole what fascinated him most was Platonism. This does not mean that Shelley made a special study of Plato; he did not live long enough for that. He took what suited him, and that was the more mystical part of the philosopher's doctrine. This, as many others had done before him, be interpreted in accordance with the later teaching of the NeoPlatonists, some of whom—not the best of them—believed in what most of us would regard as magic or necromancy. Shelley's imagination was inflamed by some of this, and, as he could turn anything into poetry, he made poetry out of that too. But in the original Greek it is sad stuff.

The most massive evidence of the inspiration drunk by Shelley from Greek poetry is *Prometheus Unbound*. It is of course only too easy to show how unlike Shelley's poem—for it is hardly a play—is to a typical Attic tragedy. To begin with, it is completely devoid of dramatic excitement or even interest, there is no plot, the spoken parts are too lyrical, the lyrical parts are given an excessive importance, the characters are altogether too shadowy. Yet when all this is said it may still be held that *Prometheus Unbound* is more essentially Greek in spirit, though less in form, than *Sanuon Agonistes,* which is really the tragedy not of Samson but of John Milton. Shelley had one necessary qualification of a dramatist which was denied to Milton—he could forget himself. *Prometheus Unbound* strikes one not indeed as like a drama of the Periclean age, but as like what the Periclean drama might have become in the hands of a great lyrical poet, who was not writing for the stage. A Greek would have been less shocked or even puzzled by it than most of Shelley's contemporaries. And *Hellas* would not have puzzled him at all. It is obviously fashioned mainly on the model of the *Persiaw* of Aeschylus, just as his Prometheus play had been modelled on the *Prometheus Bound;* but Shelley's mind is full of other Greek poetry as well, particularly Sophocles, whose *Oedipus Coloneus* has inspired an ode in *Hellas.* Its famous final chorus derives immediately from the fourth eclogue of Virgil. But the idea is Greek and was borrowed by Virgil himself.

The *Eclogues,* especially the tenth, helped to inspire *Adonais,* but the general conception of Shelley's poem is more indebted to the *Lament for Bion* of the Greek bucolic poet Moschus. Bion himself had written a *Lament for Adonis,* which also was familiar to Shelley and probably suggested the title of his own elegy. It is not clear why *Adonais* is written in the Spenserian stanza, beautifully as Shelley manages it, though there might be a reason for avoiding the appearance of direct rivalry with *Lycidas,* that supreme triumph of metrical genius. Altogether it is an interesting thing that one elegiac poet after another—Spenser, Milton, Pope, Gray, Shelley, Arnold, Swinburne—has chosen a different metre, none of them corresponding closely to the dactylic hexameters of the Greek and Latin masters of the Lament. A certain artifice is necessary to adapt the pastoral convention to modern circumstances, but it need not be ungraceful or unpoetical, and it is not so in *Adonais.* Like *Prometheus Unbound* it is not written in the Attic style, but in the later, Hellenistic manner. But it does not imitate that manner, it transcends it.

The Platonism of Shelley is not very easy to understand. There is nowhere in his works a reasoned exposition of it, although doubtless he was prepared to give this, for he was almost as fond of metaphysics as Coleridge. It seems clear that he learned most from the *Symposium* (which he translated) and the *Phaedrus.* Plato held that the visible world had no reality of itself or derived such reality as it had from an unseen world of what he called Ideas, which could not be apprehended by the senses but could be studied by pure Intellect or Reason. In the same way whatever is beautiful in the visible world has beauty only in so far as it receives this from the Idea of Beauty or Beauty Itself—Shelley calls it Intellectual Beauty. Thus his *Hymn to Intellectual Beauty* is in conception Platonic, but it is also influenced by Wordsworth *Ode on Intimations of Immortality in Childhood*, where a theory is unfolded which, though sometimes described as Platonic, is very different from anything taught in Plato, who thinks that we come nearer the truth as we grow older in study instead of going further away from it, which is the view of Wordsworth. Yet, however modified by a mystical Neo-Platonism, by Wordsworthian nature-worship, and his own conception of love, which is only partly Platonic, the strong sense of an immortal world behind the veil of the mortal (which is the essence of Platonism) operates powerfully in a great deal of Shelley's finest verse, in *Alastor*, in *Epipsychidion* and much else. Finally some of his most exquisite poetry is inspired by sheer delight in Greek mythology unperplexed by any theory. Such is the *Hymn of Pan*, the *Arethusa* poem and other things almost as good.

Keats never had the time or opportunity to learn Greek, and one may wonder if he would have written on Greek subjects at all, if he had not caught the current enthusiasm for them. He had to rely on translations, like Chapman's Homer, and on a handbook of ancient mythology. He had thus at first no means of perceiving the true quality of the best Greek art, which naturally disappears in translation, especially when done in the somewhat turbid and fantasticated style of Chapman. Nor was the influence of Leigh Hunt, which may have been useful to him in some ways, useful in this; for Hunt's own taste was, from a classical point of view, deplorable. It is not wonderful then if *Endymion* has little that is Greek about it except the story and the poet's love of beauty for its own sake. The true spiritual ancestry of *Endymion* will not be found in classical Greek, but in *The Faerie Queene*, in *Hero and Leander*, in *Venus and Adonis*. It is perhaps the main defect of Keats's lovely poetry that (to use his own expression) he 'loads every rift with ore', so that he can never permit himself any of those bare, simple, elemental lines that the greatest poets like Dante and Shakespeare, not to mention the ancients, use upon occasion with such tremendous effect. To seek richness of texture is a perfectly legitimate or rather a necessary object in writing verse, and Keats achieved it as hardly any other English poet has done; but to seek it all the time is a quest that defeats itself by creating a surfeit. That is one of the lessons of Greek art which Keats did not learn. It is not at all impossible that he would have learned it. *The Ode to a Grecian Urn* may be taken as proof of that. The style is more concentrated and inornate than is usual with Keats, and the famous last words are very Greek indeed, although they go rather beyond anything that any Greek thinker actually said. It may be objected that what the ode as a whole expresses is not a sentiment drawn from the Greek world itself, but a nostalgia for that world, that is to say a sentiment which by its very nature can be felt only by a modern. Yet the poem is singularly Greek in the restraint of its feeling and the purity of its outlines. The advance towards the understanding of classical art between *Endymion* and the ode is enormous. It was partly due no doubt to a natural maturing of taste as the poet grew older and read more; but it also looks as if he learned much by simply looking at the Elgin Marbles (which be saw when they were acquired by the British Museum) and at such a 'Grecian urn' as he addresses in his ode. True, that vessel, as described by him, seems to be made of marble with figures in relief, which suggests something quite different from the vases of the finest period of Greek ceramic art, and looks suspiciously like those products of a much later period which found their way into the houses of English gentlemen in the eighteenth and early nineteenth centuries. But he was right about the Elgin Marbles, and that was the more to his credit because it was some time before they were valued at their true worth. Most people still preferred the Belvedere Apollo and the Laocoon and the 'Dying Gladiator' (who is not a gladiator at all) and the Portland Vase and other handsome objects of that sort. This is a fact to be noted because it was part of the background not merely of the contemporaries of Keats but of the Victorians later, including Ruskin, who would almost certainly have admired Greek art more than he did if he had known the right things or known them better. But Ruskin like Keats was intoxicated by colour, and the colour has been rubbed away from the remnants of Greek art.

Tennyson

It is probably most instructive to continue our discussion of the poets into Victorian times, because Victorian poetry so clearly carries on the Georgian tradition. Tennyson is the poetical offspring of Keats. That is to say he is 'romantic' like Keats and has learned from him how to marry gorgeous colour with a subtly modulated vowel-music. But Tennyson became the scholar that Keats never had the chance to be and was able to study classical art in the classics themselves. This gave him an immense advantage from the start, but it seems possible to trace a certain progress in the understanding of classical art in Tennyson as in Keats. In his early work, such as *Oenone* or the *Lotos Eaters*, his style has all the colour and perfume of Keats; the sentiments no doubt are more in accordance with knowledge of the ancient world, but they are expressed, so to speak, in the language of romance. If however one takes a somewhat later poem by Tennyson on a classical subject, *Ulysses*, we find him coming much closer to a kind of poetry which an ancient Greek would have understood. Although the speaker is not like Homer's Ulysses, who only wanted to get home and stay there, that hardly matters. The poem does take us into the Homeric world, while the style, though it has not Homer's rapidity, has a good deal of his majestic simplicity. It may be that there is nothing in Tennyson so Greek in conception as Keats's ode to the urn, but that was an almost solitary act of divination on the part of an altogether exceptional genius. Where Keats was guessing, Tennyson knew.

From a very early period of his life Tennyson devoted himself to the creation and development of that very individual style which we associate with his name. It is as much a work of conscious art and literary scholarship as the style of Milton. It is however less classical in the restricted sense of the word-it is too mannered, too self-conscious, too pictorial to recall the Attic masters. He is much more comparable to Virgil, of whom he was all his life a devoted lover and student. It seems reasonably certain that it was from Virgil he learned to extend a little the ordinary use of words and vary a little the ordinary construction of sentences to obtain new poetic effects. It is an exquisite art, but to pursue it successfully requires an almost infinite tact and delicacy of taste. Tennyson possessed this tact in a very high degree, but it sometimes fails him, and then he seems mannered and affected. The admiration of his contemporaries induced him sometimes to attempt a higher strain than was natural to his lyrical and elegiac genius. He had no dramatic power, and his most successful work in the epic vein, *The Passing of Arthur,* is only a fragment. It is interesting to see what he made of Homer. He has translated a passage from the *Iliad* with almost literal fidelity, but the result is pure Tennyson, utterly unhomeric in its movement, but very fine in its own way and perhaps the best bit of Homeric translation we have.

But there is one ancient poet, classical though not Attic, with whom Tennyson has a remarkable affinity. This is Theocritus. What Tennyson could do in direct imitation of Theocritus is shown by the eclogue, inserted in the Princess, which begins: *'Come down, O Maid, from yonder mountain height'*. It naturally lacks a little in the freshness and originality of the Greek poet, but otherwise it is as perfect a transference of his manner as seems possible in a modern language short of mere copying. This is not accidental. The exquisite versification', the brilliant vignette-like descriptions, the extraordinary finish in the workmanship which we find in Tennyson are also found in Theocritus, where the English poet undoubtedly studied them. Tennyson must have been conscious of this when he called his most considerable work *Idylls of the King*. The real models for these are not the *Iliad* or the *Aeneid,* still less *Paradise Lort,* but the poems specifically called *epyllia* which are included among the works of

Theocritus. The *epyllia* deal in a quasi-epic manner with episodes drawn from the old mythology, just as the *Idylli of the King* deal not with the Arthurian legend as a whole but with episodes drawn from it. This is not poetry of the great age but of the later period called Hellenistic. It can be very beautiful for all that, as Tennyson felt. He has not the vigour, the dramatic sense and the humour of Theocritus, but he has other qualities which Theocritus does not reveal. To call him the English Theocritus would be misleading and inaccurate. But it is representatives of what might be called the classical tradition in our language—did not attempt any systematic defence of their principles. Even Dryden and Johnson scarcely did that, and both were too ready, although less ready than Pope in his *Essay on Criticism*, to accept the French interpretation of what Aristotle and ' Longinus' meant instead of going direct to the literature which these great critics had before them. Indeed neither Johnson nor Dryden was sufficient master of the Greek language to make so necessary a task easy for them. Landor, who had the necessary equipment and was very ready to discourse on literary matters, was too illogical and too full of crotchets to be a safe guide. Arnold had some crotchets of his own, but it is easy to discount them, and when we have done that we find a clear and consistent point of view. His main service to criticism was to insist upon the unique importance of a particular period of ancient literature, the Periclean age, whose representative poet is Sophocles. If you wished to know what classical art was at its best and purest, you must go to Sophocles. The essence of his criticism in literature as in other things was this, that we should concern ourselves only with the best and model ourselves as much as we could upon that. This best he was prepared to recognise wherever it could be found, but he thought that it was to be found most abundantly and with the least admixture of less excellent elements in Greek literature of the fifth century before Christ. In regarding this as the most classical period of classical art Arnold was no doubt right. But the question arises whether he was not too exclusive. To some extent he recognised that himself, for it is clear that he regarded Homer, who comes before the Periclean age, and Plato, who comes after it, as sufficiently classical to meet all his requirements. What he never realises, or at least admits, is the variety, even in poetry, of the Periclean age itself. In his search for the perfect style he is left isolated with Sophocles. This is the result of pursuing something that exists only in Heaven. On the other hand it can be said that Arnold was enabled by his very exclusiveness to give a new clearness and precision to our notions of the classical.

Arnold

After this it is a little surprising, though not perhaps to anyone who has perceived how little poetic inspiration is affected by a theory, to find how small a portion of Arnold's own work reminds one of Sophocles. He did compose a tragedy upon the Attic model, introducing it, in order to justify his choice of subject and style, by an important Preface. This play, *Merope,* has considerable beauty and nobility, and is written with that distinction which we expect from Arnold; but as drama it is almost totally uninteresting. This seems to show that he never asked himself why Sophocles, apart from his incomparable diction, is so exciting. It is not enough for a dramatist to choose a subject full of dramatic possibilities-Arnold has no difficulty in proving that the story of Merope is a subject of this kind—he must develop these possibilities in his play. Swinbume is just as bad as Arnold in this respect. One reads *Atalanta in Calydon* and *Erechtheus* for the poetry; nobody cares about the action. And yet Arnold says himself that in an ancient tragedy it is the action that matters most. He does not seem to have realised that the action does not act itself; it must be conducted by the dramatist. As for the style of *Merope* it does make an attempt, by no means entirely unsuccessful, to recapture the severe beauty of Attic verse. But even here Arnold is attempting the impossible. The English language is so full of colourless monosyllables and outworn metaphors that we simply cannot afford to sacrifice the advantages derived from the pictorial imagination in which the English poets have been so strong. The difference between our poetry and the Greek is like the difference between painting and sculpture. The sculptor gets his best effects by mere purity of form; the painter cannot depend on that alone. One reason why Arnold succeeds better in the lyrics than in the blank verse of *Merope* is that the odes of Greek tragedy have a much more figurative and coloured diction than the iambics used in dramatic conversation, and such a diction is natural to an English poet. And in the Greek tragic poets even the non-lyrical passages are effective poetically in proportion as they are effective dramatically, For dramatic poetry is meant to be spoken, and unless it has the qualities of spoken poetry it will not make itself felt on the stage. Neither Tennyson nor Browning, neither Arnold nor Swinburne seems to have appreciated this. At least their dramatic verse does not get across the foot-lights.

Arnold tried other classical forms besides the drama. He has attempted the epic style in *Sohrab and Rustum* and *Balder Dead*. Both, but especially *Balder Dead*, are nearer the Homeric style than the *Idylls of the King* or even *Ulysses*, although the manner of Tennyson has had some influence upon Sohrab and *Rustum*. This is a very, fine fragment, and the similes and speeches are often in very happy imitation of Homer. If it lacks the fire and rush of Homer, that no doubt was inevitable. Arnold himself however came to think that *Sohrab and Rustum* was not Homeric enough, being too romantic and ornate, so he wrote *Balder Dead* in a much severer style. The story is not so interesting as that of Sohrab, and the bleakness of the setting does not lend itself so well to warm and picturesque detail. Where there is a chance for this, as in the similes, Arnold makes the most admirable use of it—hardly any English poet has better similes. But, as in *Merope*, he does not consider sufficiently the difference in the genius of Greek and English. As he says in his fine Lectures on *Translating Homer* details which would be otherwise prosaic are made poetical by virtue of the 'grand style' that pervades the Homeric Poems. But it does not follow that the 'grand style' must be produced by the same means in English as in Greek. Arnold's own quotations prove this. Milton, he thinks, is the great master of 'the grand style' in English. But who ever thought that the style of Milton was simple or direct?

Thus *Balder Dead*, trying always to be simple and direct, becomes at times humdrum and almost prosaic. Yet it is a noble poem, the most Homeric, in style if not in effect, in the language.

Finally in *Thyrsis* and *The Scholar Gipsy* there is an approximation to the classical Pastoral, an approximation rather than an imitation, but not more remote than *Adonais*. They have stood the test of time better almost than any other part of Arnold's work, and yet for all the classical allusions in them they remind us more of Keats than of Sophocles or even Theocritus. But a man is not proved to be wrong because he cannot demonstrate his theory in practice. The greatest critics have never merely echoed the fashionable doctrines of their time; on the contrary they have generally opposed them and recalled their contemporaries to the permanent elements in literary excellence—in other words to the classics ancient or modern. Doubtless Arnold insisted too much on the negative merits of Attic art—its freedom from extravagance, from caprice, from provinciality, from false sentiment and vulgarity —and said too little about its native force and fire. But the faults just mentioned are undoubtedly such as do constantly threaten the romantic temperament, and it was a great and salutary service that Arnold performed in warning the modern world against them.

The Pre-Raphaelite poets were, with the exception of Swinburne, not greatly indebted to Greek or Latin. Rossetti Troy Town is utterly and deliberately non-classical. Morris Life and Death of Jason is saved from being as romantic as Keats Endymion only by the fact that the story of Jason and Medea is itself the most romantic of ancient tales. Morris had a greater natural sympathy with Northern saga than Greek legend, and his style, leisurely and decorative, has no affinity with the plainness and economy of classical art. Swinburne is even more voluble than Morris. But he was a better Greek scholar and had greater sympathy with the Greek spirit. This may be seen in Atalanta in Calydon, Erechtheus, Anactoria, Itylus and other poems of his inspired by Greek subjects. They reveal, or rather conceal, remarkable learning in certain parts of Greek literature, and many passages are very Greek in spirit. But Swinburne's interest in pathology is not classical, and a poem like Anactoria or Dolores is not characteristically Greek (though some people seem to think so) but characteristically modern. Nor is the style of Swinburne classical. He sometimes tried to make it so, as in the Garden of Proserpine, with fine effect. But it was not his natural manner. The extraordinary vehemence and self-propagating character of his inspiration, urging him to ever fresh variations on his theme, carried him too often beyond the bounds of a justly proportioned and duly concentrated work of art. His sense of form never leaves him, nor his purity of diction; and so far he is classical. But his inability to control his inspiration is the very opposite of classical. Nevertheless his classical background was of the utmost value to him. He is always at his best when he has a classical subject. Atalanta and Erechtheus are as undramatic as Merope, if possible more so; but they are more alive, and their choruses are not surpassed elsewhere in Swinburne's work. He also attempted the Pastoral Elegy in his poem on the death of Baudelaire, which may be compared with Thyrsis, being in a somewhat similar metre. Whatever they owe to the ancient masters, both poems are completely modern in spirit. Arnold indeed recognised that the modern world could never recapture the spiritual calm which he believed, somewhat naïvely, to have reigned in the breasts of the great classical poets. Swinburne was or tried to be frankly a Pagan in the modern world. Of course he did not really succeed, but it gives him a certain advantage when he deals with the ancient world.

PROSE

The movement of literary taste in the direction of an elaborate periodic prose which is noticeable in the later eighteenth century repeated itself in the nineteenth—repeated, not continued, for the writers of ornate prose after 1800 were more influenced by seventeenth century writers like Taylor and Browne than by any eighteenth century author, with the partial exception of Burke. The style of Landor must on the whole be called ornate, although its ornateness is chastened by his study of classical models. The style of De Quincey is ornate without qualification. No doubt he owes something to his study of ancient rhetoric, but the result is not 'Attic', it is 'Asiatic' or even 'Corinthian', which was the most florid kind of prose in the post-classical age of Greece. This is even more true of the 'Style of John Wilson ('Christopher North'), which is sometimes positively barbaric. This opulent prose however was not affected by every writer of the age. Some, like Southey and Lockhart, adopted a plainer style; others, like Lamb and Peacock, Cobbett and Borrow, invented a medium of their own not imitated from anybody or imitable by anybody. Variety is one of the notes of the nineteenth as compared with the eighteenth century. Consequently its writers have to be considered more or less individually.

Of course that cannot be done here. It is only possible to touch on one or two representative figures. A general observation of a paradoxical character may be made at once. The higher education of the nineteenth century was strongly classical; Latin and Greek, with mathematics a somewhat distant third, were the important subjects. As a result it was the rule and not the exception for a nineteenth century author to have a classical background. The exceptions were mostly women, and even many women writers had some knowledge of the ancient languages. Nevertheless the classics had nothing like the same influence on literature in the nineteenth century as they had in the seventeenth and eighteenth. Take for instance the great novelists of the first half of the nineteenth century: Scott, Jane Austen, Thackeray, Dickens. Scott is full of characters who quote Latin, and he himself had read a great deal, particularly of Scottish history, in that language; but so far as one can see the quality of his own work would have been exactly the same if he had never read a word of Latin. This may also be said of Thackeray's work. Miss Austen and Dickens are under no debt to the classics, not having read them. The case of Peacock is very different. His love for the classics, especially Greek, was matched by his knowledge of them, which was extensive and exact. But one calls Peacock a novelist only because one does not know what else to call him. The same is true of Borrow. Bulwer-Lytton *Last Days of Pompeii* is not classical but pseudo-classical. It would be unfair to say this of Kingsley Hypatia, but Egypt, the main scene of the story, is not Greece or even Pompeii, and the fact that Kingsley read a good deal of Greek in order to write Hypatia does nct make its author seem more than an Anglican clergyman who had read a good deal of Greek. (On the other hand Kingsley Andromeda, which is a poem not a novel, is as good an imitation of classical hexameters as will easily be found in English.) As for the later novelists of the century-the Brontes and Mrs. Gaskell, Anthony Trollope, George Eliot, George Meredith, Stevenson and the rest—we find them not so much unaware of the classics—Romola is almost painfully aware of them—as making no use of them.

One might expect it to be different with the historians, and to some extent it is different. You cannot write a history of Greece, like Grote or Thirlwall, or a history of Rome, like Merivale or Dr. Arnold, and not have your mind as well as your matter immersed in the subject. But these were specialists. The historians who have an eminent position in literature-Carlyle, Macaulay, Froude—are less affected by classical example than might have been looked for. Carlyle in the whole make-up of his genius is utterly unclassical. Froude is not, and his admirable style has many classical qualities. But he was engrossed in the controversies of, the Reformation and greatly under the influence of Carlyle, and all that drew him away from classical influences. His one contribution to ancient history, a volume on Julius Caesar, is of no great importance. Then there is Macaulay. Macaulay knew and loved the literature of Rome and Greece. If anyone in the century had a classical background, it was he. The Lays of Ancient Rome is only one evidence of that, for his classical knowledge is apparent all through the Essays and even makes itself felt in the *History of England*. Not that Macaulay's conception of history is that of any classical historian. He was profoundly influenced (as was Carlyle) by the *Waverley Novels*. History in the hands of Hume and Robertson and Gibbon himself was a record of the sayings and doings of certain eminent personages with generalised and almost abstract characters. Scott had peopled the past with living men and women moving in the ordinary circumstances of life. Macaulay as it were combined the method of Hume with the method of Scott. The example he gives himself is James I, who win not be truly presented by the historian unless he completes the account of James in Hume with the picture of him in *The Fortunes of Nigel*. The materials of ancient history were too scanty to admit the use of such a method, and it would be difficult to deny that it led Macaulay into a prodigality of detail which made it impossible for him to cover any considerable stretch of time. Yet doubtless he learned something from the ancient historians. It seems probable that his habit of painting characters in black and white—unrelieved black contrasted in the same person with unsullied white—was encouraged if not suggested by Tacitus, who does much the same, though with more subtlety and a deeper knowledge of human nature. He may also have learned something from the ancients of the art of narrative, in which he, like most of them, excels. Jeffrey wondered where Macaulay got his style and many other critics have wondered since. But something may surely be said about it. It is essentially rhetorical, and when one has said this one has almost said that it is classical. It is not Attic; the prose of Macaulay does not remind us of Demosthenes or even of Cicero. He has not got their rolling periods. What he does remind one of is Silver Latin. If one reads Juvenal for instance, who belongs to the age of Silver Latin-that is the Latin written under the early Roman empire—one sees a literary method at work which is very like Macaulay's. You have the sharp, antithetic, rather staccato sentences with a climax at the end of each paragraph, the shower of illustrations and parallels from history and literature, the same vivid description, the same want of light and shade. Juvenal writes in verse and Macaulay in prose, but Juvenal is more of an orator than a poet. It is most unlikely that the Englishman felt himself to be using much the same literary devices as the Roman, to whom he would justly feel himself at least morally superior. But he does, and this may be attributed to the fact that both were imbued to the lips in ancient rhetoric.

What has been said before, that nineteenth century authors while in general classically educated were in general not classically minded, may easily be tested by readers for themselves. But of course there are exceptions. Matthew Arnold was one. Newman perhaps was another. It is hardly till we come to them that the spirit of Greek culture is seized with really fine apprehension. Coleridge, Lamb, Hazlitt, who can be so illuminating on modern literature, have nothing to say on ancient literature that shows much insight. It is different with Newman. He was not a professed critic like Arnold, but he has, especially in his book called The Idea of a University, and in his Grammar of Assent, indicated what he might have done if he had cared to write at length upon Latin literature. His admiration of Cicero's style is reflected in his own, which moreover has some Attic qualities which Cicero's rather lacks. Newman's dislike of modernism and the attraction exercised upon him by Latin Christianity came to him the more easily because he already knew and loved his Virgil and his Cicero. To him certainly the classics were more than a mere background.

On the other hand Ruskin never understood or accepted the classical spirit. In him the emotional element was always predominant. He is fond enough of argument, but he cannot argue dispassionately. His prose is the efflorescence now of enthusiasm, now of indignation; unless he can express his feelings (which are nearly always very strong) he can hardly write at all. The quiet and almost detached concentration of Greek art is therefore something that he cannot quite understand. He loves Homer. But then everybody loves Homer, and besides Homer is pre-classical and has much in him to please a romantic taste. (For this reason the century rather preferred the Odyssey to the Iliad, which is a great mistake.) Ruskin did not neglect the classics. He read them diligently and even wrote books about Greek mythology. But his interpretation of that mythology is fanciful. As for Greek art —its sculpture and pottery and what is left of its architecture-it did not give him the emotional satisfaction he craved. He had an unquenchable thirst for colour, and the colour has gone from the remains of Greek art. It must be remembered however that Ruskin had not got our materials for judging. The statues now in the Acropolis Museum at Athens, the wonderful collections of Greek pottery now in the Louvre and the British Museum, were not there in his day. What confronted him as classical art was in the main Roman copies of Hellenistic sculptures. He and Browning thought this art lacked 'soul' and they considered that it was the great achievement of mediaeval art to put 'soul' into painting and sculpture. Such an opinion was natural enough, but even in Ruskin's time it could have been modified by study of the Elgin Marbles or by going to Athens and looking at the Parthenon. Towards the end of his fife there are signs that Ruskin was beginning to take more interest in Greek art, but he never liked it as he liked Tintoretto or Turner. On the other hand his belief that the artist should have a moral purpose is thoroughly Greek, though he did not learn it from the Greeks. And his style, for all its exuberance, is classical in its structure. He called it 'Johnsonian' prose himself, and, although it is not exactly that, it has the same classical ancestry.

Ruskin influenced strongly many younger writers, notably John Addington Symonds and Walter Pater, while Pater's professed disciple was Oscar Wilde. All three, but especially Symonds and Pater, were competent Greek scholars. Symonds wrote an agreeable book on Greek literature besides the immense *Renaissance in Italy,* which involved him in much reading of modern Latin as well as of the ancient literatures. If he is no longer read, as seems probable, it is because his style is florid and wordy—two very unclassical qualities—in an inordinate degree. Pater is not wordy nor even excessively florid; he is superior in those respects not merely to Symonds but to Ruskin, and his sentences are quite as beautifully formed as Ruskin's. He was naturally drawn to Greek art and literature, and he was qualified in every way to judge both. *Marius the Epicurean* and *Plato and Platonism* could not have bean written except by a scholar. But his view of antiquity seems to have been formed not by his reading in Greek, but his reading in Ruskin and the Pre-Raphaelites and the French Romantic movement. He was quite right of course to insist on those elements in the old Greek way of living which appeal to the aesthetic sensibilities, but he gives the impression of seeing nothing else—a view which would have surprised extremely any actual Greek of classical times. Wilde copies him in this false notion, with characteristic additions of his own.

SUMMARY

It is a cardinal principle, observed throughout this study, that every age looks in the classics for what it likes and takes what suits it. The eighteenth century greatly admired Homer in Mr. Pope's translation and was prepared to rank him, in virtue of his coming first, with Virgil or not far below him. To the nineteenth century the comparison seemed ludicrous. Again Horace was probably the favourite classical poet of the eighteenth century, though it was very fond too of Ovid and Juvenal. To the nineteenth century it appeared that Sappho and Pindar and Horace's own lyrical predecessor Catullus were far more truly inspired. In general Greek literature rose immensely in the judgement of critics, while Latin literature sank in proportion. No doubt the nineteenth century estimate is nearer the truth because it was based on sounder knowledge. But one reason for it undoubtedly was that Greek literature was felt to be more 'romantic' than Latin. It is easy to romanticise Catullus and to some extent even Virgil; and so these became the favourite Latin poets, although Virgil no one dreamed now of putting by the side of Homer. The greatness of Greek drama was hardly yet fully recognised except by scholars or scholarly poets like Arnold and Swinburne. On the other hand Jowett's translation of Plato revealed to the educated reader a great deal that he had not known before or knew very indistinctly. A more poetical kind of philosophy than had satisfied Cicero and the eighteenth century took possession of most minds.

It is in accordance with this bias towards Greek literature that the translators of the classics who had most influence on their contemporaries were the translators of Greek authors. We have already mentioned Jowett, whose version of Plato certainly contributed a good deal towards making Greek thought of the best period available to readers and claims recognition on its own merits as English prose. Long before Jowett, Shelley had translated Plato's *Symposium* and other Greek originals, sometimes missing the sense and sometimes omitting passages, but always with that distinction of style which was natural to him. We have already mentioned Tennyson's and Browning's translations, and we need hardly dwell upon Fitzgerald's interesting but arbitrary refashioning of the Agamemnon. More important are William Morris's translations of the Aeneid and the Odyssey. They have the merits of speed and vigour, but they produced the oddest effect upon classical scholars, who felt that Morris had turned Homer and Virgil into Scandinavians. They may be contrasted with a contemporaneous version of the Odyssey in Spenserian stanzas by Worsley, which makes Homer look as if he had read Tennyson and the Faerie Queene. This is not said in disparagement of either Worsley's or Morris's work, but to show how differently the same classical author may appear to different minds. About the same time appeared the prose version of the Odyssey by Butcher and Lang, which had a great success. The presiding spirit, so far as style goes, was obviously Lang. This translation deserved its success, and the objection that it is not written in modern English may be met by the answer that Homer was not written in modern Greek. Modernising Homer has the same effect upon him as modernising the Authorized Version has on the Bible; what you gain in one way, you lose in another. It is a more serious objection that Lang's translation is in prose, and prose of a curious Tennysonian languor of movement, very unlike the movement of Homer. He afterwards helped to translate the Iliad, which perhaps did not suit him quite so well as the Odyssey. He also found time to translate Theocritus, which perhaps suited him best of all.

There were of course other translators, some of them excellent, and the general effect of their work was to diffuse a wider and truer knowledge, especially of Greek literature, than the reading public had possessed before. There was also a large output of annotated editions of ancient classics for the use of readers who knew some Latin and Greek, but not enough to benefit by the austere commentaries of Porson and his school, which were written in Latin by professional scholars for others like themselves. The ordinary man was further aided towards the appreciation of antiquity by books like Arnold *Lectures on Translating Homer* and Sellar *Roman Poets of the Republic*, which substituted for the generalities which passed muster at the beginning of the century really detailed and illuminating criticism. The classics seemed to be flourishing as never before. Yet it was not actually so. In technical scholarship the primacy had now passed from England to Germany, and, although in a sense that is not our business, it indicates a weakness at the source. People were becoming interested in other things than the ancient classics. Even if we say nothing of science and confine ourselves to literature, we observe the appearance of dangerous rivals. The great renaissance of French literature beaded by Victor Hugo occupied more of the real interest and attention of English readers and writers than the ancients. Goethe and the German philosophers were widely studied. Above all the Middle Ages had been rediscovered. It had been presented in its most romantic aspects by Scott, and this presentation was developed in one direction by Ruskin and the Pre-Raphaelites, in another by Newman and High-Church Anglicanism. With the truth of the presentation we are not concerned; what we have to note is the enthusiasm it created. Mediaeval history and mediaeval literature were studied with a fresh ardour and increasing knowledge. The classics retained their prestige, but began to lose their influence.

11
Chapter

The Twentieth Century

INTRODUCTION

The nineteenth century passed into the twentieth without any apparent breach in the continuity of its literature. It is possible even now when it is half over to maintain that the twentieth century has not broken clear of its predecessor. There is much rebellion and shaking of chains, but the real proof that the chains have been broken, which only comes when there is a general movement of the public mind in a new direction, is scarcely evident. If it were evident, it would be easier to say in what direction the public mind has moved. There seems to be no general support for any literary school or circle that has developed entirely within the century, and until this is given the historian of literature must refrain from assigning special significance to any particular tendency. But, while that is true, it seems possible to give adequate reasons for thinking that a real change began about the end of the Boer War. Shaw, Wells, Housman—to take three typical and very different representatives of their agehad no quarrel with the literary standards and methods of the nineteenth century, but they gad a quarrel with its opinions. It is true that there was nothing novel in this. Carlyle had been a rebel against his own age, and Ruskin and Morris and others. But towards the beginning of the twentieth century it might be said that the rebels had won or were upon the point of winning. The spirit of the nation veered away from what was called Victorianism and set in a new direction or in a number of new directions. It would be difficult to define it or them, but there is one broad statement, very important for us, which we can make. The trend of contemporary literature is not classical; it is perhaps even anti-classical.

THE CHANGE

The causes of this change are numerous, and some of them have been mentioned. The chief no doubt was the appearance of formidable rivals to the classics not merely in the sciences but in the study of 'modern' subjects in general and particularly of modern languages. It is a mistake to think that pure science and classical scholarship cannot flourish together; in fact an age that has been eminent in one has generally been eminent in the other, as at the Renaissance and long before in Alexandria. What has really affected the position of the classics is the interest in other studies. The ability to read Latin or Greek with any ease or pleasure cannot be acquired except by protracted effort, for which the schools could no longer afford the time, if modern subjects were not to be neglected. To neglect our own literature, not to mention that of France or Germany, for the sake of struggling laboriously through Euripides or Virgil seemed to most people extraordinarily foolish. Something like resentment against the classics grew up in the minds of those who had been subjected to them with little or no benefit to themselves. And this feeling is perhaps now stronger than ever it was; one contemporary writer after another has given expression to it. Whether the substitutes for the study of the classics will prove any more satisfactory only time will decide. These substitutes are entitled to a fair chance, which perhaps they have not yet got. As we are concerned with English literature only, we must restrict ourselves to such remarks as appear to have some relevance. In the nineteenth century, speaking generally, a man of letters who had received a classical education was supposed to make himself acquainted with his own literature, and to acquire some knowledge of French and perhaps even German literature, as a matter of course. This assumption is made not only by Swinburne and Arnold but by Coleridge and Landor. The contrary assumption—that a man who has made a special study of English or French should as a matter of course acquire a knowledge of Greek and Latin literature in the original-cannot be made, and it would be unreasonable to make it. Consequently writers have now to address a different kind of audience. The present assumption appears to be that readersthat is to say educated readers, for the mass of readers at all times can be safely assumed to know nothing—are in the habit of reading both French and English literature, but not Latin or Greek. At the beginning of the nineteenth century and for quite a long time afterwards there was a tendency, natural enough after the wars with revolutionary and Napoleonic France, to disparage and dispraise its literature. Even Matthew Arnold, who admired its prose, writes sometimes as if he thought the French could do little or nothing in poetry. But towards the end of the century there sprang up almost a cult of French literature among English writers—it was the generation of Stevenson and Henry James, of Henley and Wilde and George Moore and Austin Dobson—and that interest has continued until the present day. Thus there is a general assumption that the reader like the author is familiar with Baudelaire and Rimbaud and Proust, just as in the eighteenth and nineteenth centuries he was expected to know his Virgil and Horace and Juvenal. How much of this was make-believe is uncertain, but it may be fairly supposed there is no more make-believe in the one case than in the other.

The change of course has been gradual. There are some authors, whose influence has been exerted mainly in the twentieth century, Bridges for instance and Housman and Gilbert Murray, who have lived all their lives with the classics. They carry on the Victorian tradition, even the metrical experiments of Bridges, like those of Sidney and Spenser, being based on classical practice. A large proportion of Bridges' work was actually on classical subjects and all of it is full of classical reminiscence. Indeed he is a good illustration of what an intense study of classical models can do for a poet who had perhaps no very strong native inspiration. In all Bridges' best work (which does not include the *Testament of Beauty*) the diction is choice and often exquisite, the form succinct and precise, so that he not rarely attains a portion of that 'Dorique delicacy' which Wotton discovered in the verses of the youthful Mlton. The poetry of Housman, even when his later pieces are added to *The Shropshire Lad*, is too narrow in compass and too monotonous in mood to give him rank as a great poet. But the finish and perfection of his verse is extraordinary, and he has the intensity which we somehow miss in Bridges. To say memorable things with clearness, brevity and simplicity is the great, though not the exclusive, aim of the most characteristic classical art. Whether the things Housman says are very memorable may be questioned, but no fair critic can deny the clearness, brevity and simplicity of his style. He is not exactly like any ancient poet, though he sometimes recalls the finer epigrams of the *Greek Anthology*; he has more of the form than the spirit of the ancients. He is more directly influenced by Heine than by any Greek or Roman. He did in English what Heine had done in German, that is he used ballad metres and diction for lyrical purposes, and infused the result with irony. But no scholar can fail to see the pervading influence of classical literature in all that Housman wrote. Indeed it could not be otherwise, for his critical work on the ancient, especially the Latin, poets is quite of the first order. Gilbert Murray is no doubt best known by his translations from the Greek dramatists, but all his writing is informed by a spirit of liberal humanism, which is characteristically Greek. His interpretation of the ancient world is necessarily coloured by his own personality, but it is based on a more exact knowledge of the ancient languages than was possessed by Pater or Arnold, although lie has contented himself mainly with translation.

These writers are in their literary qualities more typical of the nineteenth century than of the twentieth; and this is true of many other distinguished writers of the period. But, while their art is so far traditional, and the traditon has been affected and even largely moulded by classical influences, they themselves are often careless or scornful of the classical background. Consider for instance Kipling, Shaw and Wells. All three are Victorians, although none of them, not even Kipling, is typically Victorian. Kipling was by no means anti-classical. He made himself almost an authority on Roman Britain. But his vivid, jerky, highly personal way of writing, his mixture (often most effective for its purpose and quite original) of slang and Biblical English owe nothing to classical precept or example. Mr. Shaw wrote *Caesar and Cleopatra* to exercise his genius for Comedy, not to demonstrate his sympathy with the past. No one supposes that the classics mean anything to Mr. Shaw, although he was impressed by Gilbert Murray's *Euripides*. For all that his conception of Comedy is more Greek than might be supposed. It is fundamentally the conception of the old Comedy of Manners, which in the hands of Menander for example was also to a considerable extent a Comedy of Ideas. As for Wells, he used some very strong words against what he regarded as the tyranny of the classics, which would deserve greater attention if he had been able to read the literature he condemned. He admitted a debt to the *Republic* of Plato and to Plutarch. The fact is that the Greeks thought of most things that are not just mechanical inventions and we neglect what they said at our own risk. No one is bound to accept what they said, but nothing is gained by not listening. Wells however is important because of his genius and because he is symptomatic of a new spirit, not so much of criticism (for that demands knowledge) as of hostility to the classics.

Of the novelists, besides Kipling and Wells, who, born in the nineteenth century, survived into and influenced the twentieth, the most notable are perhaps Hardy, Henry James, George Moore, Conrad, Arnold Bennett, Galsworthy. There is certainly not much that is consciously classical about them. James, Moore and Bennett all expressed indebtedness to French models, but each developed a method of his own. Moore used classical material for his *Aphrodite in Aulis* and translated *Daphnis and Chloe*, for which his limpid, thin-spun style was not unsuitable. It must not be supposed from this that he knew Greek, or Latin either. No doubt that was a disability and it cannot be said that he understands the genuine classical spirit; he gallicises and Paterises it. The ancients do not go in for analytical psychology, and so had little to offer James, while Bennett was mainly content to study the novel in English, French and translated Russian. There is much more of the ancient Greek in Hardy than in the others. But this is not because he had a classical background; it is because the ancient Greeks and he had much the same background-one older than any literature. Hardy's conception of the irony of fate is neither more nor less than the primitive Greek notion of the 'Jealousy of the Gods', and has its roots not in philosophical reflection but in the hardness and precariousness of the peasant's existence. But while Greek Tragedy sought to moralise this doctrine, and Greek philosophy repudiated it altogether, Hardy appears to have found it a sufficient explanation of what happens in human life. This explains why so many of the catastrophes in Hardy seem the result of accident or divine caprice, and the element of caprice according to Greek notions has no place in a work of art. Undoubtedly there is something in *The Dynasts* and in a novel like *The Return of the Native* that makes us think of Greek Tragedy, but the inference is not that Hardy learned from the Greeks, for we may be sure he did not. Galsworthy, who, whatever his present influence, had enough in his own day to require some attention from the historian, does not seem to have been in any important way affected by such classical reading as he may have done. Conrad's method of indirect narration, through 'Marlow' or some other reporter, is used quite often in Plato's Dialogues, but we may be sure Conrad did not borrow it from Plato, but discovered or rediscovered it for himself.

THE YOUNGER GENERATION

The influence of all the writers so far mentioned has been largely discounted or disavowed by the younger generation of authors, who look more to Gerard Manley Hopkins and perhaps Samuel Butler in the nineteenth century, and in the twentieth to Yeats, T. S. Eliot, D. H. Lawrence and James Joyce, though others might be mentioned. It can be said of them as a whole that they do not submit themselves to classical influences. Hopkins indeed was no enemy of the classics, in which he was even something of a scholar; and the Roman Catholic Church with its Latin traditions meant everything to him. But his hysterical way of writing, while evidently natural to himself and productive of strange and powerful effects, was not classical, any more than his peculiar vocabulary and, disturbed metre. Samuel Butler was so far a student of ancient literature that he translated the *Odyssey* and wrote a book about it, called *The Authoress of the Odyssey*, which he himself professed to take seriously. It is at least amusing. It is likely that the influence of Buder, which became considerable when his novel, *The Way of All Flesh*, was published, is now waning. His admirably clear and succinct prose is wholly traditional; but the example he set of deriding everything that the Victorian age respected encouraged derision of the classical tradition in literature as well. Yet that was one thing he did not deride, and as far as style goes he belongs to it.

Yeats

Yeats in the earlier part of his development was essentially a traditional poet, a Pre-Raphaelite adapting a very original music to Celtic themes. It would seem that the ancient classics never suggested much to his mind, although he became early interested in mystical, or in fact magical, doctrines of the kind taught by 'Dionysius the Areopagite' and others. There is nothing classical about Dionysius, whose work, falsely attributed to the friend of SL Paul is an amalgam of Neo-Platonism or Neo-Pythagoreanism with Oriental magic. How much value Yeats (who did not know Greek) attached to it is quite uncertain, but this interest of his, which extended to Indian theosophy, has to be noted as one of the unclassical elements in his work. To the present writer it has always seemed that Yeats had a somewhat false picture in his mind of classical. antiquity, seeing it as it were through a veil of romantic mysticism. Perhaps he might have been more at home in mediaeval Byzantium (or Constantinople), which was only Greek in language. It has to be added that Yeats in his later poetry did aim at the naked grace, force and brevity of classical art, although he loved at the same time to veil his meaning in difficult or cryptic language, a practice not unknown among the ancient poets, but not characteristic of the pure classical style. He experimented a great deal with language and metre, but he was never an iconoclast breaking the old images for the sake of breaking them. His delicate sense of words and his exquisite ear perhaps kept him from that. But others without his feeling for style carried the experiments farther, while his cryptic manner was a great encouragement to those who thought that a poet should have a set of private symbols which were a secret between him and the fit reader.

T. S. Eliot

It is not very easy to discuss the classical background of Mr. Eliot, although it is very distinctly there, because he uses it. His manner, often allusive or symbolical or ironical, does not permit him to be pinned down to definite pronouncements. His earlier work appeared to show a strong sense of the futility of existence. There is something of this feeling in later antiquity, but it is not classical. In classical literature fife is often represented as tragic, or as worse in certain circumstances than death itself; but rarely as incapable of being lived if not with zest at least with dignity. On the other hand what most people are apt to suppose the distinctively modern thing about his poetry, its learned allusiveness, is of course not modern at all. There is an eminent example of it in the *Alexandra* of Lycophron, a Greek poet of the third century before Christ, though Mr. Eliot would justly condemn the *Alexandra*. It is not what manner a poet uses that is important but the use he makes of it. Eliot dislikes, one need not add with justice, the frippery of a trite poetic diction. Yet some kind of diction every poet must have when the frippery is stripped away. It is at this point that one may begin to argue that Eliot is rather for than against the classical tradition. His style is precise and concentrated;

he experiments with form, as the classics rarely did, but he is never formless, as his imitators too often are. A man who has written sympathetically of Virgil and Dryden is not hostile to the classical tradition. There are even some indications that his sympathy in that direction is increasing. Yet it must be said that his influence hitherto has rather operated towards a contrary result. The people who think distinction in writing comes from being different from everybody else have obviously found encouragement in his example.

D. H. Lawrence

There is nothing very revolutionary or specially modern about the style of D. H. Lawrence; where he is not classical is in his quarrel with society and his preoccupation with some philosophy of sex. Ancient writers took the inequalities of society and the facts of sex as matters of course; at least as public problems not as private grievances. It is improbable that any classical background (supposing him to have acquired one) would have made any difference to Lawrence, whose merits and defects are altogether his own. A deep concern with one's personal problems is one of the most notable distinctions between ancient and modern writers, at least since Rousseau, although the thing is not altogether absent from ancient literature any more than it is always present in modern times. It is more strongly present in Lawrence perhaps than in anyone else. The egotism of Joyce took another direction. It found expression in a style which ultimately no one but himself could be sure he understood. As a result we can hardly tell how far it is worth understanding. There can scarcely be a satisfactory defence of this in prose. In poetry it may be different. At least it is a common modern opinion, which seems to have been entertained by so great a scholar as Housman, that one perceives poetry by some physical sensation and not by the intellect. No classical critic, no classical poet, would have accepted that. He would have agreed rather with Dr. Johnson that poetry should always mean something. Joyce's influence then, so far as it still operates, is quite anti-classical. And, though he called his most famous book *Ulysses*, and had evidently some knowledge of the ancient languages and literatures, it is not possible to say what they really meant to Wm.

This general, though by no means universal, turning away from the long tradition of the classics has not involved much, if it has involved any, loss of interest in them. The number of books about Greece and Rome, even about their literatures, is greater than ever. It seems to be a consequence of that awakening of the historic sense, that feeling for the past, which did not become general until the nineteenth century. The main evidence however is furnished by the translations. Some of these have had an effect not only upon readers but upon writers. There is no doubt for instance that Gilbert Murray's translations drew a good deal of almost surprised attention to Greek drama, the more so as they were successfully acted. It has been objected by some that they are not close enough to the original, by others that they are not in a sufficiently modern idiom The first objection rather ignores the fact that the translator of a poet has to consider at every point whether a literal version will give not merely the sense but the poetical sense of the original. The second objection raises a more difficult problem. It may be illustrated also in the case of Homer. Thus Samuel Butler translated the *Odyssey* in prose from which he carefully excluded any trace of a poetic diction; a translation on much the same principles was made much later by T. E. Lawrence. On the other hand, between Butler and Lawrence, appeared a version by J. W. Mackail in the stanza of Fitzgerald *Rubaiyat* and in a diction which recalled Pre-Raphaelite poetry. There is no doubt that Mackail and Murray are right upon one point. Both Homer and the Greek tragic poets wrote in a traditional and very elaborate poetic diction. The question then arises whether the translator should endeavour to reproduce the effect of that diction in his own, or give up such an attempt as vain and concentrate on translating into what is called a modern idiom. If the latter method is chosen, it cannot but be found exceedingly difficult. Consider how ill one would augur of the result if a Frenchman proposed to translate *Antony and Cleopatra* or *Paradise Lost* into modern French prose or a kind of verse not very different, so far as idiom goes, from such prose. We should be apt to say that the poetry of *Antony and Cleopatra* and of *Paradise Lost* resides in the style, which uses every device of poetic ornament, and that, if quite an opposite style be tried, the poetry will probably disappear. Nevertheless every generation is entitled to translate in the way it thinks best, and the history of literature is strewn with instances in which the warnings of critics that something could not be done have been made to look foolish by some nun of genius, who came and did it. The translations that have been mentioned are by no means the only good ones that have appeared in the last half century, but they are typical enough and may stand for the rest.

SUMMARY

The influence of the ancient classics upon English literature is an historical fact. It has not ceased and it cannot cease, because it is now a vital part of our culture. It may however become greatly less. It is not at all impossible that classical education will become so impoverished as to be hardly worth while for the ordinary student, and that the reading of Homer and Virgil will be left to a handful of scholars. What the historian observes is that this has happened before. Indeed that is an understatement; it has been by far the prevalent state of affairs in the history of Western Europe. But the study of the classics always revived. So there is no reason to expect that it will disappear. There is no reason even to expect that the immediate and direct influence of the classics on authors will disappear. For a work of art like the *Odyssey* or the Aeneid is not like a scientific hypothesis; it is not disproved, it loses none of its authority from the lapse of time, rather it increases that authority.

An historical fact however needs an interpretation and is generally susceptible of many. In the case with which we have been dealing the explanations are many and they are all true. For the classics change before our eyes even as we look at them. They are changing at the present moment. An attempt has been made to show how they looked to men of the Middle Ages, to the Renaissance, to the eighteenth century, to the nineteenth, to our own. Their significance is inexhaustible or at least has not been exhausted. This perhaps ensures their permanence. At any rate their history is pan of our history. The student of the classical influence is dealing with a process to be considered not merely without prejudice but with the historical imagination. When he is reading Chaucer he must look at the classics as Chaucer looked at them, when Milton, as Milton saw them, and so with the rest. Only then will the English authors themselves be fully understood. And they have a right to be understood.

Index

B

C

D

E

F

G

H

I

J

K

L

M

E

O

P

R

S

T

U

V

W

X

Y